THE EXQUISITE CORPSE
BOOK SERIES

Publishing works from both emerging and established scholars, The Exquisite Corpse book series challenges readers with questions that are often left unasked about the human body. Like the Surrealist's parlour game, for which the series is named, these books present the body in all of its unruly and corporeal glory.

PREVIOUS BOOKS IN THE EXQUISITE CORPSE SERIES
Reading from Behind: A Cultural Analysis of the Anus,
by Jonathan A. Allan

FOR MORE INFORMATION, PLEASE CONTACT:
Karen May Clark, Acquisitions Editor
University of Regina Press
3737 Wascana Parkway
Regina SK S4S 0A2
Canada
PHONE: 306-585-4664
EMAIL: karen.clark@uregina.ca

VIRGIN ENVY

THE CULTURAL (IN)SIGNIFICANCE OF THE HYMEN

Jonathan A. Allan, Cristina Santos,
and Adriana Spahr, eds.

University of Regina Press

Printed and bound in Canada at Friesens.

Cover and text design: Duncan Campbell, University of Regina Press
Copy editor: Dallas Harrison
Proofreader: Kristine Douaud
Indexer: Patricia Furdek
Cover art: Somchaisom /iStock Photo.

Library and Archives Canada Cataloguing in Publication
Virgin envy : the cultural (in)significance of the hymen / Jonathan
A. Allan, Cristina Santos, and Adriana Spahr, eds.

(Exquisite corpse)
Includes bibliographical references and index.
Issued in print and electronic formats.
ISBN 978-0-88977-423-0 (paperback).—ISBN 978-0-88977-424-7 (pdf).
—ISBN 978-0-88977-425-4 (html)

1. Virginity—Social aspects. 2. Virginity—Political aspects. 3. Virginity—History.
4. Virginity in literature. 5. Virginity in motion pictures. 6. Hymen (Gynecology).
I. Santos, Cristina, 1972-, author, editor II. Spahr, Adriana, 1951-, author, editor
III. Allan, Jonathan A., author, editor IV. Series: Exquisite corpse (University of
Regina Press)

GN484.47.V57 2016   306.4   C2016-904760-1   C2016-904761-X

10   9   8   7   6   5   4   3   2   1

University of Regina Press, University of Regina
Regina, Saskatchewan, Canada, S4S 0A2
TEL: (306) 585-4758 FAX: (306) 585-4699
WEB: www.uofrpress.ca

We acknowledge the support of the Canada Council for the Arts for our publishing program. We acknowledge the financial support of the Government of Canada. / Nous reconnaissons l'appui financier du gouvernement du Canada. This publication was made possible through Creative Saskatchewan's Creative Industries Production Grant Program.

Canada Council   Conseil des Arts   Canada   creative
for the Arts   du Canada   SASKATCHEWAN

CONTENTS

Acknowledgements—vii

Introduction: "Our Tantalizing Double": Envious
Virgins, Envying Virgins, Virgin Envy
*Jonathan A. Allan, Cristina Santos,
and Adriana Spahr*—1

**PART 1: TOO MUCH PAIN FOR SUCH
LITTLE REWARD**

CHAPTER 1 "I Will Cut Myself and Smear Blood on
the Sheet": Testing Virginity in Medieval
and Modern Orientalist Romance
Amy Burge—17

CHAPTER 2 Between Pleasure and Pain:
The Textual Politics of the Hymen
Jodi McAlister—45

**PART 2: BLOOD, BLOOD, BLOOD . . .
AND MORE BLOOD**

CHAPTER 3 The Politics of Virginity and
Abstinence in the *Twilight* Saga
Jonathan A. Allan and Cristina Santos—67

CHAPTER 4 Lady of Perpetual Virginity: Jessica's
Presence in *True Blood*
Janice Zehentbauer and Cristina Santos—97

PART 3: MEN BE VIRGINS TOO: QUEERING VIRGINITY

CHAPTER 5 The Queer Saint: Male Virginity in Derek Jarman's *Sebastiane*
Kevin McGuiness—127

CHAPTER 6 Troping Boyishness, Effeminacy, and Masculine Queer Virginity: Abdellah Taïa and Eyet-Chékib Djaziri
Gibson Ncube—145

PART 4: F*CK: THEY ENTRAPPED US IN SOCIAL ISSUES AND POLITICS

CHAPTER 7 Bollywood Virgins: Diachronic Flirtations with Indian Womanhood
Asma Sayed—173

CHAPTER 8 The Policing of *Viragos* and Other "Fuckable" Bodies: Virginity as Performance in Latin America
Tracy Crowe Morey and Adriana Spahr—191

Contributors—233

Index—237

ACKNOWLEDGEMENTS

Jonathan Allan would like to thank his co-editors, Cristina Santos and Adriana Spahr, examples of what the academy could look like if we all collaborated a bit more, led with kindness and generosity, and continued to encourage one another. He would also like to thank the University of Regina Press, which has reminded him, time and again, that its goals are to "save the humanities from itself" and to reach a wider audience. In particular, thanks to Bruce Walsh, who continues to believe in big, bold ideas, and to Karen Clark for guiding this project from start to finish, providing rich critiques, and asking the right questions at the right times. He would also like to thank his research assistant, Morganna Malyon, for tracking down citations and reading and rereading chapters of this book. Finally, this project was undertaken, in part, thanks to funding from the Canada Research Chairs Program, and he extends his thanks to the Canadian government and Canadian taxpayers for supporting the Canada Research Chairs Program.

Cristina Santos would like to thank the Humanities Research Institute at Brock University for its financial funding for this project.

She would also like to thank her family for their unending patience and support. It was a true pleasure to come full circle with some of her students, Jonathan Allan, Janice Zehentbauer, and Kevin McGuiness. What began as an animated discussion in the master's class on monstrous women has come to fruition in this volume, and it is to you that I dedicate it. May all your future endeavours be fruitful and fulfilling.

Adriana Spahr would like to dedicate this work to Fernando and Carlina Bogado. She would also like to thank her family for their unconditional support and all the contributors to this volume (especially Cristina Santos, Tracy Crowe Morey, and Jonathan Allan). Without their hard work and commitment, this volume would not have come to fruition.

INTRODUCTION

"OUR TANTALIZING DOUBLE": ENVIOUS VIRGINS, ENVYING VIRGINS, VIRGIN ENVY

Jonathan A. Allan, Cristina Santos, and Adriana Spahr

n their 2006 collection *Defiant Deviance: The Irreality of Reality in the Cultural Imaginary*, Cristina Santos and Adriana Spahr attempted, as editors, to imagine a variety of ways in which deviance could be defiant; they were not yet thinking about virginity, certainly not about the ways in which it is developed here in *Virgin Envy: The Cultural (In)Significance of the Hymen*, and back then Jonathan Allan was still a graduate student. Today the three of us return to some of the questions first posed in *Defiant Deviance*, but now we are interested in the utter messiness of virginity—since it often appears at once as enviable and undesirable, as valuable and detrimental, as normative and deviant. We are interested too in the queering of virginity and in the questioning of the significance of the hymen when it comes to virginity in order to understand virginity in all of its different formulations.

The title that we have chosen for this collection obviously calls on and plays with the Freudian (and therefore often maligned) concept of "penis envy." As editors, we discussed the different perspectives and ideas that circulate around that concept, and that is why *Virgin Envy* seemed to be an appropriate title for this volume. The complexity, confusion, and persistence of Freud's penis envy, we agreed, are akin in many ways to how our culture thinks, talks, and writes about virginity. Definitely, our ideas about virginity—the hymen in particular—and the phallus are "cultural fantasies" that continue to inspire, provoke, and unsettle us.

In many ways, virginity also brings us to what Roland Barthes calls the "muck of language," when a concept—love in his case—is both/and. That is, when it is both "too much" and "too little."[1] On a related note, Adam Phillips, writing about sexuality and envy, notes that

> when it comes to the excesses of sexuality we can't always tell whether our morality is a cover story for our envy, or simply a rationalization of fear; we would like to be that excited, that promiscuous, that abandoned, but it is too much risk for us. . . . We don't, on the whole, tend to envy other people's appetite for food, but other people's appetite for sex—especially in a society in which sex represents health, vitality, and youth—gets to us. People are even more excessive when they talk about sexual excesses. The person who haunts us is the person who is having more pleasure than us. Our tantalizing double.[2]

As the chapters in this collection show, virginity flirts with both this "muck of language" and this "tantalizing double"; we are all haunted, it seems, by the virginity that we once had and lost or the virginity that we wish we could rid ourselves of. When we imagine our virginity loss stories, we might think back to the disappointment or the excitement of that first time; we might think back with regret, sadness, or joy. Virginity is seemingly caught forever in this double bind, in which it is something revered and wanted, yet ridiculed and unwanted. We can think here of the vestal virgins, the Virgin Mary, at the same time as we think of the sad, pathetic virgin of Steve Carrell's character in the popular film *The 40-Year-Old Virgin*.[3]

In thinking about "virgin envy" in particular, we are struck by how Phillips imagines envy as an "essential ingredient of our failures and successes."[4] Envy is never just one thing; it is always caught in the double lining of our affective lives, how we imagine that the virgin has access to something that we've lost, or how the virgin imagines that the non-virgin has gained a hitherto unattained but desired knowledge. How do we imagine virginity as either a success or a failure? Does one succeed if one fails to lose one's virginity, or does one fail if one succeeds in losing one's virginity? Many of the writers in this volume tangle with these questions of what it means to be successful in terms of one's virginity. Does it mean that one is like Joan of Arc? Or does it mean that one was virginal for long enough, lost virginity in an appropriate manner, and then moved on? Although we are all familiar with virginity—we were all once virgins or might still be virgins—questions of virginity are confusing, complicated, and curious.

Virgin Envy thus provides a unique space in which to think about the tensions between the "normal" and the "deviant." For instance, at a certain age, being a virgin is "enviable" and "normal," yet, at another age, it seems to be "deviant," "embarrassing," and "unenviable." The problem with virginity is that it can be lost too early, too late, or never—and these states of virginity then typically become deemed "abnormal." So how, then, and perhaps especially *when*, does one (or should one) lose her or his virginity? It appears as if there is but a short time when it is socially acceptable to lose one's virginity or to make one's sexual debut. And how is virginity in fact lost? And what of those who might not be sure if they are or are not virgins?

Then there are questions about how we represent and define virginity. Given that we all have had—or might still have—*it*, why does *it* prove to be difficult to define? How do we think about and respond to the ways in which virginity is lived, represented, and experienced? Most interesting is that, in trying to define virginity, many tensions are revealed between the subjective understanding of being a virgin (declaring an identity for oneself) and the limits of the word when defined by those who surround the virgin. We might have a notion of what virginity is for ourselves, but does that definition extend to others? Do we—as a culture, a subculture, a group of people, and so on—agree with *the* definition of a virgin?

For Anke Bernau, the answer seems to be fairly straightforward; she opens her book *Virgins: A Cultural History* by noting that, "although people hesitate initially when asked how one can tell whether a *woman* is a virgin or not, they usually end up remembering *the hymen* with a relieved smile."[5]

Undoubtedly, many have seemingly accepted that "female virginity becomes a universally accepted condition . . .that need not be thought about further."[6] Even though debates on the hymen and its location have spanned centuries, and even though Bernau spends pages in her book thinking further about female virginity, she herself admits that "the question of the hymen or other unquestionable physical proofs of virginity has remained uncontested until the present day."[7] Bernau confirms that we continue to be committed to the hymen as *the* signifier of virginity. But what happens when the hymen is not the measure by which a virgin is evaluated?

In *Virgin Envy*, we have gone beyond, in varying ways, the hymen: that is, we're more interested in virginity as a concept than in the archetypal narrative that so many cultural texts propagate (i.e., that girls protect virginity until marriage by keeping their hymens intact). In thinking about the archetypal narrative of virginity, we are struck by the idea that somehow we all have—or should have— a story about the loss of virginity and that these stories are easily recognizable—as if we can imagine sharing these stories and that everyone is in the know about what it means to be a virgin and to lose one's virginity. We are particularly interested in the ways that virginity has become a kind of incontestable reality that we all live with and that most of us will lose. As we began to discuss virginity, however, we realized that many of these common virginal narratives are not true. Virginity extends well beyond the girl who protects herself and her hymen until marriage. In fact, our virginal narratives—those that we tell ourselves—are often remarkably different from that archetypal narrative.

Indeed, insistence on the hymen erases all kinds of bodies save the most normative, cisgendered body of the female. Therefore, it is imperative that we go beyond the hymen and think about virginity without it. Truth be told, boys are virgins, queers are virgins, some people reclaim their virginities, and others reject virginity from the get go. Virginity is never one thing. How many virgins are not represented in popular media, let alone in scholarship? Each contributor to this volume was tasked with thinking about virginity in new ways. Specifically, we urged the contributors to think about the following question: what would happen to the study of virginity if we moved the discussion away from the hymen altogether?

Most of us would generally agree that virginity is about an "untouched" state, however complicated our definitions of touched and untouched might be. We would generally agree that it is the time *before* the first time. Virgins are in a state of sexual inexperience, by which we mean a relational sexuality (for certainly masturbation is sexual even though it might not affect one's claim to virginity). Virgins might be innocent or pure in a physical sense but not necessarily in a psychic or imaginative sense. As Eve Kosofsky Sedgwick notes in *Epistemology of the Closet*, "many people have their richest mental/emotional involvement with sexual acts that they don't do, or even don't *want* to do."[8] The more we complicated our questions, and the more the contributors responded to them, the more we realized the hermeneutic instability of terms such as "untouched," "pure," "innocent," "sexual inexperience," "celibacy," "abstinence," and "virginity." And more questions quickly emerged. Does a gay man lose his virginity the same way that a straight man does? How does a bisexual person lose virginity? Twice?

And what happens after virginity? Do non-virgins feel a sense of loss after virginity loss? If so, then what does that loss look like, feel like? Is it physical, psychic, emotional, affective? Do non-virgins *mourn* their virginities, becoming envious of those who still have theirs? We know that many have framed virginity loss as a monumental, earth-shattering event, but is this always the case? And what if the virgin's loss is disappointing, underwhelming, or entirely uninteresting? How do we think about and theorize the complexities of virginity, especially when we admit that we have a hard time defining even the most basic terms—"virginity" and its "loss"? Ultimately, virginity is a site around which some of our most basic questions about sexuality are confronted and from which we have much to learn about our central anxieties, paranoias, desires, and fears.

Divided into four parts and containing eight chapters in total, *Virgin Envy* looks at different ways that virginity is represented and used in literary texts and popular culture through different historical periods and cultures. The volume's opening section—"Too Much Pain for Such Little Reward"—contains two chapters discussing the representation of virginity in literary texts from the medieval period to the present. The first chapter, Amy Burge's "'I Will Cut Myself and Smear Blood on the Sheet': Testing Virginity in Medieval and Modern Orientalist Romance," focuses on representations of the virginity test. Burge explores six sheikh popular romance novels, all featuring virgin heroines. She positions these texts alongside two popular English medieval romances, *Bevis of Hampton* (c. 1300) and *Floris and Blancheflur* (c. 1250). She analyzes the persistent reference in all of these texts to the virginity test used to prove women's virginity. Pointing out that these tests are easily manipulated, thereby highlighting their unreliability, Burge reminds us that the sole purpose of testing female virginity is to secure male ownership of women in a heteronormatively gendered society.

In the second chapter, "Between Pleasure and Pain: The Textual Politics of the Hymen," Jodi McAlister explores the history of the representation of the hymen in Western literature romances. Her analysis ranges from the thirteenth century, with *Le roman de la rose*; to the seventeenth century, with the ballad *A Remedy for Green Sickness* (1682) and *A Dialogue between a Married Woman and a Maid* (1655); through to excerpts from "Sub-Umbra, or Sport among the She-Noodles" and "Lady Pokingham, or They All Do It" from *Pearl* (a magazine published in 1879–80); and up to examples taken from the twentieth century and twenty-first century, using *Beyond Heaving Bosoms* and recent autobiographical stories of virginity loss. By examining blood, pain, and (im)perforability—common motifs associated with the hymen—in all of these texts across such a vast array of periods, McAlister reveals the discourse over the female body across time. In doing so, she discovers that the perception of virginity loss (the rupture of the hymen) brings about a profound transformative change in women: it is the journey toward adulthood, sexual maturity, and pleasure. More so, from the earliest to the latest of these romances, McAlister argues that the role of women has greatly improved: the transformative change moves from being that imposed externally by the man to that becoming internal to the woman. Finally, and tellingly, McAlister's analysis, by moving from early literary texts to current autobiographical stories (a point of friction in her chapter between literary texts and real lives), shows that in the latter texts the hymen is less concrete: the broken hymen does not and cannot fulfill the expectation of the transformative changes long promised by our cultural imaginary.

The second part of *Virgin Envy*—"Blood, Blood, Blood . . . and More Blood"—is made up of two chapters, the first written by Jonathan A. Allan and Cristina Santos, the second written by Janice Zehentbauer and Cristina Santos.[9] Each chapter studies virginity through vampiric characters in television series, films, and literary texts, especially in the past two decades. In "The Politics of Abstinence and Virginity in the *Twilight* Saga," Allan and Santos explore vampiric and virginal characters in the popular *Twilight* series written by Stephenie Meyer. Specifically, they explore female and male virginity, particularly with respect to the two main characters: the mortal Bella and the immortal vampire Edward. The authors argue that the *Twilight* saga mirrors cultural anxieties about abstinence, purity, chastity, and virginity in both characters. Allan and Santos suggest that Bella's sexuality and desire deal not only with ideas around purity but also with ideas around erotophobia—the fear of sexuality. Abstinence, they point out, thus becomes not just a "choice" but also an ideological construct in American culture.

In "Lady of Perpetual Virginity: Jessica's Presence in *True Blood*," Janice Zehentbauer and Cristina Santos focus on the character of Jessica Hamby in HBO's cult hit *True Blood*. Jessica is a seventeen-year-old virgin who has been turned into a vampire. Through historical, sociological, and cultural approaches, the authors study Jessica alongside the phenomena of the abstinence movement, purity clubs, and (re)definition of virginity in contemporary America. The United States has witnessed the growth of what Jessica Valenti has called "the purity myth," a movement that encourages young women to remain "pure" until marriage.[10] Being a virgin in contemporary American culture is seemingly demanded by popular culture, yet the same popular culture celebrates hypersexualized femininity (and this speaks, of course, to a series of cultural anxieties about female sexuality: slut shaming, rape culture, virginity, and the demand for purity). As a vampire, Jessica can maintain the same physical condition that she had as a human; thus, she becomes an emblem of American society since she represents a forever young virgin. Her body is able to heal each and every wound quickly, which means that after sex her hymen is healed—over and over again. As the authors indicate, this situation satirizes the abstinence movement and traditional patriarchal values in regard to female sexuality, and the character's position as an eternal virgin mirrors a society that simultaneously hypersexualizes young women and demands their sexual abstinence.

The two chapters in the third part—"Men Be Virgins Too: Queering Virginity"—focus on male virginities and the ways in which they are seemingly excluded from critical thought about virginity. Both chapters draw on queer studies to account for male virginity, almost as elusive as the G-spot: we all know that it is there, but we have a hard time finding it. The authors in this part build upon a small but growing body of scholarship on male virginity and work to demonstrate that male virginity is in need of (re)consideration.

In his chapter, "The Queer Saint: Male Virginity in Derek Jarman's *Sebastiane*," Kevin McGuiness considers through the lens of psychoanalysis the 1976 film *Sebastiane*, directed by Derek Jarman. McGuiness explores how male virginity, religious ecstasy, and homoeroticism inform one another in the film. Against a lush Sardinian background, this beautifully photographed film recounts the fictionalized life of Saint Sebastian. The Christian soldier-saint, operating in the third century under the Roman Empire, was subsequently martyred for his religious beliefs. Referencing the visual vocabulary associated with the historic saint, Jarman reinvents the story of Sebastian and transforms him into a figure devoted to religious celibacy. Uncovering the latent homoerotic connotations contained within Jarman's work, McGuiness attends to the visual cues and symbolic imagery that play into virginal anxieties regarding the queer body.

In the next chapter, "Troping Boyishness, Effeminacy, and Masculine Queer Virginity: Abdellah Taïa and Eyet-Chékib Djaziri,"

Gibson Ncube pays attention to what he calls a "cavernous gap" in the research on male virginity, let alone on masculine queer virginities, in Arab Muslim societies of North Africa. Ncube posits that masculine queer virginity is a significant marker of dissidence and destabilization of the status quo on sexuality and identity construction. Drawing on Kathryn Bond Stockton's theoretical perspectives on the "proto-gay child," as well as on Lucas Hilderbrand's notion of "queer boyhood," Ncube argues that the juvenile queer protagonists of Djaziri and Taïa play important roles in mapping and negotiating gay sexuality in the Arab Muslim and patriarchal societies of North Africa. Queer virginity is intrinsically linked to the development of a sexual identity considered deviant and undesirable in these communities. In this way, traditional forms of gender and sexuality are undermined by the emergence of alternative modes of being.

The volume's fourth and final part—"F*ck: They Entrapped Us in Social Issues and Politics"—contains chapters that explore the intersection of virginity and sociocultural concerns. The authors here reveal how virginity becomes a tool for political concerns, especially at the level of political nationalism, by controlling female bodies.

In "Bollywood Virgins: Diachronic Flirtations with Indian Womanhood," Asma Sayed discusses the role of Bollywood films in perpetuating a nation's patriarchal values in a number of ways. Portraying women in submissive roles and happy households after marriage, the films perpetuate nationalist and populist views to the detriment of not only women but also marginalized peoples. Providing an overview of the representations of virginity in the context of female identity politics in Bollywood cinema, Sayed focuses primarily on the films of the past two decades. Some post-1990s films have made superficial attempts to present strong female characters. Although these films have showcased seemingly liberated female characters trying to make independent life choices, most still end with the characters concluding that they love the men to whom they lost their virginity. Thus, these films typically end with the female protagonist marrying her first lover—a perpetuation of the patriarchal status quo that has historically restricted women's opportunities. This chapter offers important observations on the ways in which national identities and virginities become enmeshed in one another and once more demonstrate how female bodies are controlled by the patriarchy.

In the closing chapter, "The Policing of *Viragos* and Other 'Fuckable' Bodies: The Politics of Virginity in Latin American Women's Testimony," Tracy Crowe Morey and Adriana Spahr devote attention to female virginity and changing political contexts. Taking the recent case of virginity testing on politically active women in Tahrir Square, the authors ask about other "political" bodies and the ways in which virginity has been tested, performed, and challenged. They seek to demonstrate the conditions and repercussions of such strict controls of the vagina through an examination of particularized cases of "unruly" women, often defined as either *viragos* or the third sex in the Latin American context.[11] The *virago* creates a new space centred not on virginity or the lack of it but on her capacity to perform as a male—a *virago*—in the public sphere. Historically, *viragos* who dared to enter such areas were denigrated (raped), subjugated (not only physically but also psychologically), and often reconstituted in virginal roles defined by the heteronormative confines of their society. The figure of the *virago* seems to be intermittent and appears to have succumbed under the force of patriarchal society and much more within the Latin American context, the primary focus of this chapter. The reality is that, after being defeated, their stories have been modified by the official, state-sanctioned "history" in order to preserve the status quo. The intention of the authors is to demonstrate how these women refused to live under the shadow of virginity and the subsequent efforts of society to destroy them. The analysis includes, among others, Catalina de Erauso, *soldaderas* or female soldiers during the Mexican Revolution (1910–17), and guerrilla women from Chile and Argentina during the military dictatorships of the 1970s and 1980s.

Taken together, the chapters in this volume highlight what Judith Halberstam calls "queer methodology," a kind of "scavenger methodology that uses different methods to collect and produce information on subjects who have been deliberately or accidentally excluded from traditional studies of human behaviour."[12] This approach to the question of virginity immediately calls the reader's attention to the complexity of the question itself: where is virginity represented? Seemingly, the answer is everywhere. Virginity, like air, surrounds us and finds its way into texts that cut across centuries, genres, cultures, and forms of authorship, ranging from the canonical texts of medieval literature, to the popular romance novels, and up to the recent turn to "virginity confessions" or "first-person accounts of virginity loss." These chapters affirm what we had suspected, that the study of virginity demands a rejection of "disciplinary coherence" because virginity cannot be contained within the tight walls of a discipline that governs, protects, and affirms its contents.[13]

At the same time, despite this "scavenger methodology" that ranges far and wide, we as editors regret that this collection does not contain much about lesbian or trans virginities—important areas of research that need to be attended to, especially within the realm of popular culture. Truthfully, virginity studies remains, in many ways, an untouched field of study, especially when it tries to move beyond the traditionally defined subject of the female. It is surprising that, though virginity studies is a field dominated by the idea that virginity is female, lesbian experiences of virginity are unaccounted for in the scholarship. As Paige Averett, Amy Moore, and Lindsay Price have noted, "literature on LGBT virginity [is] very limited": "there is a need for *any type of virginity studies* that have LGBT youths in the sample."[14] We note these absences from this collection not to absolve ourselves of them, but to encourage ourselves and others to begin to undertake this important work. Without a doubt, the volume represents just the beginning of a much-needed excavation of what is an eclectic archive of virginity representations. We genuinely hope that future studies of virginity will continue to challenge "disciplinary coherence," precisely because the question of virginity—as a lived practice, as an ideology, as a religious tenet, and so on—surely cannot be contained.

In closing, we note that we have purposefully "refuse[d] the academic compulsion toward disciplinary coherence,"[15] precisely because "traditional disciplinary boundaries become inadequate containers for subjects whose lives and utterances traverse the categories meant to contain them."[16] We thus invite the reader to witness how the chapters in this volume struggle with the question of virginity, the matter of virginity, the impossibility of virginity.

Virginity is at once all encompassing, an identity imposed on the body, and entirely intangible, untouchable. When we think about the untouched nature of virginity, we quickly realize how complicated it is: can virginity, the thing that makes us virginal, be touched, and if so what and where is it? But if it were to be touched, just touched, nothing more, a light tickle or a soft caress, would it still be untouched? And beyond this immediate touch, how do we think about the touching intimacy of the sexual scene in which we "lose" our virginities? All of these questions flirt with the binary that sustains them: that is, to speak about virginity is to confront, once and again, the "muck of language," the ways in which language fails us in our most real and lived lives. Perhaps, at the end of the day, the envy that sustains this volume seeks a language that can be reconciled with the complexity of virginity.

NOTES

1   Roland Barthes, *A Lover's Discourse: Fragments*, trans. Richard Howard (New York: Hill and Wang, 1978), 99.

2   Adam Phillips, *On Balance* (New York: Farrar, Straus and Giroux, 2010), 35.

3   *The 40-Year-Old Virgin*, dir. Judd Apatow (Universal Pictures, 2005).

4   Adam Phillips, *On Flirtation* (Cambridge, MA: Harvard University Press, 1994), 57.

5   Anke Bernau, *Virgins: A Cultural History* (London: Granta Books, 2007), 1; emphasis added.

6   Ibid.

7   Ibid., 6.

8   Eve Kosofsky Sedgwick, *Epistemology of the Closet* (Berkeley: University of California Press, 1990), 25.

9   These two chapters also highlight the editors' commitment to mentorship and collaboration since both are products of a collaborative authorship between Cristina Santos and her former students.

10   Jessica Valenti, *The Purity Myth: How America's Obsession with Virginity Is Hurting Young Women* (Berkeley: Seal Press, 2010).

11 Diana Taylor, *Disappearing Acts: Spectacles of Gender and Nationalism in Argentina's "Dirty War"* (Durham: Duke University Press, 1997).

12 Judith Halberstam, *Female Masculinity* (Durham: Duke University Press, 1998), 13.

13 Ibid.

14 Paige Averett, Amy Moore, and Lindsay Price, "Virginity Definitions and Meaning among the LGBT Community," *Journal of Gay and Lesbian Social Services* 26, 3 (2014): 274, 276; emphasis added.

15 Halberstam, *Female Masculinity*, 13.

16 Juana María Rodríguez, *Queer Latinidad: Identity Practices, Discursive Spaces* (New York: New York University Press, 2003).

REFERENCES

Averett, Paige, Amy Moore, and Lindsay Price. "Virginity Definitions and Meaning among the LGBT Community." *Journal of Gay and Lesbian Social Services* 26, 3 (2014): 259–78.

Barthes, Roland. *A Lover's Discourse: Fragments.* Translated by Richard Howard. New York: Hill and Wang, 1978.

Bernau, Anke. *Virgins: A Cultural History.* London: Granta Books, 2007.

The 40-Year-Old Virgin. Directed by Judd Apatow. Universal Pictures, 2005.

Halberstam, Judith. *Female Masculinity.* Durham: Duke University Press, 1998.

Phillips, Adam. *On Balance.* New York: Farrar, Straus and Giroux, 2010.

———. *On Flirtation.* Cambridge, MA: Harvard University Press, 1994.

Rodríguez, Juana María. *Queer Latinidad: Identity Practices, Discursive Spaces.* New York: New York University Press, 2003.

Santos, Cristina, and Adriana Spahr, eds. *Defiant Deviance: The Irreality of Reality in the Cultural Imaginary.* New York: Peter Lang, 2006.

Sedgwick, Eve Kosofsky. *Epistemology of the Closet.* Berkeley: University of California Press, 1990.

Taylor, Diana. *Disappearing Acts: Spectacles of Gender and Nationalism in Argentina's "Dirty War."* Durham: Duke University Press, 1997.

Valenti, Jessica. *The Purity Myth: How America's Obsession with Virginity Is Hurting Young Women.* Berkeley: Seal Press, 2010.

PART 1:
TOO MUCH PAIN
FOR SUCH LITTLE
REWARD

CHAPTER 1

"I WILL CUT MYSELF AND SMEAR BLOOD ON THE SHEET": TESTING VIRGINITY IN MEDIEVAL AND MODERN ORIENTALIST ROMANCE

Amy Burge

A bloody sheet, a shaky goblet, an enchanted fountain—the virginity or chastity test has long been a persistent and imaginative literary motif. Indeed, some of the most fantastic tests are drawn from medieval romance, the most popular secular genre in late medieval Europe.[1] Today the virginity test is increasingly associated with cultures in Africa, the Middle East, and Asia, where vigorous debates about virginity examinations have attracted national and international attention. Both the literary virginity test and its current association with Asian and African cultures have found their modern-day expression in the Orientalist sheikh romance novel: a consistently popular subgenre of contemporary romance publishing that details a cross-cultural love story between a Western heroine and a Middle Eastern or North African sheikh or sultan hero.

This chapter explores the representation of the virginity test in English Orientalist romance literature from two distinct historical moments: the late Middle Ages and the twenty-first century.

This cross-period approach takes a long view of the virginity test, considering how current romance ideologies contrast with those of medieval romance. It antagonizes exactly what is at stake in persistent reference to the virginity test in romance literature, focusing on articulations of certainty and uncertainty, loss and possession. My focus throughout is on the test as it applies to women, echoing the deeply gendered discourses that surround virginity testing: there are no virgin sheikhs. Through close readings of six popular sheikh romances featuring virgin heroines published by the genre's biggest publisher, Harlequin Mills & Boon[2]—Lynne Graham's *The Arabian Mistress* (2001), Lucy Monroe's *The Sheikh's Bartered Bride* (2004), Penny Jordan's *Possessed by the Sheikh* (2005), Sarah Morgan's *The Sultan's Virgin Bride* (2006), Lynne Graham's *The Desert Sheikh's Captive Wife* (2007), and Chantelle Shaw's *At the Sheikh's Bidding* (2008)—alongside two popular English medieval romances, *Bevis of Hampton* (c. 1300) and *Floris and Blancheflur* (c. 1250), I consider how the test is positioned in each text and what it reveals about the importance of virginity. To put the testing in context, I offer a brief overview of virginity testing in European culture before examining the role of virginity in these romances. Then I focus on the test itself, indicating how testing for virginity in these romances is inherently unstable. Finally, I explore how testing for virginity ultimately functions to secure male ownership of women as part of the romance genre's heteronormative gender system. Ultimately, I encourage a deeper interrogation of the easy association of virginity and the East in these popular Western texts.

"IF SHE IS CORRUPT, SHE WILL URINATE IMMEDIATELY": METHODS OF TESTING

As long as women's virginity has been of social, cultural, or political importance, the virginity test has existed. Daniel Pollack defines the virginity test as, simply, "an old custom designed to check if a young girl's hymen is intact,"[3] revealing the gendered cultural assumptions made about virginity testing. However, methods of testing for virginity have been more varied than Pollack indicates, perhaps a reflection of the fact that the word *hymen* was not used in its modern meaning until the fifteenth century.[4] A range of historical texts—the Bible, medical treatises, romances, folk tales, court records—describes the myriad ways in which a woman's chastity can be tested. Kathleen Coyne Kelly helpfully separates such testing into two genealogies: mythical (in folklore and literature) and historical (in treatises and court records).[5] Laurie Maguire further categorizes virginity tests into four main groups: "textile proof of bleeding; gynaecological examination by a jury of women; proof by magical ability on the part of the virgin; and somatic responses to ingested fluid or inhaled fumes."[6]

All virginity tests ultimately look for the same thing: signs of virginity rather than virginity itself.[7] Deuteronomy details "tokens of . . . virginity," which Hanne Blank reasons are likely to be bloodied bed sheets.[8] Tuccia, a Roman vestal virgin, famously proved her virginity by carrying water in a sieve.[9] In the Middle Ages, tests incorporated varied signs such as bleeding following penetration, tightness or difficulty on penetration, examination of urine, and physical examination by a midwife.[10] Although checking the sheets for blood was not an authentic practice in fourteenth-century England, according to Kelly it is an old custom for communities in North Africa, the Middle East, and the Mediterranean whose continued usage into modernity she notes.[11] The thirteenth-century medical treatise *De secretis mulierum* (Secrets of Women) suggests giving ground lilies to a woman to eat, upon which, "if she is corrupt, she will urinate immediately."[12] A medieval woman's virginity could also be discerned by how loudly she urinated, how long it took her to urinate,[13] and whether, upon fumigation of the vagina with coal, she "perceive[d] the odor through her mouth and nose."[14] Folk stories and medieval romances present a multitude of magical tests, including a horn from which only virgins can drink without spilling, a mantle that will not fit an unchaste woman, and a harp that plays out of tune when a non-virgin approaches.[15] Equally, as Sarah Salih indicates, "an intact body is inferred from outward signs."[16] Virginity (or its lack) is also externally visible; breasts have been indicators of virginity since the second century,[17] and *De secretis mulierum* catalogues behavioural indicators of virginity, such as avoiding eye contact with men and speaking and acting modestly.[18]

More recently, the virginity test has been the focus of negative scrutiny in certain Middle Eastern and African countries.[19] In Jordan and Palestine, imposed virginity testing in cases of reported sexual assault has been criticized as a tool of female oppression.[20] In Turkey, despite national and international pressure to outlaw the practice, virginity testing was performed up to the late 1990s,[21] fuelled by widespread notions of female sexual honour, shame, community, and tradition.[22] Indeed, well into the twenty-first century, it is still relatively common in parts of Turkey to display blood-stained sheets to prove the bride's virginity following the wedding night.[23] In South Africa, virginity testing has become conflated with contemporary debates on the HIV/AIDS epidemic; in KwaZulu-Natal province, virginity testing has enjoyed a revival since the mid-1990s.[24] Initially intended to protect family status,[25] the practice has been firmly connected, in recent years, with the discourse of HIV/AIDS via claims that virginity testing offers a "culturally appropriate solution" to problems caused by the epidemic,[26] effectively functioning as a mechanism of abstinence.[27]

Yet, despite this diversity, there are some aspects common to all virginity tests. For a start, they are unreliable. For as long as there have been virginity tests, there have been ways to cheat them. *De secretis mulierum* cautions that a non-virginal woman can simulate modesty and that there are multiple methods to conceal a lack of virginity; bleeding can be faked by inserting a dove's intestine filled with blood into the vagina or by carefully applying a leech to the labia.[28] Ultimately, as Blank points out, "the simple fact is that short of catching someone in the act of sex, virginity can be neither proven nor disproven."[29]

What's more, virginity testing is an almost exclusively female discourse. Long-standing and persistent patriarchal structures that require reproductive exclusivity to secure primogeniture support the idea that women, rather than men, should be tested to provide "proof" of virginity. Kelly admits that almost all medieval virginity tests are aimed at women, and this gendered prejudice is echoed in the romances examined in this chapter, all of which focus on female virginity.[30] Historical and contemporary discourses of virginity testing are drawn across the boundaries of fiction and fact; the "reality" of such testing draws on and feeds into the fantasy of testing. It is precisely this collocation of myth and reality that perpetuates inclusion of the test in romance, a genre similarly positioned at the juncture of fact and fantasy. Popular romance is thus perfectly placed to explore representations of the virginity test.

VIRGINITY IN MEDIEVAL AND MODERN ROMANCE

Virgins are fundamental to contemporary romance. The "sexually unawakened heroine"[31] remains a persistent trope of many romances. Yet a large-scale analysis of Mills & Boon Modern Romance[32] novels reveals that female virginity is particularly pronounced in romance novels with "foreign heroes": the ubiquitous Greeks, Italians, Spaniards, Brazilians, Argentines, and, of course, sheikhs.[33] Of the 931 Modern Romance novels published in the United Kingdom from 2000 to 2009, 458 feature virgin heroines, and 281 of them (approximately 61 percent) have foreign heroes. This simultaneously reveals Western preoccupation with virginity and its situating of it "elsewhere." Sheikh romances do not contain significantly more virgin heroines than other foreign hero romances; proportionally, there are at least as many virgin heroines in novels with Greek heroes, and there are proportionally more virgin heroines in novels with Spanish heroes.[34] However, when considering the titles of Modern Romance novels, an interesting distinction emerges in sheikh romance novels.

In romance titles, the words *virgin*, *innocent*, and *innocence* are used to signal that the heroine of the romance is a virgin. The majority of romances with titles featuring one or more of these words contain foreign heroes: of a total of eighty-four romances with titles containing these words, sixty have foreign heroes. But when we look at those romances more carefully, the number of sheikh romances that contain these words in the titles is proportionately higher per romance published than any other type of foreign hero romance (see Table 1.1), suggesting a fundamental link between signifiers of the East—sheikh, sultan, desert—and signifiers of virginity. Thus, though sheikh romance novels might not contain more virgin heroines than romances with Spanish and Greek heroes, in terms of their marketing and appeal via their titles virginity can be considered a prominent trope associated with the sheikh genre. The created Eastern world of the sheikh romance—what I term the "romance East"—is thus explicitly connected with virginity.

Table 1.1: The Words *Virgin* and *Innocent/Innocence* in Modern Romance Titles of Novels with Foreign Heroes*

Type of Hero[†]	Number of Titles Containing Virgin	Number of Titles Containing *Innocent/ Innocence*	Total Number of Novels	Proportion of Virgin, *Innocent/Innocence* Titles (%)
Sheikh	9	3	57	21
Greek	12	2[‡]	115	15
South American	2	2	29	14
Spanish	7	2	69	13
Italian	15	3	189	9.5
French	1	0	22	4.5

* Some titles did not make it clear whether the heroine was a virgin or not. I have included them in the count, assuming that their heroines are non-virgins, meaning that the number of virgin heroines might be slightly higher than noted here. The novels in which it is unclear whether the heroine is a virgin are as follows: sheikh (1), Spanish (3), Italian (16), Greek (12), French (1), South American (1).

† In addition to the heroes mentioned here, and included in my count of romances with foreign heroes, are four romances with Russian heroes and Penny Jordan's *Virgin for the Billionaire's Taking* (2008), which has an Indian hero (apparently the first Indian hero in Harlequin Mills & Boon romance).

‡ Two romances with Greek heroes feature the words *innocent* and *virgin* in the title, which I have counted only once under *virgin*.

Source: Amy Burge, *Representing Difference in the Medieval and Modern Orientalist Romance* (New York: Palgrave Macmillan, 2016), 91.

In the romance East, female virginity is of great cultural importance. Sheikh romances repeatedly highlight the importance placed on virginity in Eastern culture; in *The Arabian Mistress*, the sheikh hero tells the heroine "you do not appear to understand how high is the regard for a woman's virtue in my culture."[35] In this instance, it is clear that "virtue" is used as a synonym for "virginity," yet indicators of virtue elsewhere in the sheikh genre—downcast eyes, modest dress, and meek behaviour—map directly onto signs of virginity, indicating the privileging of virginity within this discourse. Such a cultural valuing is connected to ideas of tradition often glossed as "medieval." One heroine demurs that, "had she not been a virgin, she had the awful feeling even a pity date would not have occurred. It was medieval and felt like the worst kind of betrayal."[36] In *Possessed by the Sheikh*, the hero says that "it is my duty to do as my brother commands me and, besides, since I took your virginity, . . . " to which the heroine responds "you're marrying me because of that! But that's . . . that's archaic . . . medieval. . . . "[37] By suggesting that the romance East, where virginity is prized, is somehow premodern in its views on female virginity, these romances engage with the conflict between tradition and modernity that characterizes contemporary debates over virginity and virginity testing in various cultures.

Contrarily, the West is assumed to be a place where virginity is no longer either valued or present. In most sheikh romances, the sheikh hero initially considers the Western heroine to exemplify a promiscuous femininity, leading him to conclude that she cannot possibly be a virgin.[38] This misunderstanding usually persists until the moment the couple have sex for the first time. In *At the Sheikh's Bidding*, the hero Zahir tells the heroine Erin that "you can drop the act of maidenly virtue now . . . . Qubbah may be rooted in tradition, but I'm a modern guy and I'm happy to accept that you may have had lovers."[39] The hero of *The Arabian Mistress* similarly acknowledges that "every other western woman I had been with was only interested in fun, sex and what I could buy,"[40] connecting Western femininity with promiscuity and lack of virginity. The more advanced age of the heroine can also contribute to an assumption of sexual experience; the heroines of the six sheikh novels are all in their early to mid-twenties (twenty-two to twenty-four), several years beyond the age of consent in Europe, North America, and Australia (roughly fifteen to eighteen, though it is lower in several European countries). This is in contrast to the Middle East, where the age of consent ranges from eighteen to twenty-one, and in some countries sex outside marriage is not permitted. Although it is not uncommon for the hero of a romance novel to wrongly assume that the heroine is more sexually experienced than she is, in sheikh romance sexual experience is explicitly associated with the West, thus firmly aligning virginity and its cultural value with the East.

Virginity is also valued in medieval romance, though the distinction between its value in the East and West is not as pronounced.[41] The two romances discussed here, *Floris and Blancheflur* (hereafter referred to as *Floris*) and *Bevis of Hampton* (hereafter referred to as *Bevis*), were among the most popular late medieval romances in England and are extant in the comprehensive and important Auchinleck manuscript (c. 1330).[42] *Floris*, thought to have been composed around 1250, tells the story of Floris, the pagan son of the king of Spain, who travels to Babylon to rescue his beloved, Blancheflur, the Christian daughter of a slave woman, who has been sold to the emir of Babylon and is being kept in his harem. *Bevis*, written around 1300, is an expansive tale concerning the adventures of Bevis, a knight exiled from his Southampton home and raised by a Saracen king in fictional Ermony. Bevis eventually marries the king's daughter, Josian.

In *Floris*, virginity is valued monetarily. The monetary and social worth of virginity in the Middle Ages has been documented. Kim M. Phillips, in her analysis of court records from the late thirteenth century to the mid-fifteenth century, writes that "evidence . . . indicates that premarital virginity was commonly believed to have a value which could be matched in money."[43] This is reflected in *Floris*, in which women are referred to as "merchandise."[44] Blancheflur's value is expressed monetarily; the parents of Floris expect "much property and goods"[45] in return for selling her, and they receive a valuable and ornate cup in return. Even Floris alludes to a monetary valuing of Blancheflur since, on his quest to find her, he tells people that he is seeking his "merchandise." The emir similarly regards

Blancheflur financially, paying for her "seven times her weight in gold / For he intended, without doubt / To take that fair maiden as his queen."[46] Although his purchase does not explicitly refer to Blancheflur's virginity, the emphasis on female virginity through-out the romance might suggest that her worth is tied to her status as a "clean maiden [virgin]."[47] By assessing Blancheflur's body in monetary terms, literally measuring the worth of her body's weight, the emir can be said to be simultaneously valuing the virginity of that body.

In *Bevis*, on the other hand, virginity is presented as a Christian ideal and as vital for issues of heritage; Bevis needs a wife and heirs in order to regain his lands and rejoin the system of primogeniture. Kelly points out that "both virginity and paternity are essential to the workings of a feudal society that held the bulk of its wealth in private, aristocratic hands and passed on such wealth from father to son."[48] Following a spell of imprisonment and separation from Josian, Bevis visits the patriarch[49] in Jerusalem, who "forbid[s] him upon his life, / That he should take a wife, / Unless she were a virgin."[50] Bevis later repeats these words to Josian, underscoring the link between Christianity and virginity. The main threat to Josian throughout *Bevis* is sexual; a previous suitor, Brademond, threatens to "lay her by my side at night," after which he will give her "to a carter, who is worn out!," and Miles, a suitor to whom Josian is briefly married, intends to have Josian "under the covers" and tries to "get her drunk [to get her] into bed" in order to "have his will."[51]

Even Bevis is initially figured as a sexual threat to Josian; when her father is told that Bevis has allegedly "deflowered his daughter," he considers this a crime so serious that he sends Bevis, whom he "loved" and raised in his household, to be punished by Brademond, a "Saracen king."[52] Sexual threat is taken seriously in *Bevis*. Up to the point of her marriage to Bevis, Josian's romantic adventures centre on maintaining her virginity for the knight whom Josian chooses to give it to: Bevis.[53] So it is perhaps unsurprising that, in romances in which virginity is emphasized and valued to this extent, virginity testing should feature so prominently.

"THROUGH CUNNING AND ENCHANTMENT":
TESTING AND AMBIGUITY

When it comes to testing, it is generally agreed that virginity is intrinsically difficult to test. Sarah Salih, Anke Bernau, and Ruth Evans argue that "virginity is a paradoxical condition . . . defined by both absence and presence."[54] Kelly concurs, writing that virginity is "something that counts only when it is thought lost."[55] It is difficult to test for something that you cannot see. However, this does not prevent virginity tests from being deployed in romance. Indeed, extrapolating from Kelly's argument about virginity in twentieth-century film, neither modern sheikh romance nor medieval romance contests that virginity can be tested or verified.[56] As outlined above, a virginity test might typically involve an examination of a woman by a medical practitioner to establish the unbroken state of her hymen or otherwise ascertain her virginal or non-virginal status. In romance literature, on the other hand, virginity testing is more "romantic," with little or no reference to the hymen or medical procedures and, in Middle English romance, the use of magic.

Floris contains a detailed description of a two-part virginity test. Every year the emir of Babylon selects a new wife from among his harem in a ritual with a virginity test at its core. The maidens are brought down from the harem into the emir's fabulous garden, "the fairest on earth."[57] In the garden is a fountain "of such awesome quality"[58] that,

If any woman approaches [the fountain] who has slept with a man
And she kneels on the ground
To wash her hands,
The water will scream as though it were mad,
And turn as red as blood.
Whichever maiden causes the water to act thus
Shall soon be put to death.
And those that are clean maidens [virgins],
They may wash themselves in the stream.
The water will run silent and clear
It will not cause them any harm.[59]

The test is uncompromising and dramatic. Kelly has noted the parallel between the fountain that runs with blood and screams and the moment that a virgin is penetrated, arguing that the fountain is "capable, apparently, of impersonating the young woman at the precise moment of penetration . . . : that is, what caused her to shed the blood of virginity."[60] The test also indicates that, though the emir appears to be unconcerned about ensuring virginity for the purposes of lineage, as evidenced by the complete lack of children in Babylon, he is careful to test his prospective wives to ensure that they are "clean" and punishes those women who are not with death.[61]

In *Bevis*, Josian is repeatedly put into situations that threaten her virginity, and the tricks and bargains that she uses either to protect her virginity or to prove that she is still a virgin feature prominently in the romance. When forced into an unwanted marriage with Yvor, a suitor chosen by her father, Josian wears an enchanted ring "of such virtue" claiming that, "while I am wearing that ring, / No man shall sexually desire me."[62] After reuniting with Josian after his escape from imprisonment, Bevis discovers that she has been married to Yvor for seven years and asks her "for seven years you have been a queen / And every night a king [lay] next to you / How might you then be a virgin?"[63] Although the narrative has made it clear that Josian is a virgin through use of the ring, Bevis does not know about it (and apparently she does not tell him). Her virginity is not evident, so a test is proposed.

Bevis, with the patriarch's advice to marry a "clean maiden" fresh in his mind, has been told that Josian is married "to be at table and in bed," suggesting that she has been a wife in every sense of the word.[64] She proposes a solution to "prove" her virginity to Bevis, saying "and if you do not find me to be a virgin, / According to what any man can say, / Send me back to my enemies / All naked in only my smock!"[65] Unlike the emir's virginity test, the one proposed by Josian relies not on physical signs of virginity but on verbal testimony; if she can prove beyond any slander or gossip that she is a virgin, then Bevis will accept it. The romance provides further evidence of Josian's virginity in her taming of two lions that attack her and Bevis: a lion not harming virgins is a common trope. Both *Bevis* and *Floris* then, in their insistence on testing virginity, promote the assumption that women *need* to be tested since their virginal status cannot be taken for granted.

The virginity test persists into the modern sheikh romance. A particular test that occurs in at least three sheikh romances is that of visibly proving virginity on a blood-stained sheet following intercourse, a practice referred to in historical and contemporary accounts of virginity testing. The hero of *The Desert Sheikh's Captive Wife* "went very still when he saw the evidence of her lost innocence on the white sheet,"[66] and "the bloodstain on the sheet where he had lain with her"[67] informs the hero of *The Arabian Mistress* that the heroine was a virgin. In *Possessed by the Sheikh*, a bloody sheet is an archaic and traditional aspect of Eastern life; the hero informs the heroine that "it is a tribal custom amongst the nomad population that a blood-stained sheet is produced on the morning after a young woman is married as proof of her virginity."[68] The ultimate virginity test for heroines in sheikh romance, paradoxically, is sex with the hero. In *At the Sheikh's Bidding*, as Erin "was forced to accept the awesome length of his erection," "[Zahir] felt the unmistakeable barrier of her virginity."[69] What the sheikh feels is presumably (and gynecologically suspiciously) her hymen.[70] In *The Sultan's Virgin Bride*, the sign of virginity is more uncertain but still apparent: Tariq apparently realizes that the heroine, Farrah, is a virgin through her body's "instinctive" tightening.[71] This virginity test is paradoxical because the moment that the sheikh realizes that the heroine is a virgin is precisely the moment that she *ceases* to be a virgin. As Kelly states, "in any given narrative, at the very moment virginity can be asserted, it can also be denied."[72] Any proof of virginity identified by penetration during a sex act can only be retrospective, for at the moment that virginity is identified it can simultaneously be disavowed. Encoded in the basis of the penetrative sex act as virginity test, then, is a fundamental ambiguity, since virginity is something that exists only as it is lost.

Virginity tests in medieval romance can be similarly ambiguous and open to interpretation. Kelly suggests that the virginity test in *Floris*, as with many methods of testing virginity, is perhaps not as reliable as it might appear. She draws attention to the second part of the emir's selection process, immediately following identification of virginity in the fountain, in which a flower from the "Tree of Love" falls onto the woman whom the emir will select as his wife.[73] The narrative reveals that this part of the test can and will be manipulated by the emir:

if there is any maiden [there]
Whom the Emir holds in greater value
The flower shall be made to fall onto her
Through cunning and through enchantment.
Thus he [the emir] chooses via the flower
And ever we expect to hear that it shall be Blancheflur [whom he chooses].[74]

Kelly argues that "the two signifiers, fountain and tree, participate in a destabilizing exchange by virtue of their narrative juxtaposition. That a signifier can be so patently false as the tree casts doubt on the signifier immediately preceding it—namely, the fountain."[75] In other words, if the emir can manipulate the second part of the selection process, then the first part might also be manipulated and the maidens' virginity faked.

The virginity test proposed by Josian in *Bevis* seems to be similarly abstruse. Her virginity test hinges not on physical evidence but on a lack of verbal testimony: she is reliant on people *not* saying that she is *not* a virgin. The test is thus something of a reversal: Josian does not propose to prove her virginity actively but asserts that others should try to prove that she is not a virgin. Presumably, even if she had sex with Yvor, she would pass the test if no one spoke up to proclaim that her marriage to him was consummated. This is a test that invites silence. This is not the first time in *Bevis* that verbal testimony has been associated with the proving or disproving of sexual relations. The terms of the proposed test—that Josian should be proven a non-virgin *"according to what any man can say"*—echo the accusation of illicit sex for which Bevis is punished following their first sexual encounter. Although accused of having had "illicit sexual relations" with Josian, "he did nothing but kiss her once," the text declares: *"/ There was nothing else about them that anyone knew."*[76] This rather odd line highlights what is at stake in her virginity test: the sexual state of a body can be verbally discerned. In this romance, sexual encounters seem to be provable (or not) according to the accounts of others, emphasizing the performative nature of sexuality; the state of the sexual body is constructed and hidden or exposed according to verbal testimony.

The test is referred to twice more at significant moments in the romance. In the first moment, Bevis accepts Josian's proposed virginity test: "I willingly concede to that agreement!"[77] Later in the romance, he wins a tournament at Aumberforce, and the maiden there proposes that he live chastely with her as her "lord" for seven years.[78] Bevis replies using the same words that he used earlier to agree to Josian's virginity test. This uncommon reference to male chastity thus collocates directly with female virginity, supporting Kelly's point that male virginity is "made intelligible only by reference to an elaborate feminized and feminizing signifiying system."[79] That we should be so forcefully reminded of Josian's strange virginity test at a moment when Bevis's own chastity is under threat cannot be coincidental. Perhaps the repetition serves to remind us of her promise at a moment when Bevis himself makes a similar vow. However, I suggest that, because Josian's test relies on the unstable testimony of others, which has already been shown to be unreliable in the false accusation of her "deflowering," the repetition of Bevis' words imbues this new chastity agreement with the same instability to which Josian's was subjected, casting doubt on his own promise of chastity.

The second moment when Josian's virginity test is alluded to occurs after Josian has killed Miles, her unwanted third husband, and is condemned to be burned to death. As Bevis rides up to rescue her, she is described on the pyre, where "she stood naked in her smock," an almost direct reference to her earlier proposed punishment for *not* being a virgin.[80] Aside from the original virginity agreement, this is the only time that the word *smock* is used in the entire romance. I am not arguing that the text suggests here that Josian is not a virgin. But by drawing our attention back to her original virginity test at a moment when her virginity can be perceived by Bevis to have been at risk once again (from her marriage to Miles), *Bevis* underscores the importance of virginity while revealing that the terms of the agreement, like many virginity tests, elude clear interpretation. In modern sheikh romance, too, virginity tests can be cheated. On some occasions, believing that the heroine is not a virgin, the hero will attempt to fake the proof by bleeding onto a sheet himself. In *Possessed by the Sheikh*, the hero cuts his arm and holds the sheet "against the cut,"[81] and the hero of *The Arabian Mistress* murmurs "I will cut myself and smear blood on the sheet."[82] The sheikh's falsifying of the virginity test is ironic since the heroine in each case is a virgin yet; as Kelly points out, just as the loss of virginity can be faked, so too can a sexually experienced woman simulate virginity.[83] This is precisely what the sheikh hero believes the heroine is doing; as I pointed out earlier, he does not believe that she is a virgin because she is Western.

Furthermore, if virginity is performative, enacted through visible signs on the body, then it is possible for false virginity to be displayed. Tamar Jeffers McDonald highlights the precariousness of having sexual experience or inexperience legible on the female body, for once virginity is legible it can be counterfeited.[84] According to the sheikh, the heroine is performing promiscuous, Western sexuality and therefore *cannot* be a virgin. Although he is pleasantly surprised to discover that she actually *is* a virgin, the fact that he misinterprets her earlier sexual performance suggests that it can equally be possible to misread the performance of virginity: in other words, for someone who is *not* a virgin to believably perform virginity. Kelly argues that, "in the end, all tests for verifying virginity are inherently flawed."[85] Certainly, the tests in *Bevis*, *Floris*, and these six modern sheikh romances seem to be rooted more in uncertainty than in certainty.

VIRGINITY AS LOSS AND POSSESSION

If virginity tests are fundamentally unreliable—if their primary function of identifying the presence or absence of virginity cannot be relied on—then they must have another function in these romances. I suggest that, though these retrospective, liminal tests might not be reliable as clear indicators of virginity, they do indicate what is at stake in a discourse that positions women as the possessions of men to whom they have "lost" their virginity. Virginity testing in these romances is part of a system whereby men control female sexuality. In *Floris* and *Bevis*, it is men who threaten and demand virginity and, in the case of the emir's manipulation of the test, men who control it. Equally, in modern romance, it is the sheikh's responsibility to confirm or deny virginity; it is the sheikh who proposes faking the test by bleeding onto a sheet, and it is the penetrative intercourse that he proposes that ultimately reveals the heroine's virginity.

Loss is integral to virginity in sheikh romance; deploying penetrative intercourse as a test indicates how the test for virginity and the loss of virginity are one and the same. Doreen Owens Malek suggests that virgins are so persistent in romance because their transition into womanhood, in other words their loss of virginity, is what is fascinating and appealing about the romance.[86] The revelation of virginity goes hand in hand with an assumption of male possession of the heroine. Some romance heroes express a desire for virginity that connects the loss of virginity at the moment of testing with male possession. Although they do not expect heroines to be virgins, sheikhs are "very pleased" when they are.[87] For Tariq, "the knowledge that he'd been the first and only man to experience the seductive passion of Farrah Tyndall brought a soft smile of masculine satisfaction to his face."[88] Similarly, Zahir feels "primitive possessiveness" following his discovery of Erin's virginal status.[89]

Losing her virginity means that the heroine is now positioned within the romance as a potential wife, mother, or lover; in other words, the virginity test is the means of her transition both into womanhood and into a subordinate position within the heteronormative matrix of the romance, within which the hero maintains hegemonic power. As Susan Gubar indicates in her analysis of "the blank page," bloodstains, representative of the loss of virginity, are a "testimony to the woman . . . as a silent token of exchange"[90] in a discourse in which a bride is property passed from father to husband. For Anke Bernau, the loss of virginity is the mechanism by which a man imprints onto a woman: it is through this imprinting that ownership is transferred from father to husband.[91] This is explicit in *Bevis* and *Floris*: the emir's monetary valuing of Blancheflur's virginal body echoes the wealth in property and lineage that Bevis will gain via Josian's virginity, indicating the value of female virginity in a world of male primogeniture. Although heterosexuality might not have been an organizing principle for gender in the same way that it is considered to be for modern sexuality, medieval gender roles of masculine and feminine were still defined by a social structure in which they were considered oppositional and wielded different levels of power: a structure that resembles the modern institution of heterosexuality. At root, then, virginity matters more to the men in these romances than to the women.

Romance narratives "are crucial sites for the operation of patriarchal ideology"; "the hero, as representative of the phallus and patriarchal power, instigates and controls the heroine's desire, forcing her to recognise and take her place in opposition to his subjectivity—in the place of not-male of the female other."[92] Although Jan Cohn claims that romance novels go some way toward redistributing power between hero and heroine, she simultaneously admits that romances retain "the essential structure of sexual ideology"[93] within which the heroine's virginity and its loss to male virility function as mutually reinforcing signifiers. This reveals that what makes one a woman in romance is the loss of virginity, and it is precisely this loss, I argue, that allows the hero to possess the heroine: she is possessed not because she *is* a virgin but because she is an *ex*-virgin. It is the virginity test's revelation of loss that fundamentally confirms masculine power over female sexuality and, ultimately, over the heroine herself. Thus, the virginity test, in its retrospective inscribing of gender identity in Middle English and modern popular sheikh romance, functions according to a heterosexual model of difference, emphasizing differentiated gender behaviour and upholding a hegemonic system of gender dominance and submission.

CONCLUSION

Romance values virginity. Both medieval romance and modern romance place cultural and, in some cases, monetary worth on female virginity and make a strong case for testing it. Yet both public tests—magical fountains, tame lions, blossom trees, and bloody sheets—and more private tests—penetrative sexual inter-course—are liminal, unstable, or retrospective; some tests indicate virginity only after it is lost, and others can be manipulated, casting doubt on their ability to function as reliable indicators of virginity. Ultimately, testing for virginity functions, in both medieval ro-mance and modern romance, to secure male ownership of women as part of the romance genre's heteronormative gender system; the importance of family and lineage in romance values virginity as part of a system of patriarchal family relations in which the loss of female virginity positions women as brides, wives, and mothers: submissive roles within patriarchal gender relations. This is finally what the discourse of possession in virginity is all about: ensuring ownership of women's bodies and their potential progeny.

Moreover, the connections made in these sheikh romances among virginity, the medieval, and the East is revealing of popular attitudes toward each. Virginity is medieval, both in the parallels between testing in medieval romance and modern romance and in the emphasis on virginity in the romance East as anti-modern and retrograde. In this way, these romances are engaging with precisely the traditional/modern dichotomy that frames contemporary de-bates over virginity testing in parts of Asia and Africa; as Ayse Parla notes in the case of Turkey, virginity exams "are either tolerated, or even championed, for protecting the traditional values of honor, chastity, and virtue; or alternatively, they are condemned as proof of our failure in attaining the desirable degree of modernity."[94] For a series called Modern Romance to dwell so persistently on virginity while, paradoxically, emphasizing the *lack* of modernity in valuing virginity suggests a deeply conflicted attitude toward virginity and virginity testing in contemporary Western romantic fiction.

For contemporary popular romance fiction to construct the "romance East" as a space in which "medieval" virginity can be celebrated echoes the similar practice of situating practices or at-titudes inappropriate today—such as sexual violence—in a distant space, such as the historical past or, indeed, the East.[95] Relegating the valuing and testing of virginity to the East might be in line with current popular ideas about the East, but it also reveals some of the romance genre's motivations for situating this valuing in the fictional romance East. In other words, for the romance genre to celebrate the unequal traditions of heteronormativity, the virginity testing that upholds these traditions must be situated "elsewhere." As much as many Western readers, indicated through countless news and comment pieces, might condemn "foreign" cultures for continuing to conduct virginity tests, the gender hegemony that these tests uphold is clearly evident and even celebrated in our own romantic cultural imagination, as revealed in the pages of some of the most popular contemporary Western fiction.

ACKNOWLEDGEMENT

Parts of this essay have appeared in Amy Burge, *Representing Difference in the Medieval and Modern Orientalist Romance*. New York: Palgrave Macmillan, 2016. Reprinted here with permission from the publisher.

NOTES

1   Roberta L. Krueger, "Introduction," in *The Cambridge Companion to Medieval Romance*, ed. Roberta L. Krueger (Cambridge, UK: Cambridge University Press, 2000), 1.

2   For more on the publishing company, see Jay Dixon, *The Romance Fiction of Mills & Boon, 1909–1990s* (London: UCL Press, 1999), and Joseph McAleer, *Passion's Fortune: The Story of Mills & Boon* (Oxford: Oxford University Press, 1999).

3   Daniel Pollack, "Virginity Testing: International Law and Social Work Perspectives," *International Social Work* 51, 2 (2008): 262.

4   Kathleen Coyne Kelly, *Performing Virginity and Testing Chastity in the Middle Ages* (London: Routledge, 2000), 45.

5   Ibid., 64.

6   Laurie Maguire, "Virginity Tests," in *The Oxford Companion to the Body*, ed. Colin Blakemore and Sheila Jennett (Oxford: Oxford University Press, 2003), http://www.oxfordreference.com/view/10.1093/acref/9780198524038.001.0001/acref-9780198524038-e-999.

7   Hanne Blank, *Virgin: The Untouched History* (New York: Bloomsbury, 2007), 77.

8   Ibid., 90.

9   Kelly, *Performing Virginity*, 63.

10 Anke Bernau, *Virgins: A Cultural History* (London: Granta, 2007), 7; Blank, *Virgin*, 85; Esther Lastique and Helen Rodnite Lemay, "A Medieval Physician's Guide to Virginity," in *Sex in the Middle Ages: A Book of Essays*, ed. Joyce E. Salisbury (New York: Garland, 1991), 59–61.

11 Kelly, *Performing Virginity*, 128–29.

12 Ibid., 30.

13 Blank, *Virgin*, 82.

14 Lastique and Lemay, "A Medieval Physician's Guide to Virginity," 63.

15 Stith Thompson, *Motif-Index of Folk-Literature*, vol. 3 (Bloomington: Indiana University Press, 1996), 411–15.

16 Sarah Salih, *Versions of Virginity in Late Medieval England* (Cambridge, UK: D. S. Brewer, 2001), 21.

17 Blank, *Virgin*, 80.

18 Kelly, *Performing Virginity*, 30. For further descriptions of the variety of testing, see ibid., 63–64, and Blank, *Virgin*, 74–95.

19 I am grateful to Dr. Ebtihal Mahadeen for generously sharing her expertise in this area.

20 Nadera Shalhoub-Kevorkian, "Imposition of Virginity Testing: A Life-Saver or a License to Kill?," *Social Science and Medicine* 60, 6 (2005): 1195.

21 Martina W. Frank et al., "Virginity Examinations in Turkey: Role of Forensic Physicians in Controlling Female Sexuality," *Journal of the American Medical Association* 281, 5 (1999): 485.

22 Ayse Parla, "The 'Honor' of the State: Virginity Examinations in Turkey," *Feminist Studies* 27, 1 (2001): 84.

23 Altan Eşsizoğlu et al., "Double Standard for Traditional Value of Virginity and Premarital Sexuality in Turkey: A University Students Case," *Women and Health* 51 (2011): 138.

24 Louise Vincent, "Virginity Testing in South Africa: Re-Traditioning the Postcolony," *Culture, Health, and Sexuality* 8, 1 (2006): 17.

25 Charles Sylvester Rankhotha, "Do Traditional Values Entrench Male Supremacy?," *Agenda: Empowering Women for Gender Equity* 59 (2004): 85.

26   Suzanne Leclerc-Madlala, "Virginity Testing: Managing Sexuality in a Maturing HIV/AIDS Epidemic," *Medical Anthropology Quarterly* 15, 4 (2001): 535.

27   Erika R. George, "Virginity Testing and South Africa's HIV/AIDS Crisis: Beyond Rights Universalism and Cultural Relativism toward Health Capabilities," *California Law Review* 96 (2008): 1449–50.

28   Kelly, *Performing Virginity*, 35, 32; Blank, *Virgin*, 85–87, 91.

29   Blank, *Virgin*, 76.

30   Some attention has been paid to male virginity in romance; Kelly, *Performing Virginity*, 91–118, has explored male virginity in relation to female virginity in some medieval literature, and Jonathan A. Allan has considered male virginity in modern popular romance in "Theorising Male Virginity in Popular Romance Novels," *Journal of Popular Romance Studies* 2, 1 (2013), http://jprstudies.org/2011/10/theorising-male-virginity.

31   Sarah Wendell and Candy Tan, quoted in Allan, "Theorising Male Virginity in Popular Romance Novels."

32   The Modern Romance series is Harlequin Mills & Boon's flagship series in the United Kingdom, equivalent to North America's Harlequin Presents . . . and Australia's Sexy series. The first Modern Romance titles were published in July 2000, and in 2010 the series accounted for 28 percent of current sales in Britain. Jenny Hutton, "Re: Query about Sheikh Modern Romance," email message to the author, January 5, 2010.

33   I follow the romances themselves here in defining a "foreign" hero as one who hails from a country other than Britain, the United States, Canada, or Australia.

34   Of the 115 Modern Romance novels published with Greek heroes, at least sixty-five have virgin heroines, and from a total of sixty-nine novels with Spanish heroes a minimum of forty-five feature heroines who are virgins.

35   Lynne Graham, *The Arabian Mistress* (Richmond: Harlequin Mills & Boon, 2001), 92.

36   Lucy Monroe, *The Sheikh's Bartered Bride* (Richmond: Harlequin Mills & Boon, 2004), 94.

37   Penny Jordan, *Possessed by the Sheikh* (Richmond: Harlequin Mills & Boon, 2005), 153.

38   This draws on contemporary Middle Eastern attitudes that consider the West as "both the home and exporter of vice"; Derek Hopwood, *Sexual*

Encounters in the Middle East: The British, the French, and the Arabs (Reading, UK: Ithaca Press, 1999), 277.

39 Chantelle Shaw, *At the Sheikh's Bidding* (Richmond: Harlequin Mills & Boon, 2008), 116.

40 Graham, *The Arabian Mistress*, 179.

41 A significant difference between medieval and modern romance is the emphasis on religion. In Middle English romance, the difference between East and West is centred on religion (the West is Christian, the East is Muslim). Contemporary romance novels, however, elide any overt reference to religion, preferring to indicate difference through references to ethnicity or culture. For an extended discussion, see Burge, *Representing Difference in the Medieval and Modern Orientalist Romance*.

42 *Floris* is extant in four manuscripts, none of which is complete, that date from the late thirteenth century and the early fourteenth century. Erik Kooper, ed., *Sentimental and Humorous Romances:* Floris and Blancheflour, Sir Degrevant, *the* Squire of Low Degree, *the* Tournament of Tottenham, *and the* Feast of Tottenham (Kalamazoo, MI: Medieval Institute Publications, 2006), 13. *Bevis* is extant in an extraordinary eight manuscripts; for a comprehensive list of extant manuscript and print versions of *Bevis* to 1711, see Jennifer Fellows, "The Middle English and Renaissance *Bevis*: A Textual Survey," in *Sir Bevis of Hampton in Literary Tradition*, ed. Jennifer Fellows and Ivana Djordjević (Cambridge, UK: D. S. Brewer, 2008), 80–113. A full facsimile of Edinburgh, National Library of Scotland, Advocates 19.2.1 (the Auchinleck manuscript), which was produced in London in the 1330s and contains an unusual number of romances in Middle English, is available on the website of the National Library of Scotland, http://auchinleck.nls.uk/.

43 Kim M. Phillips, "Four Virgins' Tales: Sex and Power in Medieval Law," in *Medieval Virginities*, ed. Anke Bernau, Ruth Evans, and Sarah Salih (Cardiff: University of Wales Press, 2003), 86.

44 Kooper, *Sentimental and Humorous Romances*, 484, 584. All references to *Floris* are from the Auchinleck version (with 366 early lines supplemented from London, British Library, Egerton 2862) in Kooper, and all translations are my own. Casting women as goods and men as merchants is a trope that has been analyzed by Kathleen Coyne Kelly in "The Bartering of Blauncheflur in the Middle English *Floris and Blauncheflur*," *Studies in Philology* 91, 2 (1994): 101–10.

45 "muche catell and goode"; Kooper, *Sentimental and Humorous Romances*, 150.

46 "sevyn sythes of gold her wyght, / For he thought, without weene, / That faire mayde have to queene" (ibid., 196–98).

47 "mayde clene" (ibid., 59).

48 Kelly, *Performing Virginity*, 8.

49 *The Middle English Dictionary* explains that a patriarch was "the bishop of one of the chief sees of Antioch, Alexandria, Constantinople, Rome, or Jerusalem." See "Patriarke," in *Middle English Dictionary* (Ann Arbor: University of Michigan, 2001), http://quod.lib.umich.edu/cgi/m/mec/med-idx?type=id&id=MED32636.

50 "forbed him upon his lif, / That he never toke wif, / Boute she were clene maide"; Ronald B. Herzman, Graham Drake, and Eve Salisbury, eds., *Four Romances of England:* King Horn, Havelock the Dane, Bevis of Hampton, Athelston (Kalamazoo, MI: Medieval Institute Publications, 1999), 1967–69). All references to *Bevis* are from the Auchinleck version edited by Herzman et al., and all translations are my own.

51 "lay hire a night be me side" (ibid., 924); "to a weine-pain, that is fordrive!" (ibid., 926); "under covertour" (ibid., 3184); "make hire dronke a bedde" (ibid., 3190); "have is wille" (ibid., 3161).

52 "[his] doughter . . .forlain" (ibid., 1209); "lovede" (ibid., 569); "king of Sarasine" (ibid., 1071).

53 We could apply here the idea of "temporary virginity" that Felicity Riddy reads in *Le Bone Florence of Rome*—neither romance is about the heroine preserving her virginity forever but about protecting it long enough to lose it to the correct person. Felicity Riddy, "Temporary Virginity and the Everyday Body: *Le Bone Florence of Rome* and Bourgeois Self-Making," in *Pulp Fictions of Medieval England: Essays in Popular Romance*, ed. Nicola McDonald (Manchester: Manchester University Press, 2004), 197–216.

54 Sarah Salih, Anke Bernau, and Ruth Evans, "Introduction: Virginities and Virginity Studies," in *Medieval Virginities*, ed. Anke Bernau, Ruth Evans, and Sarah Salih (Cardiff: University of Wales Press, 2003), 2.

55 Kelly, *Performing Virginity*, 133.

56 Ibid., 134.

57 "the fairest of al middelhard"; Kooper, *Sentimental and Humorous Romances*, 649.

58 "of so mochel eye" (ibid., 664).

59   "Yif ther cometh ani maiden that is forleie, / And hi bowe to the grounde / For to waschen here honde, / The water wille yelle als hit ware wod, / And bicome on hire so red so blod. / Wich maiden the water fareth on so, / Hi schal sone be fordo. / And thilke that beth maidenes clene, / Thai mai hem wassche of the rene. / The water wille erne stille and cler, / Nelle hit hem make no daunger" (ibid., 665–75).

60   Kelly, *Performing Virginity*, 9.

61   There are several examples of wells or fountains being used to measure virginity. They include two wells (one muddy, one clear) being used as a chastity index; a well that, if an unchaste woman were to dip her arms into it, would boil her skin away; and a spring that wells up if the woman is not a virgin; Thompson, *Motif-Index of Folk-Literature*, 412. The association of wells with virginity is also present in *Bevis*, in which the hero is healed in well water in which a virgin had bathed.

62   "of swiche vertu"; "while ichave on that ilche ring, / To me schel no man have welling"; Herzman et al., *Four Romances of England*, 1470–72. Kelly, *Performing Virginity*, 66–67, notes that magic rings were commonly used in literature for the preservation of virginity.

63   "thow havest seve year ben a quene, / And everi night a king be thee: / How mightow thanne maide be?"; Herzman et al., *Four Romances of England*, 2198–2200.

64   "bothe to bord and to bedde" (ibid., 2012).

65   "boute thee finde me maide wimman, / Be that eni man saie can, / Send me aghen to me fon / Al naked in me smok alon!" (ibid., 2203–06).

66   Lynne Graham, *The Desert Sheikh's Captive Wife* (Richmond: Harlequin Mills & Boon, 2007), 151.

67   Ibid., 94.

68   Jordan, *Possessed by the Sheikh*, 101.

69   Shaw, *At the Sheikh's Bidding*, 125.

70   For a critique of the representation of the hymen in romance, see Sarah Wendell and Candy Tan, *Beyond Heaving Bosoms: The Smart Bitches' Guide to Romance Novels* (New York: Fireside, 2009), 27, 37–40.

71   Sarah Morgan, *The Sultan's Virgin Bride* (Richmond: Harlequin Mills & Boon, 2006), 126.

72   Kelly, *Performing Virginity*, 1.

73   "Tree of Love"; Kooper, *Sentimental and Humorous Romances*, 678.

74 "And yif ther ani maiden is / That th'Amerail halt of mest pris, / The flour schal on here be went / Thourh art and thourgh enchantement. / Thous he cheseth thourgh the flour, / And evere we herkneth when hit be Blauncheflur" (ibid., 684–89).

75 Kelly, *Performing Virginity*, 9.

76 "forlain"; Herzman et al., *Four Romances of England*, 1209; "he dede nothing, boute ones hire kiste, / *Nought elles bi hem men ne wiste*" (ibid., 1213–14; emphasis added).

77 "in that forward I graunte wel!" (ibid., 2208).

78 "lord" (ibid., 3836).

79 Kelly, *Performing Virginity*, 93.

80 "in hire smok she stod naked"; Herzman et al., *Four Romances of England*, 3289.

81 Jordan, *Possessed by the Sheikh*, 101.

82 Graham, *The Desert Sheikh's Captive Wife*, 93.

83 Kelly, *Performing Virginity*, 128.

84 Tamar Jeffers McDonald, "Introduction," in *Virgin Territory: Representing Sexual Inexperience in Film*, ed. Tamar Jeffers McDonald (Detroit: Wayne State University Press, 2010), 6.

85 Kelly, *Performing Virginity*, 18.

86 Doreen Owens Malek, "Loved I Not Honor More: The Virginal Heroine in Romance," in *Dangerous Men and Adventurous Women: Romance Writers on the Appeal of the Romance*, ed. Jayne Ann Krentz (Philadelphia: University of Pennsylvania Press, 1992), 118.

87 Graham, *The Arabian Mistress*, 104.

88 Morgan, *The Sultan's Virgin Bride*, 127.

89 Shaw, *At the Sheikh's Bidding*, 127.

90 Susan Gubar, "'The Blank Page' and the Issues of Female Creativity," *Critical Inquiry* 8, 2 (1981): 254.

91 Bernau, *Virgins*, 78–79.

92 Teresa L. Ebert, "The Romance of Patriarchy: Ideology, Subjectivity, and Postmodern Feminist Cultural Theory," *Cultural Critique* 10 (1998): 21, 40.

93 Jan Cohn, *Romance and the Erotics of Property: Mass-Market Fiction for Women* (Durham: Duke University Press, 1998), 36.

94 Parla, "The 'Honor' of the State," 66.

95　See Amy Burge, "Do Knights Still Rescue Damsels in Distress? Reimagining the Medieval in the Mills & Boon Historical Romance," in *The Female Figure in Contemporary Historical Fiction*, ed. Katherine Cooper and Emma Short (Basingstoke: Palgrave Macmillan, 2012), 95–114.

REFERENCES

Allan, Jonathan A. "Theorising Male Virginity in Popular Romance Novels." *Journal of Popular Romance Studies* 2, 1 (2013), http://jprstudies. org/2011/10/theorising-male-virginity.

Bernau, Anke. *Virgins: A Cultural History*. London: Granta Books, 2007.

Blank, Hanne. *Virgin: The Untouched History*. New York: Bloomsbury, 2007.

Burge, Amy. "Do Knights Still Rescue Damsels in Distress? Reimagining the Medieval in the Mills & Boon Historical Romance." In *The Female Figure in Contemporary Historical Fiction*, edited by Katherine Cooper and Emma Short, 95–114. Basingstoke: Palgrave Macmillan, 2012.

———. *Representing Difference in the Medieval and Modern Orientalist Romance*. New York: Palgrave Macmillan, 2016.

Cohn, Jan. *Romance and the Erotics of Property: Mass-Market Fiction for Women*. Durham: Duke University Press, 1998.

Dixon, Jay. *The Romance Fiction of Mills & Boon, 1909–1990s*. London: UCL Press, 1999.

Ebert, Teresa L. "The Romance of Patriarchy: Ideology, Subjectivity, and Postmodern Feminist Cultural Theory." *Cultural Critique* 10 (1988): 19–57.

Eşsizoğlu, Altan, Aziz Yasan, Ejder Akgun Yildirim, Faruk Gurgen, and Mustafa Ozkan. "Double Standard for Traditional Value of Virginity and Premarital Sexuality in Turkey: A University Students Case." *Women and Health* 51 (2011): 136–50.

Fellows, Jennifer. "The Middle English and Renaissance *Bevis*: A Textual Survey." In *Sir Bevis of Hampton in Literary Tradition*, edited by Jennifer Fellows and Ivana Djordjević, 80–113. Cambridge, UK: D. S. Brewer, 2008.

Frank, Martina W., Heidi M. Bauer, Nadir Arican, Sebnem Korur Fincanci, and Vincent Iacopino. "Virginity Examinations in Turkey: Role of Forensic Physicians in Controlling Female Sexuality." *Journal of the American Medical Association* 282, 5 (1999): 485–90.

George, Erika R. "Virginity Testing and South Africa's HIV/AIDS Crisis: Beyond Rights Universalism and Cultural Relativism toward Health Capabilities." *California Law Review* 96 (2008): 1447–1518.

Graham, Lynne. *The Arabian Mistress*. Richmond: Harlequin Mills & Boon, 2001.

———. *The Desert Sheikh's Captive Wife*. Richmond: Harlequin Mills & Boon, 2007.

Gubar, Susan. "'The Blank Page' and the Issues of Female Creativity." *Critical Inquiry* 8, 2 (1981): 243–63.

Herzman, Ronald B., Graham Drake, and Eve Salisbury, eds. *Four Romances of England:* King Horn, Havelock the Dane, Bevis of Hampton, Athelston. Kalamazoo, MI: Medieval Institute Publications, 1999.

Hopwood, Derek. *Sexual Encounters in the Middle East: The British, the French, and the Arabs*. Reading, UK: Ithaca Press, 1999.

Jordan, Penny. *Possessed by the Sheikh*. Richmond: Harlequin Mills & Boon, 2005.

———. *Virgin for the Billionaire's Taking*. Richmond: Harlequin Mills & Boon, 2008.

Kelly, Kathleen Coyne. "The Bartering of Blauncheflur in the Middle English *Floris and Blauncheflur*." *Studies in Philology* 91, 2 (1994): 101–10.

———. *Performing Virginity and Testing Chastity in the Middle Ages*. London: Routledge, 2000.

Kooper, Erik, ed. *Sentimental and Humorous Romances:* Floris and Blancheflour, Sir Degrevant, *the* Squire of Low Degree, *the* Tournament of Tottenham, *and the* Feast of Tottenham. Kalamazoo, MI: Medieval Institute Publications, 2006.

Krueger, Roberta L. "Introduction." In *The Cambridge Companion to Medieval Romance*, edited by Roberta L. Krueger, 1–9. Cambridge, UK: Cambridge University Press, 2000.

Lastique, Esther, and Helen Rodnite Lemay. "A Medieval Physician's Guide to Virginity." In *Sex in the Middle Ages: A Book of Essays*, edited by Joyce E. Salisbury, 56–79. New York: Garland, 1991.

Leclerc-Madlala, Suzanne. "Virginity Testing: Managing Sexuality in a Maturing HIV/AIDS Epidemic." *Medical Anthropology Quarterly* 15, 4 (2001): 533–52.

Maguire, Laurie. "Virginity Tests." In *The Oxford Companion to the Body*, edited by Colin Blakemore and Sheila Jennett. Oxford: Oxford University Press, 2003. http://www.oxfordreference.com/view/10.1093/acref/9780198524038.001.0001/acref-9780198524038-e-999.

McAleer, Joseph. *Passion's Fortune: The Story of Mills & Boon*. Oxford: Oxford University Press, 1999.

McDonald, Tamar Jeffers. "Introduction." In *Virgin Territory: Representing Sexual Inexperience in Film*, edited by Tamar Jeffers McDonald, 1–14. Detroit: Wayne State University Press, 2010.

Monroe, Lucy. *The Sheikh's Bartered Bride*. Richmond: Harlequin Mills & Boon, 2004.

Morgan, Sarah. *The Sultan's Virgin Bride*. Richmond: Harlequin Mills & Boon, 2006.

Owens Malek, Doreen. "Loved I Not Honor More: The Virginal Heroine in Romance." In *Dangerous Men and Adventurous Women: Romance Writers on the Appeal of the Romance, edited by Jayne Ann Krentz, 115–20. Philadelphia: University of Pennsylvania Press, 1992.

Parla, Ayse. "The 'Honor' of the State: Virginity Examinations in Turkey." Feminist Studies 27, 1 (2001): 65–88.

"Patriarke." In Middle English Dictionary. Ann Arbor: University of Michigan, 2001. http://quod.lib.umich.edu/cgi/m/mec/med-idx?type=id&id=MED32636.

Phillips, Kim M. "Four Virgins' Tales: Sex and Power in Medieval Law." In Medieval Virginities, edited by Anke Bernau, Ruth Evans, and Sarah Salih, 80–101. Cardiff: University of Wales Press, 2003.

Pollack, Daniel. "Virginity Testing: International Law and Social Work Perspectives." International Social Work 51, 2 (2008): 262–67.

Rankhotha, Charles Sylvester. "Do Traditional Values Entrench Male Supremacy?" Agenda: Empowering Women for Gender Equity 59 (2004): 80–89.

Riddy, Felicity. "Temporary Virginity and the Everyday Body: Le Bone Florence of Rome and Bourgeois Self-Making." In Pulp Fictions of Medieval England: Essays in Popular Romance, edited by Nicola McDonald, 197–216. Manchester: Manchester University Press, 2004.

Salih, Sarah. Versions of Virginity in Late Medieval England. Cambridge, UK: D. S. Brewer, 2001.

Salih, Sarah, Anke Bernau, and Ruth Evans. "Introduction: Virginities and Virginity Studies." In Medieval Virginities, edited by Anke Bernau, Ruth Evans, and Sarah Salih, 1–13. Cardiff: University of Wales Press, 2003.

Shalhoub-Kevorkian, Nadera. "Imposition of Virginity Testing: A Life-Saver or a License to Kill?" Social Science and Medicine 60, 6 (2005): 1187–96.

Shaw, Chantelle. At the Sheikh's Bidding. Richmond: Harlequin Mills & Boon, 2008.

Thompson, Stith. Motif-Index of Folk-Literature. Vol. 3. Bloomington: Indiana University Press, 1996.

Vincent, Louise. "Virginity Testing in South Africa: Re-Traditioning the Postcolony." Culture, Health, and Sexuality 8, 1 (2006): 17–30.

Wendell, Sarah, and Candy Tan. Beyond Heaving Bosoms: The Smart Bitches' Guide to Romance Novels. New York: Fireside, 2009.

CHAPTER 2
BETWEEN PLEASURE AND PAIN: THE TEXTUAL POLITICS OF THE HYMEN

Jodi McAlister

n "The Double Session" in *Dissemination*, Jacques Derrida theorizes the hymen as a "protective screen, the jewel box of virginity, the vaginal partition, the fine, invisible veil which stands *between* the inside and the outside of a woman, and consequently between desire and fulfilment."[1] He uses the term "hymen" in two senses: first, as a barrier; second, as a consummation. As such, the hymen becomes both the barrier to consummation and consummation itself: it stands between these two things yet is somehow part and not part of both of them—a fusion as well as an obstruction. It is at once permanently on the brink of destruction and somehow indestructible, a sort of reification of absence, at once a literal object and a melting or melding together of two disparate ideas. In this sense, it functions, as it so often has in cultural discourse, as a literal representation of female virginity, that cultural idea so often thought of as an object yet also an identity based upon *not* doing.[2]

Because Derrida's notion of the hymen at once stands between (presumably male) desire and fulfillment and represents the blurring of these two things, it is unsurprising that Derrida does not devote a great deal of space to the possibility of the hymen being broken.

He writes that the hymen only takes place when it does not take place, when there is a consummation without violence, when a veil that does not exist is torn.[3] In this sense, the hymen, for him, is not only undecidable but also imperforate: if it is penetrated, he seems to argue, it never really existed in the first place.

Essentially, the Derridean hymen is elusive, being both there and not there. I do not want to rely heavily here on the double meaning of the hymen that Derrida employs, but I have begun with his theorization for a reason: it highlights a sort of slipperiness in the discourse that surrounds the hymen. Even if we remove this idea of the hymen as consummation and think of it simply as a membrane covering the vaginal opening, it remains problematic. Kathleen Coyne Kelly writes that "the hymen is notoriously an unstable and ambiguous concept, with an anxious and uncertain history,"[4] and she is correct: although it can theoretically offer proof of a woman's virginity, in practice it is more fraught. In "conventional" understanding, the hymen is supposed to be broken upon the first experience of penetrative heterosex, thus constituting female virginity loss. Although the physical reality is more complex (and, perhaps more importantly, idiosyncratic, for some women do not possess hymens at all), it is arguably the spiritual or emotional dimension that is more problematic. Virginity loss is figured in Western literature and culture as intrinsically transformative: that is, breaking the hymen should have a tangible effect on the woman, and her virginity loss should be written not only on her body (usually via bleeding) but also on her psyche. As Tassie Gwilliam writes, there is supposed to be a "congruence between the crossing of a physical border—the hymen—and the crossing of a spiritual or metaphorical border—the move from innocence to experience or from innocence to degradation."[5] Similarly, the notion of virginity as an entity that can be bought and sold seems to signal that there is an innate worth in the hymen that disappears once it has been broken, transforming the (now ex-)virgin's worth. But the hymen's elusiveness reflects anxieties about the readability of the female body that have persistently plagued Western culture and literature: how can one really determine if a woman is a virgin or not? Virginity loss is regularly figured in popular discourse as something deeply transformative for the woman, but the instability of the hymen is a reflection of the instability of this idea. The cultural and literary idea of the hymen does not reflect its reality, to the extent that, when it is represented in literature, it is regularly located in an anatomically incorrect position.[6]

The hymen has not always functioned as the locus around which anxieties over proving female virginity have revolved. In the medieval period in Europe, the female body was still considered readable, but it was largely the uterus that was considered the signifier of virginity. The blood of first intercourse was considered the sign *par excellence* of virginity loss, but it was figured not as hymeneal blood but as blood resulting from a reshaping of the uterine passage.[7] Other virginity tests also existed in both literature and life. Some were pseudo-medical, involving an examination of the shape of the uterus, of the direction in which the woman's breasts pointed, or of the colour of her urine. Some were pseudo-magical: she might have been asked, for example, to drink from a magic cup or carry a sieve full of water.[8] These magical tests demonstrate the idea that virginity was more than just physical in this period; it was also a spiritual condition.

This began to change in the sixteenth and seventeenth centuries as virginity increasingly became a medicalized (and commercialized) phenomenon. The word *hymen* was first used in the fifteenth century by Michael Savonarola, who wrote that "the cervix is covered by a subtle membrane called the hymen, which is broken at the time of deflowering, so that the blood flows."[9] The precise nature and even existence of the hymen were not agreed on; however, it began to appear increasingly in medical texts of the sixteenth and seventeenth centuries.[10] Humoral medicine was in fashion during this period. This kind of medicine regularly required the evacuation of fluid from the body.[11] Some virgins were said to be affected by chlorosis or "green-sickness," for which marriage was recommended as the cure,[12] reasoning that fluids such as menstrual blood were being obstructed by the hymen, and thus the cure was its destruction. We can see this represented in the sections below from the 1682 ballad "A Remedy for the Green Sickness":

A handsome buxom lass lay panting on her bed,
She looked as green as grass, and mournfully she said:
Except I have some lusty lad to ease me of my pain,
I cannot live, I sigh and grieve,
My life I now disdain.
. . .

A gallant lively lad that in the next room lay,
It made his heart full glad to hear what she did say.
Into the room immediately this youngster he did rush,
Some words he spoke,
Love to provoke,
But she straight cried out, Hush!

My father he will hear and then we're both undone,
Quoth he, love do not fear, I'll venture for a son.
The coverlet he then threw off and jumped into the bed,
And in a trice,
He kissed her twice,
Then to his chamber fled.

And blushing all alone this damsel sweating lay,
Her troubles they were gone, thus softly did she say:
Had I but known that lover's bliss
Had been so sweet a taste,
I'd ne'er have stayed,
Nor begged nor prayed,
That so much time did waste.[13]

We can see represented here not only the cure for green-sickness but also the pathologization of maintained virginity that existed during the sixteenth and seventeenth centuries.[14] Hanne Blank notes that it is an interesting coincidence that green-sickness was so often diagnosed during the period in which Protestantism, with its emphasis on marriage as the ideal state, became popular in Europe.[15] We can also see ideas of virginity loss as transformative: not only is the girl in question immediately cured of her green-sickness, but also her sexual appetite immediately becomes voracious. The poem ends with her dreaming about the boy who has deflowered her and planning to offer him money to sleep with her again. (This notion of the deflowered virgin who immediately becomes a nymphomaniac is one of the most common articulations of the idea of virginity loss as transformative: it became a common motif in eighteenth- and nineteenth-century pornography, the hymen functioning as a literal barrier between the virgin and pleasure.)

In the eighteenth century, as ongoing virginity once again became idealized and semi-spiritualized, green-sickness became a fashionable illness from which to suffer.[16] Corrinne Harol suggests that in this period virginity began to disappear from medical texts, only to reappear in fiction, as evidenced by the "defloration mania" that began to bloom in novels in the mid-eighteenth century and continued into the nineteenth century. This is not to say that the hymen disappeared from medical understanding entirely, because that was not the case. As Harol notes, though virginity as a notion was somewhat demedicalized, the hymen remained a subject of "profound interest."[17] She suggests that in this period "fiction is the appropriate mode for discursive representations of virginity, because epistemological and semiotic authority over virginity can be, at least at this time, only an act of the imagination."[18] It would be simplistic to suggest that the demedicalization of virginity was the *only* contributing factor to the popularity of virgins in eighteenth- and nineteenth-century literature (an argument that also ignores the fact that virgins appeared regularly in texts before this period), but it is certainly fascinating to note the discursive shift that occurred. Gwilliam notes that there was an "uneasy conflict between two concepts of virginity. . . . Virginity as a quality competes with the idea of virginity as a body part—the elusive and reclusive hymen."[19] If virginity is a spiritual rather than a medical condition, then the hymen becomes an unstable signifier of virginity loss. In 1730, a letter published in the *Universal Spectator* bemoaned the female practice of reading romances, especially those written by Eliza Haywood and Delarivier Manley: "It grieves me to say it, they [romances] ruin more Virgins than *Masquerades* or *Brothels*. They strike at the very Root of all Virtue, by corrupting the Mind: And tho' every *Romance-reading-Nymph* may not proceed to Overt-Acts,

I hope you do not think her excusable."[20] The idea that virginity, at least in part, is a mental state is reflected here: it can be ruined by reading. As Bernau writes, "loss of virginity begins in the soul and is finalised in the body."[21] Although the hymen is still important here, its penetration still considered a concrete medical sign of virginity loss, it is also a site of anxiety. Even if a woman is *virgo intacta*, what is to say that she is *virgo integra*? Even if virginity can be physically proven, how is it to be proven spiritually? And can it even be physically proven? The fact that the hymen can readily be counterfeited was a pervasive source of cultural angst.[22]

As Harol notes, virginity was a popular trope in eighteenth- and nineteenth-century fiction.[23] However, ideas of the hymen appear in literature much earlier. Although it might not have been explicitly referred to as the hymen, the idea of a physical barrier within a woman that needs to be breached for virginity loss to occur has been reproduced in Western literature for many centuries. For example, in the thirteenth-century romance *Le roman de la rose* (The Romance of the Rose), the male Lover is on a quest to pluck the Rose at the centre of an enchanted garden. It is an unsubtle allegory of defloration:

> I kissed the image very devoutly and then, to enter the sheath safely, wished to put my staff into the aperture, with the sack hanging behind. Indeed I thought that I could shoot it in at the first try, but it came back out. . . . By no effort could it enter there, for, I found, there was a paling in front, which I felt but could not see. . . . I had to assault it vigorously, throw myself against it often, often fail. . . . When I could not immediately break the barrier, I struggled so hard and with such violence that I was drenched in sweat. . . . However, I continued my assault until I noticed a narrow passage. . . . Nothing could have prevented me from sliding my staff all the way in. . . .[24]

The image of the virginal body as closed has been repeated over history. Anke Bernau notes that it is continually referred to as "an enclosed garden, a shut door, a sealed fountain, a fortified castle,"[25] and Kelly notes that this idea might have its roots in the Song of Songs, in which the female body is figured as both a wall and a door, "produced through a series of mystifications as closed, sealed, intact."[26] As the hymen as a textual figure developed, it increasingly became the weak point in this female fortress, the barrier that must be battered down for the deflowerer to reach the treasure within, whether it is an allegorical treasure like the rose or the woman's virginity as an item of commercial value, which became much more common in the eighteenth century.[27] As seen in the excerpt above, breaking this barrier is often a difficult task for the deflowerer, so apparently imperforate is this hymen.

Missing from that text, however, is the virgin's perspective. It can be found in abundant detail in erotic texts published a few hundred years later, texts that eroticize the experience of virginity loss for the woman (presumably for a male audience). In the seventeenth century, pornography often took the form of dialogues between two women.[28] In *A Dialogue between a Married Woman and a Maid* (1655), married woman Tullia describes female anatomy to her curious virginal cousin Octavia:

> Under them [labia minora] about a Finger's Breadth, or more, within, are in Virgins, as thou art, four little rising Buds, which, joining together, and leaving only a little Hole between, stop up the best Part of the Passage into the Womb, and gives all the Trouble Men meet with in deflouring [sic] us, and all the Pain we feel, is upon the breaking thro' them with Violence, for then they fall a Bleeding and smart exceedingly.[29]

Tullia identifies here three ubiquitous things in pornographic defloration scenes: the trouble that men have penetrating the hymen, the extreme pain that it causes the virgin, and blood. The virgin's pain and blood appear to be guarantors of her virginity and mark her transformation from virgin to non-virgin. This is a transformation that the hero has to work hard to effect. In *Memoirs of a Woman of Pleasure*, John Cleland's 1749 pornographic novel, it takes Charles a considerable amount of time to deflower Fanny Hill. He attempts to penetrate her, but "after several vigorous pushes . . . which hurt [her] extremely . . . he made not the least impression." They pause, and he tries again ("he tried again, still no admittance, still no penetration; but he had hurt me yet more") until "at length, after repeated fruitless trials," he is finally successful:

> At length, the tender texture of that tract giving way to such fierce tearing and rending, he pierced something further into me: and now, outrageous and no longer his own master, but borne headlong away by the fury and over-mettle of that member, now exerting itself with a kind of native rage, he breaks in, carries all before him, and one violent merciless lunge, sent it, imbrued, and reeking with virgin blood, up to the very hilt in me. . . . Then! then all my resolution deserted me: I screamed out, and fainted away with the sharpness of the pain; and, as he told me afterwards, on his drawing out, when emission was over with him, my thighs were instantly all in a stream of blood, that flowed from the wounded torn passage.[30]

Fanny's hymen and the hymens of other virgins resist penetration. Even when the virgin in question actively consents to her defloration, virginity does not want to be lost. It must be torn from the body. Virginity loss becomes a battle, and inevitably it is the woman who is wounded, conquered by the man. This casts the hymen as her defence mechanism. In *Making Sex: Body and Gender from the Greeks to Freud*, Thomas Walter Laqueur argues that medical understandings of gender changed greatly over the eighteenth century as men and women came to be understood as different rather than women being understood as flawed versions of men.[31] One of the casualties of this shift was the idea of female pleasure: in the new model, women were generally understood to be relatively passionless.[32] *Memoirs of a Woman of Pleasure* was published before the new understandings of sexuality that Laqueur discusses became prevalent, but the enduring popularity of this incredibly imperforate hymen in literature is certainly interesting when we think about this new image of the woman, who is virtually asexual, devoid of sexual desire, and considered abnormal if she does experience it. The hymen becomes a literalization of this idea: the female body does not want to be penetrated. However, though the deflowerer might have to struggle hard, he is ultimately successful (and, if he is not, he is somehow unmanned). The hymen yields, the feminine yielding to the masculine, and the social gender hierarchy is endorsed. In this sense, the man is still the Lover of *Le roman de la rose*, and the woman's body is still a fortress: something that he must conquer to pluck the Rose within.

The image of the painful, bloody defloration of the virgin with the iron hymen endured into nineteenth- and twentieth-century literature. The following excerpts come from virginity loss scenes in the *Pearl*, a pornographic magazine published in 1879–80. The first is from "Sub-Umbra, or Sport among the She-Noodles," the second from "Lady Pokingham, or They All Do It":

> I kept my affair straight to the mark; then pushing vigorously, the head entered about an inch, till it was chock up to the opposing hymen. She gave a start of pain, but her eyes gazed into mine with a most encouraging look. . . . I gave a ruthless push, just as her bottom heaved up to meet me, and the deed was done. King Priapus had burst through all obstacles to our enjoyment. She gave a subdued shriek of agonized pain, and I felt myself throbbing in possession of her inmost charms.[33]

> Clenching her teeth firmly, and shutting her eyes, she gave another desperate plunge upon William's spear of love, the hymen was broken, and she was fairly impaled to the roots of his affair. But it cost her dear, she fell forward in a dead faint, whilst the trickling blood proved the sanguinary nature of Love's victory.[34]

These passages are interesting in that they use the word *hymen*—the idea was familiar enough to have passed into common parlance, it seems—but otherwise there are considerable similarities between the virginity loss experiences represented in these pornographic texts and

Fanny's virginity loss in *Memoirs of a Woman of Pleasure* more than 100 years earlier. The virgin still experiences a considerable amount of pain, she still bleeds (though it is not mentioned in the passage cited from "Sub-Umbra," the hero keeps a handkerchief soaked in the virgin's blood), and it is still difficult for the deflowerer to break her hymen. This last feature of the pornographic defloration scene seems to be the most variable—sometimes, as in the passages above, the deflowerer has considerable trouble, whereas other times it is relatively easy. The following passage is also from "Lady Pokingham": "His onset was too impetuous to be withstood, and she lay in such a passive favourable position that the network of her hymen was broken at the first charge, and he was soon in full possession up to the roots of his hair."[35] This is the element of virginity loss that seems to have changed the most over time. It seems to be nearly impossible for Charles to deflower Fanny, so resistant is her body to his penetration. The virginal body still seems to resist invasion in these later texts (even when, as in the first passage from "Lady Pokingham," the virgin in question actively attempts to break her hymen), but the fortress's defences seem to have been weakened. The Lover no longer has to struggle so hard to pluck the Rose. The body of the late-nineteenth-century virgin, it seems, is more willing to be deflowered—interesting, given the Victorian idea of the woman being "not very much troubled by sexual feeling of any kind,"[36] but perhaps not surprising, for motherhood (and thus defloration) were considered to be the woman's ideal state.

In the twentieth and twenty-first centuries, the popular romance genre has been one of the most common homes for explicit defloration scenes. This is a genre written largely by women for women,[37] whereas the pornographic texts I have hitherto discussed were written by men presumably for men. The significance of this fact should not be overlooked and deserves considerably more space than I can give it here. However, perhaps despite this fact, scenes of virginity loss bear considerable similarities to those that came before them. Although there is a huge variation in the ways in which virginity loss is portrayed across the popular romance genre (varying not only between authors and subgenres but also over time as the genre evolved and changed), the hymen is regularly represented, its penetration causing the virgin heroine pain and often making her bleed. The former is perhaps the most ubiquitous element, as demonstrated in the excerpts below, which come from Harlequin Mills & Boon romances from the 2000s:

> She felt him push into her, felt her inner muscles contract around him, felt the glorious fullness moving slowly onward, meeting the resistance of her virginity, pausing. . . . He surged through the thin barrier—only the slightest sense of tearing, swiftly soothed by the fierce satisfaction of feeling him move past it, going deeper, deeper, filling the empty ache, replacing it with an ecstatic sense of completion.[38]

> [She was] stunned by the stretch, the sting of pain.
> He pressed harder and again she felt him pull and stretch her. Was this how it felt for everyone? Did it always hurt like this?
> Fighting panic, Joelle took a breath, exhaled, tried to relax. And as she . . .told herself to relax, this was normal, he was just breaking through the hymen, she felt him thrust forward hard. Harder than she expected. Hard enough her eyes smarted, tears suddenly welling.[39]

> His groan of pleasure was cut short when she gave a sharp cry of pain.
> Raul stilled, paralysed with shock. *Dio!* It was impossible. He must have imagined the sensation of pushing through a fragile barrier. But she felt so tight around him. . . . But she could *not* be a virgin, his brain pointed out, the idea was inconceivable.[40]

All of these heroines feel pain (like many other—though not all—heroines in the genre), but it is not the pain of the earlier pornographic virgins, who regularly passed out because of the agony of their virginity loss. There is nowhere near as much emphasis on blood—Joelle, the heroine of the second passage, bleeds, but it is nothing more than a "faint red stain."[41] Other virginal heroines of the romance genre bleed more, but generally virginity loss episodes in modern romances are nowhere near as gory as their earlier pornographic counterparts, perhaps largely because of the difference in audience. The most noticeable change, however, is in the effort that it takes the man in question to deflower the virgin. The hymen here is a "fragile" and "thin" barrier. It exists—and the hero is literally able to feel its existence—but it is so ephemeral that he can almost convince himself that it is imaginary. Although the heroine's virginity is important, and her hymen is a major textual presence, her body no longer resists penetration in any major way.

Perhaps this is because the text is focused on the female experience: the heroine is ready for sex and has consented to it in a meaningful way, her mental state translated into her physical one. These texts are also contemporary, written in a time period in which social consequences of virginity loss are not as potent as they were for eighteenth- and nineteenth-century virgins. In these modern texts, the heroine's ongoing virginity is often portrayed as more socially taboo: "How pathetic to still be a virgin!" one heroine moans, calling her virginity a "humiliating, futile hangover from the past."[42] This is particularly interesting if we read these texts alongside erotic historical romances, especially those written in the early days of the genre (the 1970s and 1980s). In these texts, in which the heroine faces greater social consequences for virginity loss, often there is more emphasis on blood, and her hymen seems to be more imperforate. Such scenes are ubiquitous enough that Sarah Wendell and Candy Tan parody them in their book *Beyond Heaving Bosoms: The Smart Bitches' Guide to Romance Novels*:

> Suddenly he felt the tip of his eager manhood brush against her maidenhead. . . . "It will only hurt but a moment, and then it will be gone," he said. Then he reared back as if he and his man-staff were jumping hedges at full gallop, and thrust himself deep within her.
>
> Eleanora screamed as if she'd been impaled upon a pikestaff, beating his shoulders with her fists and crying out from the pain.[43]

Interestingly, in these historical romances, even though the hymeneal barrier is more imperforate, the idea that the hero has to exert a considerable amount of effort to penetrate it does not regularly appear. Perhaps this is because of the new focus on the female experience. We might also read it as a sign that, though he is the one who deflowers her, he is somehow less involved in her transformation. He no longer has to work to effect a change in her: that change is internal to the virgin in question rather than being effected on her from the outside. Interestingly, in romance, there is considerably less emphasis on the virgin being transformed than there is on the hero being transformed. The romance is focused more on transforming him into an ideal husband as she teaches him to love.[44]

This is not to say that there is no element of transformation for the heroine in the romance genre. The most notable transformation is from pain to pleasure: all of the virginity loss scenes here result in multiple orgasms for the heroine. The hymen must be broken for this pleasure to occur. If we return briefly to Derrida, then we can argue that the hymen becomes the barrier between desire and fulfillment not just for the hero but also for the heroine. Pain is transformed into pleasure, and as such the transformation from virgin to non-virgin becomes both painful and pleasurable. This is the guarantee of the literary hymen. However, there is an important emphasis here on "literary," because this hymen does not reflect reality. It is regularly located in an anatomically incorrect place (partway up the vaginal passage instead of outside the vaginal opening), it is omnipresent in virgins, and its destruction can be felt by both virgin and deflowerer. However, in autobiographical stories of virginity loss, the hymen becomes far less concrete. In my doctoral thesis, I survey several books in what I have termed the "virginity loss confessional genre,"[45] in which people tell their own virginity loss stories. Across this genre, hymeneal experiences vary wildly. Here are some excerpts:

> We had the hymen problem. Took hours, finally we made progress with that in the morning because at one point in the evening we stopped and were exhausted from trying. In the morning we made the "break-through."[46]

My wife, my soul mate, had been with five guys before me. We've been together five years and I kid you not, I just popped her cherry three weeks ago. It wasn't in the normal spot. It was up high on the top wall. I fucking nailed it and it said, "*Boom*," the hymen split. That hymen is fucking smashed.[47]

I loved the feelings. Of course, the initial tear of the hymen hurt a bit but the feelings that happened before and after were amazing. I had never felt anything like it.[48]

One thing that has always stood out about that first time was that there was no blood. . . . Did my hymen break from horseback riding, wearing tampons, or had I perhaps been sexually abused in the past and just blocked it? I don't know the answer, but I was disappointed, because I expected to see proof.[49]

Even in these "real-life" stories of virginity loss, the hymen remains elusive.[50] Sometimes, as in the first excerpt, it is practically imperforate, and at other times, as in the last excerpt, it does not exist. Anxieties over the hymen in these autobiographical stories regularly mirror anxieties over virginity more broadly. Conventionally, as I have discussed, virginity loss has been figured as intrinsically transformative for women. Although sexual scripts have evolved, this idea has not disappeared. Laura M. Carpenter argues that three major metaphors through which virginity loss is conceptualized have developed: as a gift, as a stigma, and as a process or rite of passage.[51] In the first two, virginity becomes a literal object that can be given (or thrown) away, presumably resulting in a deep change in the (now ex-)virgin. In the latter, virginity loss is a step on a journey toward adulthood and sexual maturity: not quite as overtly transformative but something that still changes the individual. One of the major attitudes expressed in autobiographical virginity loss stories is a kind of disappointment: virginity loss has been represented in culture and literature as intrinsically transformative, but the newly deflowered person often does not find herself transformed. Pain is not satisfactorily transformed into pleasure: the literary promise of the hymen is not fulfilled. The narrative of virginity loss is somehow incomplete. Although the hymen has been established in literature as a concrete sign of virginity loss, in autobiographical stories it remains uncertain and undetermined, in a state of flux. It remains, like the Derridean hymen, both there and not there, mirroring, in many ways, anxieties about the intangibility of virginity loss, which cannot be read on the woman's body: how, exactly, does one "lose" something that technically is a lack in the first place?

NOTES

1   Jacques Derrida, "The Double Session," in *Dissemination*, trans. Barbara Johnson (1972; reprinted, London: Continuum, 2004), 212–13.

2   Jamie Mullaney, "Like a Virgin: Temptation, Resistance, and the Construction of Identities Based on 'Not Doings,'" *Qualitative Sociology* 24, 1 (2001): 3.

3   Derrida, "The Double Session," 212–13.

4   Kathleen Coyne Kelly, *Performing Virginity and Testing Chastity in the Middle Ages* (London: Routledge, 2002), 9–10.

5   Tassie Gwilliam, "Female Fraud: Counterfeit Maidenheads in the Eighteenth Century," *Journal of the History of Sexuality* 6, 4 (1996): 547.

6   This is so ubiquitous in romance fiction that it is regularly the subject of (gently) mocking commentary. See, for example, the post "Where Is the Hymen?" on the romance review website Smart Bitches, Trashy Books, in which author Sarah Wendell says that "it is not up the canal by any means! It's not a portcullis halfway to the cervix! It's not a barrier up the valley, a logjam obstructing the path of the river of love, a dam in the reservoir of passion. IT IS NOT INSIDE ANYTHING. THE HYMEN IS EXTERNAL." Sarah Wendell, "Where Is the Hymen?," Smart Bitches, Trashy Books, January 2, 2012, http://smartbitchestrashybooks.com/blog/where-is-the-hymen.

7   Kelly, *Performing Virginity*, 12.

8   Ibid., ix.

9   Danielle Jacquart and Claude Thomasset, *Sexuality and Medicine in the Middle Ages* (Cambridge, UK: Polity Press, 1988), 44.

10   Anke Bernau, *Virgins: A Cultural History* (London: Granta Books, 2007), 2–4.

11   Corrinne Harol, *Enlightened Virginity in Eighteenth-Century Literature* (New York: Palgrave Macmillan, 2006), 60–61.

12   Hanne Blank, *Virgin: The Untouched History* (New York: Bloomsbury, 2007), 66.

13   Anonymous, "A Remedy for the Green Sickness," in *Poetica Erotica: A Collection of Rare and Curious Amatory Verse*, vol. 1, ed. Thomas Robert Smith (New York: Crown Publishers, 1927).

14   Harol, *Enlightened Virginity*, 59.

15   Blank, *Virgin*, 67.

16   Harol, *Enlightened Virginity*, 63.

17   Ibid., 83.

18   Ibid.

19   Gwilliam, "Female Fraud," 526.

20   Cited in Bradford Keyes Mudge, *The Whore's Story: Women, Pornography, and the British Novel, 1684–1830* (Oxford: Oxford University Press, 2000), 75.

21   Bernau, *Virgins*, 32.

22   Gwilliam, "Female Fraud," 547.

23   Harol, *Enlightened Virginity*, 78.

24   Guillaume de Lorris and Jean de Meun, *The Romance of the Rose: Guillaume de Lorris and Jean de Meun*, trans. Charles Dahlberg (Princeton: Princeton University Press, 1995), 351–52.

25   Bernau, *Virgins*, 137.

26   Kelly, *Performing Virginity*, 42.

27   Jon Stratton, *The Virgin Text: Fiction, Sexuality, and Ideology* (Norman: University of Oklahoma Press, 1987), 18.

28   Russell J. Ganim, "Aretino's Legacy: *L'Ecole des filles* and the Pornographic Continuum in Early Modern France," *French Language and Literature Papers*, University of Nebraska Digital Commons (2007): 162, http://digitalcommons.unl.edu/cgi/viewcontent.cgi?article=1034&context=modlangfrench.

29   Nicholas Chorier, *A Dialogue between a Married Lady and a Maid* (abridged adaptation in English; London: n.p., 1740), 12–13, http://books.google.com.au/books?id=ocRNAAAAcAAJ&printsec=frontcover&dq=A+Dialogue+between+a+Married+Lady+and+a+Maid/.

30 John Cleland, *Memoirs of a Woman of Pleasure* (1749; reprinted, Oxford: Oxford University Press, 1999), 41.

31 Thomas Walter Laqueur, *Making Sex: Body and Gender from the Greeks to Freud* (Cambridge, MA: Harvard University Press, 1990), 5–6.

32 Ibid., 150.

33 Anonymous, "Sub-Umbra, or Sport among the She-Noodles," *Pearl*, August 1879, http://www.horntip.com/html/books_&_MSS/1870s/1879-1880_the_pearl_journal/issue_02_-_aug_1879/index.htm.

34 Anonymous, "Lady Pokingham, or They All Do It," *Pearl*, September 1879, http://www.horntip.com/html/books_&_MSS/1870s/1879–1880_the_pearl_journal/issue_03_-_sep_1879/index.htm.

35 Ibid.

36 William Acton, "The Functions and Disorders of the Reproductive Organs in Childhood, Youth, Adult Age, and Advanced Life, Considered in Their Physiological, Social, and Moral Relations" (London, 1857).

37 Although there are men who read and write romance, the overwhelming majority of romance authors and readers are women. This is an identity often mobilized by defenders of the genre: for example, Jayne Ann Krentz describes romance authors as "part of an unbroken female line dedicated to passing on an ancient tradition of literature written by women for women." Jayne Ann Krentz, ed., *Dangerous Men and Adventurous Women: Romance Writers on the Appeal of Romance* (Philadelphia: University of Pennsylvania Press, 1992), xi.

38 Emma Darcy, *The Bedroom Surrender* (London: Harlequin Mills & Boon, 2003), 95–96.

39 Jane Porter, *The Italian's Virgin Princess* (London: Harlequin Mills & Boon, 2005), 62.

40 Chantelle Shaw, *Untouched until Marriage* (London: Harlequin Mills & Boon, 2010), 127.

41 Porter, *The Italian's Virgin Princess*, 71.

42 Robyn Donald, *The Virgin and His Majesty* (London: Harlequin Mills & Boon, 2010), 10–11.

43 Sarah Wendell and Candy Tan, *Beyond Heaving Bosoms: The Smart Bitches' Guide to Romance Novels* (New York: Simon and Schuster, 2009), 39.

44 Catherine Roach, "Getting a Good Man to Love: Popular Romance Fiction and the Problem of Patriarchy," *Journal of Popular Romance Studies* 1, 1 (2010): 9.

45 Jodi McAlister, "Romancing the Virgin: Female Virginity Loss and Love in Popular Literatures in the West" (PhD thesis, Macquarie University, 2015).

46 Shawn Wickens, *How to Lose Your Virginity (. . .and How Not To): Real Stories about the First Time* (Charleston, SC: BookSurge Publishing, 2010), 122.

47 Ibid., 212.

48 Kimberley A. Johnson and Ann Werner, eds., *The Virgin Diaries* (Charleston, SC: Ark Stories in cooperation with CreateSpace, 2010), 184, digital edition.

49 Karen Bouris, *The First Time: What Parents and Teenage Girls Should Know about "Losing Your Virginity"* (Newburyport, MA: Conari Press, 1993), location 1665, digital edition.

50 Stories in the virginity loss confessional genre must be taken with a grain of salt, so to speak, for there is no guarantee that they are truthful, and some are clearly false. However, they still provide a fascinating site of analysis since they highlight the ways in which people think about virginity even if they do not always reflect actual experience.

51 Laura M. Carpenter, *Virginity Lost: An Intimate Portrait of First Sexual Experiences* (New York: New York University Press, 2005), 11.

REFERENCES

Acton, William. "The Functions and Disorders of the Reproductive Organs in Childhood, Youth, Adult Age, and Advanced Life, Considered in Their Physiological, Social, and Moral Relations." London, 1857.

Anonymous. "Lady Pokingham, or They All Do It." *Pearl*, August 1879, http://www.horntip.com/html/books_&_MSS/1870s/1879-1880_the_pearl_journal/issue_02_-_aug_1879/index.htm.

Anonymous. "Lady Pokingham, or They All Do It." *Pearl*, September 1879, http://www.horntip.com/html/books_&_MSS/1870s/1879-1880_the_pearl_journal/issue_03_-_sep_1879/index.htm.

Anonymous. "A Remedy for the Green Sickness." In *Poetica Erotica: A Collection of Rare and Curious Amatory Verse*, vol. 1, edited by Thomas Robert Smith. New York: Crown Publishers, 1927.

Anonymous. "Sub-Umbra, or Sport among the She-Noodles." *Pearl*, August 1879, http://www.horntip.com/html/books_&_MSS/1870s/1879-1880_the_pearl_journal/issue_02_-_aug_1879/index.htm.

Bernau, Anke. *Virgins: A Cultural History*. London: Granta Books, 2007.

Blank, Hanne. *Virgin: The Untouched History*. New York: Bloomsbury, 2007.

Bouris, Karen. *The First Time: What Parents and Teenage Girls Should Know about "Losing Your Virginity."* Newburyport, MA: Conari Press, 1993. Digital edition.

Carpenter, Laura M. *Virginity Lost: An Intimate Portrait of First Sexual Experiences*. New York: New York University Press, 2005.

Chorier, Nicolas. *A Dialogue between a Married Lady and a Maid*. An abridged adaptation in English. London: n.p., 1740. http://books.google.com.au/books?id=ocRNAAAAcAAJ&printsec=frontcover&dq=A+Dialogue+between+a+Married+Lady+and+a+Maid/.

Cleland, John. *Memoirs of a Woman of Pleasure*. 1749; reprinted, Oxford: Oxford University Press, 1999.

Darcy, Emma. *The Bedroom Surrender*. London: Harlequin Mills & Boon, 2003.

de Lorris, Guillaume, and Jean de Meun. *The Romance of the Rose: Guillaume de Lorris and Jean de Meun*. Translated by Charles Dahlberg. Princeton: Princeton University Press, 1995.

Derrida, Jacques. *Dissemination*. Translated by Barbara Johnson. 1972; reprinted, London: Continuum, 2004.

Donald, Robyn. *The Virgin and His Majesty*. London: Harlequin Mills & Boon, 2010.

Ganim, Russell J. "Aretino's Legacy: *L'Ecole des filles* and the Pornographic Continuum in Early Modern France." *French Language and Literature Papers*, University of Nebraska Digital Commons (2007): 161–73. http://digitalcommons.unl.edu/cgi/viewcontent.cgi?article=1034&context=modlangfrench.

Gwilliam, Tassie. "Female Fraud: Counterfeit Maidenheads in the Eighteenth Century." *Journal of the History of Sexuality* 6, 4 (1996): 518–48.

Harol, Corrinne. *Enlightened Virginity in Eighteenth-Century Literature*. New York: Palgrave Macmillan, 2006.

Jacquart, Danielle, and Claude Thomasset. *Sexuality and Medicine in the Middle Ages*. Cambridge, UK: Polity Press, 1988.

Johnson, Kimberley A., and Ann Werner, eds. *The Virgin Diaries*. Charleston, SC: Ark Stories in cooperation with CreateSpace, 2010. Digital edition.

Kelly, Kathleen Coyne. *Performing Virginity and Testing Chastity in the Middle Ages*. London: Routledge, 2000.

Krentz, Jayne Ann, ed. *Dangerous Men and Adventurous Women: Romance Writers on the Appeal of the Romance*. Philadelphia: University of Pennsylvania Press, 1992.

Laqueur, Thomas Walter. *Making Sex: Body and Gender from the Greeks to Freud*. Cambridge, MA: Harvard University Press, 1990.

McAlister, Jodi. "Romancing the Virgin: Female Virginity Loss and Love in Popular Literatures in the West." PhD thesis, Macquarie University, 2015.

Mudge, Bradford Keyes. *The Whore's Story: Women, Pornography, and the British Novel, 1684–1830*. Oxford: Oxford University Press, 2000.

Mullaney, Jamie. "Like a Virgin: Temptation, Resistance, and the Construction of Identities Based on 'Not Doings.'" *Qualitative Sociology* 24, 1 (2001): 3–24.

Porter, Jane. *The Italian's Virgin Princess*. London: Harlequin Mills & Boon, 2005.

Roach, Catherine. "Getting a Good Man to Love: Popular Romance Fiction and the Problem of Patriarchy." *Journal of Popular Romance Studies* 1, 1 (2010): n. pag. http://jprstudies.org/2010/08/getting-a-good-man-to-love-popular-romance-fiction-and-the-problem-of-patriarchy-by-catherine-roach/.

Shaw, Chantelle. *Untouched until Marriage*. London: Harlequin Mills & Boon, 2010.

Stratton, Jon. *The Virgin Text: Fiction, Sexuality, and Ideology*. Norman: University of Oklahoma Press, 1987.

Wendell, Sarah. "Where Is the Hymen?" Smart Bitches, Trashy Books, January 2, 2012, http://smartbitchestrashybooks.com/blog/where-is-the-hymen.

Wendell, Sarah, and Candy Tan. *Beyond Heaving Bosoms: The Smart Bitches' Guide to Romance Novels*. New York: Simon and Schuster, 2009.

Wickens, Shawn. *How to Lose Your Virginity (. . .and How Not To): Real Stories about the First Time*. Charleston, SC: BookSurge Publishing, 2010.

PART 2:
BLOOD, BLOOD, BLOOD . . . AND MORE BLOOD

CHAPTER 3

THE POLITICS OF VIRGINITY AND ABSTINENCE IN THE *TWILIGHT* SAGA

Jonathan A. Allan and Cristina Santos

Virgins are everywhere in popular culture, yet we still struggle with how we understand virginity, who gets to be a virgin, when one loses virginity. In this chapter, we focus our attention on the blockbuster *Twilight* saga, which includes both a virgin heroine, Bella Swan, and a virgin hero, Edward Cullen. When one thinks about the first time and virginity in *Twilight*, it is important to read not only the representations and performances of virginity but also the politics behind these virginities that extend far beyond the Mormon identity of the text's author, which all too often has been used as a kind of "shorthand" explanation. Carrie Anne Platt, for instance, speaks to the question of abstinence in the saga and provides a feminist critique:

> Although the *Twilight* series is progressive in its recognition of the reality of adolescent female sexuality, the sexual politics of the saga are decidedly conservative. Far from being sexually empowered, Bella is rendered a perpetual victim of her own uncontrollable desires, desires that get her into

more and more trouble as the series progresses. The overall ideological message is clear: to be young, female, and sexual is to court danger, destruction, or even death.[1]

It is certainly hard to disagree with Platt's perspective, but it does not recognize the totality of those "decidedly conservative" sexual politics at play in the saga; however, we must recall, as Janice Irvine has noted, that "not all of those promoting abstinence-only education are social conservatives or evangelical Christians."[2] The sexual politics of the *Twilight* saga are about commitment to a purity that extends far beyond the hymen and, as this chapter works to demonstrate, toward a deeply erotophobic culture in which all sexuality always leads to trouble and bad things for otherwise good people and good bodies.

COMPLEX VIRGINITIES

More often than not, discussions of virginity focus exclusively on the female body, a woman's virginity, and her experiences of it and its loss. Indeed, if one looks at Hanne Blank's *Virgin: The Untouched History*, the most "untouched" history is that of the male virgin.[3] The same holds true, unfortunately, for Anke Bernau's *Virgins: A Cultural History*, which suggests that it offers a plurality of virgins but ultimately focuses on female virgins.[4] Although it seems that we all "know" what virginity is and whether we have it or not, we have a difficult time, we must admit, articulating it or thinking about it. Virginity fascinates the imagination in numerous ways, probably because it has been turned into a myth: that is, much time is spent safeguarding it and deciding how and to whom to lose it. Does it have to be penetrative vaginal intercourse only? What about fellatio? Anal sex? Non-heterosexual sex? We believe that virginity and its loss affect people's lives in perpetuity. Even for those who will never lose their virginities, for any number of reasons, they know about these myths. They are everywhere. Television. Movies. Magazines. Harlequin romance novels. Websites. Social media. We are inundated with stories about the virgin's first time.[5]

In thinking about virginity, we position the virgin as someone who has yet to have sexual relations—intercourse or interaction—with another consenting person. We consider enthusiastic consent to be absolutely essential for all participants in the sexual act. Definitions of sexual interaction or intercourse will vary, and thus we understand them as being fluid insofar as the virgin can and will determine for himself or herself what constitutes "virginity loss." As much as we might appreciate our definition of virginity, we must also contend with a historical tradition that has largely and squarely focused on female virginity in the heterosexual sense and its definition as being dependent on the presence of the hymen. However, as Jocelyn Wogan-Browne notes, "the hymen is not a constant of bodily knowledge, but appears and disappears at various periods from the Greeks to twentieth-century medicine."[6]

But what can be said of male virginity, the virginity of boys and men? Scholarship on male virginity, it must be admitted, is a nascent area of interest that boasts but a handful of articles—indeed, *Virgin Envy* might well double the number of articles on male virginity. Earlier studies of virginity have almost uniformly addressed, as noted, female virginity,[7] and only infrequently have scholars seriously considered male virginity,[8] and often when male virgins are considered it is in a clinical sense of accounting for biological or sexual functions and failures (e.g., premature ejaculation).[9] We also find brief narratives about male virginity in therapeutic or anecdotal sources.[10] In the context of cultural texts, we have limited resources. When we do encounter narratives of male virgins, Sandra L. Caron and Sarah P. Hinman observe, "the typical story is a boy who desires to be rid of his virginity, along with the peer pressure and stigma associated with male virginity."[11] These narratives, more often than not, do not account for the complexity of male virginity, particularly having an identity that one is not supposed to have and that can threaten society's concept of masculinity (i.e., how can a man be a virgin?). Finally, we also see discussions of male virginity in the space of comedy, for instance scholarly work on the movie *The 40-Year-Old Virgin*.[12] Female virginity, in contrast, is pervasive; it is *how* virginity has come to be defined. The standard role of men in virginity, if any, is less about being virgins than about *deflowering* virgins.

Virginity among men, then, becomes an impossibility; simply put, there is no signifier—imagined, real, or otherwise—that confirms a man's virginity: that is, the male body cannot prove its purity. J. H. Arnold, for instance, notes that "it is far from clear how virginity could be distinguished from chastity for medieval men. There is no clear marker, no hymen (however culturally construed or imaginary) to be breached, no pregnancy to be avoided. If the signs of purity were problematic for women, they were equally so for men."[13] The problem for the medieval man still occurs for the modern man. What, for instance, could prove a man's purity?[14] Where would we find proof of his virginity? In the words of Northrop Frye, male virginity is "bloody confusing."[15]

Accordingly, we admit that a great deal of work remains to be done with the male virgin. And matters are even more complicated if we are to consider questions of identity, difference, and language. When we contemplate representations of male virginity in culture, we usually choose terms—"chastity," "celibacy," "abstinence"— other than "virginity."[16] Such a rhetorical gesture does a disservice to the complexities of virginity, and surely we must admit that an experience denied language (i.e., male virginity) is detrimental to our understanding of those complexities that we have uncovered in female virginity and its institutionalized androcentric control as a method of restoring the moral fibre of the country.[17] In a sense, then, we are taking virginity out of the metaphorical closet and admitting that in the closet we find many other virginities worthy of consideration alone and in relation to each other. For that purpose, a case study of Stephenie Meyer's successful novel franchise the *Twilight* saga serves as the backdrop to the discussion of virginal problematics in the twenty-first century—a complicated issue involving discussions not only of virginity but also of abstinence and purity for both males and females. Moreover, we are very interested in the representation of the first time of two first timers: that is, both Edward and Bella are virgins during their quintessential first time, their wedding night. It is the relationality of male and female virginity that reveals and openly explores the gendered power dynamics of the first time and the anxieties of and expectations for the heterosexual participants. The *Twilight* saga captures the attention and sympathy of its readers "with the supernatural main characters . . . as well as . . . the sexual titillation of the romance novel."[18] The saga revolves around numerous virgins but most notably the hero, Edward Cullen, a century-old virgin, and Bella Swan, an adolescent girl. As readers, we witness the development of virgins over three books, totalling nearly 2,000 pages; we go with them to the altar and on their honeymoon, and we live through the loss of virginity and what follows. We are treated to the full complexity of virginity and its loss, particularly for Edward and Bella, when negotiating the erotic tensions between them. The saga in many ways inverts the sexual script by foregrounding and complicating virginal identities and positioning the virgins alongside one another. Erotic tensions overwhelm the narrative. It is perhaps surprising, then, that in a culture in which "sex is pervasive [and] . . . leaks across the covers of magazines marketed *at both men and women*"[19] virginity is so central to the saga.

Curiously, however, though much has been said about Bella's virginity, little has been said about Edward's virginity, and even less has been said about how these virginities are constructed and represented, and little to nothing has been said about these virginities together. This chapter intervenes, therefore, in a number of discussions about virginity in the *Twilight* saga and shows the complexities of the construct of virginity. We argue that the virginities as represented here by Edward and Bella cannot be studied in isolation, and we demonstrate that the text highlights the anxieties surrounding virginity and its various cultural performances and meanings at the beginning of the twenty-first century.

TWILIGHT AND VIRGINITY

In her study of the saga, Anna Silver writes that "part of what makes the *Twilight* series so popular and so unusual is Edward and Bella's old-fashioned courtship in which only kisses are exchanged before the wedding," and she contends that, "for Edward and [author] Meyer, marriage is the only moral arena for sexual desire."[20] Because of this, Victoria E. Collins and Dianne C. Carmody observe that

"Christian publications have heralded the book series, noting that the characters restrain from engaging in sexual intercourse until they are married and portray themes of immense self-control in the face of temptation."[21] Throughout the saga, Edward, more often than Bella, demands abstinence and purity in their relationship. Silver argues that his values are "uncommon in popular, mainstream secular discourse about young adult sexuality today."[22] Although there is a seeming discourse toward sexuality rather than away from it, there is an entire industry dedicated to ensuring sexual purity, which, though having a religious affiliation, is also very much a part of secular culture. But why does Edward strive to protect both his and Bella's purity? Why is purity so essential to the *Twilight* saga?

Relatively little has been said about virginity in the *Twilight* saga. Caryss Crossen frames her study as follows: "The characters I have chosen to examine—with the *possible exception* of Edward Cullen of *Twilight*—have had some experience of sexual intercourse, despite their current celibacy."[23] Crossen seems to be uncertain whether or not Edward is a virgin. Why? What does it mean for scholarship that scholars choose not to articulate or frame him as a virgin? Likewise, Ann V. Bliss tends to speak in terms of "abstinence" rather than "virginity" in her study of *Twilight*. For Bliss, her use of the term "abstinence" is twofold because Edward abstains from both sex and the consumption of blood: "While the fundamental manifestation of abstinence in the *Twilight* series is the Cullen family's refusal to drink human blood, references to abstinence resonate throughout Edward's relationship with Bella."[24] Again, we have to ask, why are both Crossen and Bliss reluctant to refer to Edward as a virgin? Are we witnessing a kind of "virgin-phobia"? Critics seem to be uneasy in thinking of him in terms of his virginity, and the reason might well be that to call him a virgin would seemingly undercut his claim to masculinity, as if the romance hero cannot and should not be a virgin. Of course, however, this is not the case, and popular romance fiction contains numerous examples of virgin heroes, all of whom still maintain their claims to masculinity.

Even though we have seen a renewed (was it ever otherwise?) interest in virginity, whether at purity balls or at mumblecore films that appear in the cinema every summer, we have not witnessed an overarching "coming out" of virginity. Instead, the "uncovering [of virginity] seems if anything heightened in surprise and delectability, rather than staled, by the increasingly intense atmosphere of and about [virginity]."[25] We are appropriating Eve Kosofsky Sedgwick's language from *Epistemology of the Closet* because we want to highlight how virginity rides the slippery slope between the "public" and the "private." We can speak about virginity as a private identity that can also carry a public weight not only of performance but also of worth in the sociocultural marketplace. Likewise, Bliss and Crossen speak "around" virginity rather than naming it as such, as if naming it would reveal too much: that is, bring something seen as quintessentially private to the forefront of public space and discussion. This kind of gesture is full of problems because it highlights a discomfort or fear that needs to be accounted for by critical voices. Too often we have left certain subjects behind because, simply put, we are uncomfortable with them or because they distress us. In many ways, this is precisely how virginity works.

The twenty-first century has witnessed a renewed interest in virginity, abstinence, and sexual purity, which in turn has made their "revelation" all the more important. We are dealing with a kind of virginity paradox: although "it" is "out," virgins might not be. In the case of the *Twilight* saga, the term "virgin" is rarely uttered, yet readers attuned to virginity will note that it is present on nearly every page of the saga. The challenge that we face is about *how* we read virginity in the saga and to what ends. In what follows, we treat Bella and Edward separately, and ultimately we bring them together to explore the ways in which virginity informs their subjectivities and their relationship and how it ultimately presents contemporary views of and anxieties about male and female virginities. Virginity, in many ways, haunts not only their subjectivities but also the development and ultimately the totality of their personal relationship and their relationships with their sociopolitical and familial environments.

BELLA'S VIRGINITY IN WAITING

Throughout the *Twilight* saga, Bella is not prudish when it comes to her sexuality, and she is described as the prototypical heterosexual teenage girl: interested in boys, curious about sexuality. Although virginal, she is not, to be certain, naive about sexuality and its social dynamics, always aware of virginity's presence and the possible ramifications of its loss. Her sexual desires are never fully satisfied, however, since Edward not only represents the threat to her virginity (and her life) but also functions as the subject who controls her sexuality and pleasure until she acquiesces to his conditions: that is, marrying him. Her virginity is prized enough to be lost only within the confines of marriage: that is, Bella loses her virginity to Edward on their marriage bed, and it is through his bite that the vampire virus is transmitted to her on her hospital bed, thus saving her from the imminence of her human death and leading to her rebirth as a vampire. Even though it is often repeated throughout the saga that ultimately it is her decision to be turned into a vampire, the same principle of choice does not apply to her virginity. As a result, her agency is never actualized but always in flux, and in a paternalistic manner the question of her purity (and her humanness) is left to her bridegroom, seemingly charged with safeguarding it not only from himself but also for himself: "I just want it to be official," Edward declares, "that you belong to me and *no one else*."[26] His conquest of Bella's virginity emphasizes his role as the subject who not only initiates her transition to womanhood but also does so by placing Bella as the object of his introduction into manhood. Yet it is clear that her sexual initiation reinforces the notion of female virginity *loss*, wheras his own sexual dawning is one of heroic *penetration* and *marking* of virginal territory that no other man has ever conquered.

There is much more to this than just mere safeguarding; not only is her virginity commodified, but also Bella herself becomes a commodity fought over by two alpha males: Edward and Jacob. Her body and its virginity are essentially trafficked between men. If we accept, as Gayle S. Rubin suggests, that, "if it is women who are being transacted, then it is the men who give and take them who are linked, the woman being a conduit of a relationship rather than a partner of it,"[27] then we can see how this quickly lends itself to a reading of the *Twilight* saga since Bella, the woman in this negotiation, is being exchanged between these men over the course of the saga. Her commodification reaches a new level when we admit that the trafficking is twofold: first, it is about Bella; second, it is about virginity. That is, her body, like her virginity, is commodified and traded by men and for men. Moreover, as Rubin has noted, the trafficking of women is "far from being confined to the 'primitive' world, [and] these practices seem only to become more pronounced and commercialized in more 'civilized' societies."[28] The *Twilight* saga, of course, is one of the most commercially successful book and movie franchises. Throughout the saga, readers and viewers witness the blending of the "primitive" (Jacob) and the "civilized" (Edward), and they observe the drawn-out trafficking of Bella's body and virginity.

Edward and Jacob, individually and collectively, become a kind of "patriarchal censor" determining what Bella can and cannot do, and they push and pull her in different and competing ways: "And I realized that I'd been wrong all along about magnets. It had not been Edward and Jacob that I'd been trying to force together, it was the two parts of myself, Edward's Bella and Jacob's Bella. But they could not exist together, and I never should have tried."[29] Bella recognizes the exchange happening between men, but she is depicted as missing the larger point, that this is the value placed on female virginity. Ultimately, she ends up with Edward, though she admits that "Jacob had become a part of me, and there was no changing that now."[30] But the larger point here is how her virginity and her body are commodified and participate in the political economy of sexuality, and how this becomes eroticized by way of a romantic narrative.

Considering the social dynamics of the commodification of and market value placed on Bella's virginity within her personal social environment, her sexuality is not a hollow issue; rather, it is complex both for Bella and for literary critics and readers. While she is perceived as something to be won over by either Edward or Jacob within the romantic narrative, she does not always choose abstinence (she is very much in touch with her sexuality and attempts to have Edward engage with her), although it is often required by her environment that she adopt a virginal identity that supports abstinence. Edward, however, is not alone in concerning himself with her abstinence: "'Ugh!' [Bella] groaned. 'I really wish you were not forcing me to say this out loud, Dad. *Really*. But . . . I am a . . . virgin, and I have no immediate plans to change that status.' We both cringed, but then Charlie's face smoothed out."[31] Thus, even though much of the criticism has focused on the Cullen family, particularly Edward, with regard to Bella's abstinence, both the vampires and the humans (especially her father) share a paternalistic concern for her virginity.

In the *Twilight* saga, Bella is made abstinent because she is denied pleasure, though a question that needs to be asked is why does she not simply seek out pleasure elsewhere, for instance with Jacob? Bonnie Mann writes that

> the most surprising thing about Bella's romance with Edward is not that Edward has to resist the urge to perforate her pulsing jugular vein, but that he, not she, puts the brakes on their erotic encounters. Knowing that any loss of control spells death for his beloved, Edward's restraint allows Bella to be the one consumed by desire. She is regularly physically rebuffed by him as she longs to tear off his clothes. In the end, he is pushed into agreeing to sex while she is still human, only by forcing Bella to agree to marry him.[32]

The question of power and manipulation here is problematic because both Bella and Edward impose a certain power on the other for their own personal physical/emotional/moral gain.

Bella thus becomes aware of her virginity and its value, which necessarily implies the risk of loss—of virginity and by extension of her value in the patriarchal marketplace. In her case, losing her virginity occurs twice: her deflowering on her honeymoon and her genesis as a vampire. In each case, it is ostensibly presented as "her choice," but it is a choice greatly influenced by her fear of losing Edward. One can read her thoughts and fears regarding her transformation into a vampire in tandem with her virginity loss:

"It's not that you're afraid you won't . . . like me as much when I'm different—when I'm not soft and warm and I don't smell the same? You really do want to keep me, no matter how I turn out?" . . .

There was something about him being the one to make the choice—to want to keep me enough that he wouldn't just allow me to be changed, he would act to keep me. . . . I wanted *his* venom to poison my system. It would make me belong to him in a tangible, quantifiable way.[33]

In each case, Bella's loss of virginity and humanity is a choice made possible only by Edward's participation. Even though Carlisle offers to be the one to change Bella, it is Edward who chooses to be the vehicle through which she can transform into a twice-bitten vampire.

In examining Bella's own loss of virginity and humanness, one cannot do so without having understood, to some degree, Edward's own fixation on safeguarding her virginity, since it might have been his own virginity that he feared losing (a point that we will discuss below):

"You make me feel like a villain in a melodrama—twirling my mustache while I try to steal some poor girl's virtue." . . ."That's it, isn't it?"

The short laugh that escaped me [Bella] was more shocked than amused. "You're trying to protect your virtue!" . . .

"No, silly girl. . . . I'm trying to protect *yours*."[34]

It is within this dichotomous relationship between the puritanical Edward and the sexually awakening yet still virginal Bella that some patriarchal and Christian traditions would paint her as the stereotypical temptress/Eve.[35] This question of her agency is a theme repeated throughout the *Twilight* saga and a topic directly linked to her choice to lose her virginity. Even though still human throughout their "courting," Bella might actually have more power over Edward because she can make him lose control and compromise his virtue while also sacrificing her own virginity to their "monstrous" impulses.

Nevertheless, Bella fulfills the patriarchal and cultural code of saving her virginity for the marriage bed, which leads to a honeymoon pregnancy—inherently enforcing the traditional idea of sexual intercourse primarily for the purpose of procreation. Although in her virginal state Bella exercised a "sexual" power over men, here she acquires true power only upon giving birth and not necessarily in the consummation of the marriage.

EDWARD'S VIRGINITY

The narrative that unfolds in the saga shows the queerness and strangeness of male virginity precisely because it contradicts stereotypes and ideals often associated with male sexuality: "'This is unbearable. So many things I've wanted to give you—and *this* is what you decide to demand. Do you have any idea how painful it is, trying to refuse you, when you plead with me this way?'"[36] Edward is clearly the one who is demanding virginity and purity for both himself and her. Bella, on the other hand, demands an answer: "Give me one good reason why tonight is not as good as any other night."[37] It's certainly a good question and deserves an answer in a relationship of equals, but theirs is not that kind of relationship.

The sexual history of the Cullens perhaps offers some indications of the *hysteria* that prefigures Edward's virginal identity. In her article, Silver notes, for instance, that

> pre-marital sex in *Twilight* is risky, life-threatening, and brutal for everyone involved, both men and women. The most obvious case of men being harmed by premarital sex is the case of Rosalie's fiancé and his friends, but Edward's brother Jasper is another example. Jasper is turned into a vampire after encountering "the three most beautiful women I had ever seen" (*Eclipse* 213), whose angelic faces and appreciation for his "lovely" smell cloud his awareness of danger.[38]

We could add that Rosalie also suffers a traumatic rape at the hands of her fiancé and his friends before being turned by Carlisle. Thus, the men in the *Twilight* saga have all had traumatic experiences of sexuality. Accordingly, it stands to reason that Edward—given the experiences of those around him—would be anxious about sexuality. In answering his hysterical question, he opts to hold on to the last bastion of purity, and of humanity, contained within him: his virginity.

Edward is terrified by the possibility of losing his virginity and what it would mean for his identity. He has been a virgin for over a century. What then happens after sex? His virginity is complex, and his relationship to it needs to be understood as part of the cultural framework in which he finds himself. His refusal to partake in sexuality and blood can be interpreted as part of the erotophobic culture in which he finds himself. And these values are then spread to the reader, who ultimately learns that sex always leads to pregnancy, which, of course, is the same lesson of abstinence-only education (to which we will devote attention below). Nonetheless, we have questions about Edward the virgin. What does it mean for readers that he is a virgin? Why would the author choose to reify male virginity in the construction of an apparently "dangerous" and non-human hero? Indeed, readers have noted that Edward the vampire is not really a "vampire" so much as a "vegetarian vampire": "So Edward sucks blood. So he lives on blood. So he kills people. No wait, unlike vampires in most stories, Edward doesn't kill people, does he? Edward confines himself to animals in the woods. He never kills any humans and he never hurts their pets. He's a good vampire, with a soul."[39] He is surely one of the least threatening vampires in the history of vampire literature. Edward, for all of his sparkle, is barely monstrous at all, at least in terms of vampirism. Lois H. Gresh, for instance, calls him a "reformed vampire."[40] Although his vampirism might be reformed, his gender politics surely are not; they are at best, perhaps, troubled.

Where Edward is at his most interesting is at the level of gender and sexuality, and arguably this is where he becomes most "monstrous," by which we mean defying the norm. His claims to monstrosity are tenuous because they do not meet our general ideas about monstrosity; he is not threatening in the same way as earlier manifestations of the vampiric. Indeed, we argue, his prolonged virginity—he is, after all, a 107-year-old virgin—renders Edward (more) monstrous, deviant, anomalous. It is through virginity that he both "protects" and "oppresses" Bella. There is a problematic paradigm unfolding here that needs to be thought about carefully and critically. Many critics[41] have noted the ways in which Edward is a "stalker" or an "abusive partner," and we do not dispute these claims, for we largely agree with the bulk of them, especially in light of *Midnight Sun*, the apocryphal first novel of the *Twilight* saga told from his perspective.[42] We suggest, however, that without recognizing his complicated and puritanical relationship to sexuality, particularly his own sexuality, these studies miss an important part of his subjectivity and initiation into manhood.

In *New Moon*, readers learn—as though they had not already learned it in *Twilight*—of the importance of purity or abstinence to Edward: "He scooped me [Bella, narrating] off the bed with one arm, and pulled the cover back with the other. He put me down with my head on my pillow and tucked the quilt around me. He lay down next to me—*on top of the blanket* so I wouldn't get chilled—and put his arm over me."[43] Admittedly, there is no announcement of his virginity (or her virginity, for that matter), but the point to be noted here is that the two, despite being in an amorous relationship, are not sleeping under the same covers. There must be a cover—a metaphorical hymen—between the two that protects them from virginity loss. Later, in *Breaking Dawn*, his virginity is affirmed when readers learn that Edward has not yet experienced "physical gratification": "He started to pull away—that was his automatic response whenever he decided things had gone too far, his reflex reaction whenever he most wanted to keep going. Edward spent most of his life rejecting any kind of physical gratification. I knew it was terrifying him to change those habits now."[44] The word that best describes Edward here is *abstinence*, for he has merely abstained from pleasure—for over a century. His abstinence is in accordance with American abstinence philosophies of the nineteenth century, Jessica Warner explains:

> Nineteenth-century perfectionists had an almost morbid
> fear of leisure, and that fear was writ large in the fripperies
> that proscribed . . . drinking, masturbating, copulating for
> purposes other than procreation, dancing, overeating, read-
> ing novels, using tobacco in any form. Each idle moment
> was a truce in the ongoing war against sin, an opportunity
> for the enemy to steal a march on the unwary and open
> the floodgates to perdition.[45]

It seems that Edward is very afraid of that "idle moment" that would
expose him to damnation and all the evils that pleasure often affords.
After all, in *Breaking Dawn*, readers are told that he "spent most of
his life rejecting any kind of physical gratification," and this certainly
seems to be in line with nineteenth-century perfectionists. When
one considers the age of Edward, born June 20, 1901, it seems to be
entirely plausible that his attitudes toward sexuality—and indeed
physical gratification—are marked by his, rather than contemporary
readers', sociocultural framework.

Throughout the saga, we find persistent discussions of his abstinence (from human blood) and virginity, and ultimately this comes
to a climax in the third volume of the saga. In *Eclipse*, readers are
finally rewarded with the engagement of Edward and Bella, and
in this scene they are alone in his bedroom, where once more she
urges him to have sex, and once more he recants. "'Edward,' she says,
'There's something I want to do before I'm not human anymore,'"[46]
which is to say that she wants to experience carnal pleasure *as a human*; we will recall here that her virginity is intimately tied to her
humanity. "He grabbed my wrists and pinned them to my sides, 'I
said we're not.'"[47] Bella admits that "rejection washed through me,
instinctive and strong."[48] She is also speaking here about shame,
perhaps even a kind of slut shaming. Sedgwick has noted that "shame
floods into being as a moment, a disruptive moment, in a circuit
of identity-consuming identificatory communication,"[49] and this
is precisely what Bella means when she speaks of "washing through
me"; rejection is a shameful experience that Edward imposes on her.

Edward, however, does not frame this in terms of "shaming"
(though it certainly is). He imagines this condescending gesture

as "protective," explaining that "'it's not possible now. Later, when you are less breakable. Be patient, Bella.'"[50] In this instance, then, the general patrimonious notion seems to be that female virginity, particularly Bella's virginity, is "breakable." But, as we note, in the latter part of this excuse—"be patient, Bella"—she is shamed by Edward and made to doubt her carnal desires, and he being the pure virgin, always worried about (his) celibacy. There is, to be certain, a great deal of sexual shame for him that needs to be explored in greater detail. Both his virginity and his lack of sexual experience are sites of masculine shame and confusion, a cluster of negative affects that needs to be thought about carefully.

As Gilles Deleuze quips, "the shame of being a man—is there any better reason to write?"[51] The study of masculinity is full of examples of shame that become central to masculine identity. In his work, Michael Kimmel observes that "throughout American history American men have been afraid that others will see us as less than manly, as weak, as timid, frightened." For Kimmel, "American men define their masculinity, not as much in relation to women, but in relation to other men. Masculinity is largely a homosocial enactment."[52] If a man is not living up to the expectations of masculinity, then other men will tell him so. Not to be masculine, or not masculine enough, is to become worthy of shame. Men shame one another in a constant competition over who can claim to be the most manly. Yet, and surprisingly, contrary to contemporary cultural practices, Edward's drawn-out virginity is never questioned as a threat to his masculinity; however, we should note that romance fiction, written by women for women, in many ways provides the most complex treatment of male virginity.[53]

EROTOPHOBIA, HEGEMONIC MASCULINITY, AND THE PURSUIT OF PURITY

Throughout the saga, readers find abstinence, especially sexual abstinence. Many critics have related this to Meyer's Mormonism.[54] Truth be told, however, this is part of American sexual culture, which continues to value virginity, especially female virginity. Abstinence-only education is deeply enmeshed in notions of being a "good sexual citizen"—that is, "heterosexual, married, and monogamous,"[55] three virtues that *Twilight* espouses throughout its narrative. What we hope to argue here is that abstinence-only education, though tied to the idea of avoiding unplanned pregnancies, is also intimately tied to the erotophobia—"negative feelings about sex"[56]—of the state.[57]

Moral panic, especially about adolescence and sexuality, has "significant implications for policies affecting young people, including those surrounding sexuality education,"[58] which has been a long and fraught debate, precisely because it highlights an inherent paradox regarding youth and sexuality. Anastasia Powell argues that, "in defending the concept that children and young people need protection from sexual exploitation, Western society has become invested in the idea that we cannot simultaneously allow them any sexual agency at all."[59] The *Twilight* saga, in many ways, can be located in the same paradoxical space, on the one hand recognizing adolescent sexuality, on the other trying to shut it down and limit it to the confines of marriage. After all, as some abstinence-only education programs teach, "don't be a louse, wait for your spouse."[60] Claire Greslé-Favier notes that "the idea that sexual abstinence before marriage is desirable has achieved an almost hegemonic status in contemporary debates around sexual education in the United States."[61] Abstinence and virginity become the modus operandi for the *Twilight* saga, but it is the inversion of these terms—concerning males rather than females—that is important to note.

Although abstinence-only education speaks about avoiding pregnancy, it also speaks about the fears that run tangential to sexuality, such as sexually transmitted infections. As Elia and Eliason observe, historically "a major purpose of sexuality education has been to prevent the spread of sexually transmitted diseases," and it certainly seems that the historical claim holds true today.[62] Abstinence-only education works to establish and affirm good sexual citizenship. The rise of such education can be traced alongside the HIV/AIDS crisis. It was not until the 1980s that the American government was involved in sexuality education. In 1981, the Adolescent Family Life Act was passed. Its goal was "to prevent teen pregnancy through the use of strong abstinence-only-until-marriage messages. It received $11 million its first year and funding has increased or stayed steady since, with $28.9 million in funding in fiscal year 2009."[63] For Fields and Hirschman, abstinence-only education is partly "a response to teenage pregnancy, HIV, and sexual activity."[64] Critics largely agree that abstinence-only education is very much a response to fears about the sexuality of adolescents and its potential effects: pregnancy and disease.

Twilight, then, might well be read in terms of the erotophobic perspective of abstinence-only education, which often positions all sex outside marriage as risky. In essence, these educational programs have advocated a "conservative, sex negative approach" in which any sexuality outside heterosexual, monogamous marriage is treated with suspicion.[65] Edward's virginity and abstinence invert the model or popular and stereotypical vision of abstinence education in the United States. It has become common to think of abstinence education, purity movements, and the pursuit of virginity as concerning girls rather than boys. Silver, however, contends that "Meyer's avowal of abstinence is not to every contemporary reader's taste, but she is clear on one point: abstinence is the model for both boys and girls. Love and lust, for both sexes, should be intertwined and should be made permanent by marriage."[66]

Abstinence and virginity become the modus operandi for the *Twilight* saga, but it is the inversion of these terms—concerning males rather than females—that is important to note. Why does Meyer seem to privilege male virginity over female virginity? That is, why is the male always responsible for his and his love interest's abstinence in her novels? What happens when men have sex? And why is Edward ultimately afraid of sex?

As noted above by Silver, the men in the *Twilight* saga have all had traumatic experiences of sexuality. Accordingly, Edward, given the experiences of those around him, is anxious about it. And it is only once Edward (who remains a virgin) is "turned into a vampire" (though through an act of generosity) that he begins to question whether he is a monster. He becomes a vampire not because of sexuality, like Jasper, and thus he is perpetually forced to contend with a problematic identity, still rendered pure in terms of his virginity but monstrous in terms of his vampirism. But, as already demonstrated, his vampirism is hardly monstrous.

The sexual politics of *Twilight* should not be lost on us, for after Edward and Bella have sex, after she becomes pregnant, the fetus, like a disease or virus, quickly begins to feed on her body, rendering her weak, feeble, and incapable of surviving—yet must be carried to term despite the risk to her life. In a sense, *Twilight* engages with a duplicitous fear/fantasy about sex in a culture that embraces and relishes virginity: pregnancy and disease. Of course, we know that "it is not monogamy [or] abstention per se that protects one from the AIDS infection," Paula A. Treichler writes, but these are "practices that prevent the virus from entering the blood stream."[67] That is, we need to separate the fantasies from the facts: monogamy and abstinence are merely modalities through which students have been taught that they can protect their bodies from HIV/AIDS—just as female bodies can be protected from pregnancy by practising abstinence. In the fantasy of virginity purists, then, the virginal body is freed from these fears because it refuses to participate, which is true of course, but what else does it mean, especially if we think through the lens of feminist and queer theories? And this point should not be lost on readers of the *Twilight* saga; it is, at bottom, a fantasy of what happens when adolescents have sex: pregnancy, disease, death. As much as this narrative has been critiqued for being an abortion[68] allegory, it is also a remarkably erotophobic work.

We are struck by how often Bella's virginity is framed as a site of anxiety and fear that revolves around much more than a girl having sex; indeed, we argue that much of the time the narrative fetishizes purity as a site where nothing bad can happen. In a particularly telling scene in the novel, Bella discusses sexuality with her father, assuring him that he does not need to have the "talk," but he insists: "I am your father. I have responsibilities."[69] During this scene, she imagines that "this was beyond the seventh circle of Hades,"[70] which of course is the circle of hell for violence, which includes, unsurprisingly, sodomites who commit violence against nature. We cannot, and want to insist on this, separate Meyer's pursuit of purity from erotophobia inherent to abstinence-only education. Bella's father admits, "I know the times have changed," which surely can be read, once more, as a comment on the rise of HIV/AIDS. And this is confirmed when he says, "Just tell me you are being responsible."[71] We note that "responsibility" becomes a repeated term that speaks to the ideas of "safe sex," which safeguard the sexual subjects from both pregnancy and HIV/AIDS and other sexually transmitted infections. It is imperative that we, as critical scholars, recognize how virginity is being used as the ultimate form to safeguard oneself from these "bad" things.

In recent years, readers have witnessed the rise of the *Twilight* saga (2005–10) into mainstream popular culture. Each of these books and films reflects cultural anxieties about abstinence, chastity, and virginity in the twenty-first century. Even though both Bella and Edward, the chief protagonists, are virginal characters, much of the focus has been on her virginity, and relatively little has been said about his virginity. Even less has been said about how these virginities are constructed not only alongside one another in the saga, but also as representative of a larger cultural paradigm of contemporary constructions and interpretations of female and male virginities. Using Edward and Bella as examples, one can posit male and female virginities alongside one another and best understand the poetics and politics of virginity in the *Twilight* saga, and, by extension, in the current wave of abstinence and purity education. These virginities cannot be studied in isolation, and their relationality highlights the anxieties still prevalent in society about virginity and its various cultural performances at the beginning of the twenty-first century.

NOTES

1   Carrie Anne Platt, "Cullen Family Values: Gender and Sexual Politics in the *Twilight* Series," in *Bitten by* Twilight*: Youth Culture, Media, and the Vampire Franchise*, ed. Melissa A. Click, Jennifer Stevens Aubrey, and Elizabeth Behm-Morawitz (New York: Peter Lang, 2010), 80.

2   Quoted in Jessica Fields and Celeste Hirschman, "Citizenship Lessons in Abstinence-Only Sexuality Education," *American Journal of Sexuality Education* 2, 2 (2007): 4.

3   Hanne Blank, *Virgin: The Untouched History* (New York: Bloomsbury, 2007).

4   Anke Bernau, *Virgins: A Cultural History* (London: Granta Books, 2007).

5   This chapter builds upon earlier work that we have written individually and revises some of our initial ideas in light of continued thinking about the *Twilight* saga and with new readings on the saga. We think here of books by Rebecca Housel and J. Jeremy Wisnewski, eds., Twilight *and Philosophy: Vampires, Vegetarians, and the Pursuit of Immortality* (Hoboken, NJ: John Wiley and Sons, 2009); Melissa A. Click, Jennifer Stevens Aubrey, and Elizabeth Behm-Morawitz, eds., *Bitten by* Twilight: *Youth Culture, Media, and the Vampire Franchise* (New York: Peter Lang, 2010); Amy M. Clarke and Marijane Osborn, eds., *The* Twilight *Mystique: Critical Essays on the Novels and Films* (Jefferson, NC: McFarland Press, 2010); Giselle Liza Anatol, ed., *Bringing Light to* Twilight: *Perspectives on the Pop Culture Phenomenon* (New York: Palgrave Macmillan, 2011); Natalie Wilson, *Seduced by* Twilight: *The Allure and Contradictory Messages of the Popular Saga* (Jefferson, NC: McFarland Press, 2011); and Maggie Park and Natalie Wilson, eds., *Theorizing* Twilight: *Critical Essays on What's at Stake in a Post-Vampire World* (Jefferson, NC: McFarland Press, 2011).

6   Jocelyn Wogan-Browne, "Virginity Always Comes Twice: Virginity and Profession, Virginity and Romance," in *Maistresse of My Wit: Medieval Women, Modern Scholars*, ed. Louise D. D'Arcens and Juanita Feros Ruys (Turnhout: Brepols, 2004), 4.

7   Bernau, *Virgins*; Anke Bernau, Ruth Evans, and Sarah Salih, eds., *Medieval Virginities* (Toronto: University of Toronto Press, 2003); Blank, *Virgin*.

8   Laura M. Carpenter, *Virginity Lost: An Intimate Portrait of First Sexual Experiences* (New York: New York University Press, 2005. Indeed, when male virginity is considered, it is often displaced and referred to as chastity, celibacy, or abstinence rather than virginity as such. Such a rhetorical or terminological turn does a disservice to the complexities of male virginity, which have remained understudied, and thus many of these complexities can only ever be known at anecdotal levels. See Sandra L. Caron and Sarah P. Hinman, "'I Took His V-Card': An Exploratory Analysis of College Student Stories Involving Male Virginity Loss," *Sexuality and Culture* 17, 4 (2013): 525–39; and Kate Monro, *The First Time: True Tales of Virginity Lost and Found (Including My Own)* (London: Icon Books, 2011).

9   Pekka Santtila, N. Kenneth Sandnabba, and Patrick Jern, "Prevalence and Determinants of Male Sexual Dysfunctions during First Intercourse," *Journal of Sex and Marital Therapy* 35, 2 (2009): 86–105.

10   Caron and Hinman, "'I Took His V-Card'"; Monro, *The First Time*.

11   Caron and Hinman, "'I Took His V-Card,'" 526.

12   Celestino Deleyto, "The New Road to Sexual Ecstasy: Virginity and Genre in *The 40-Year-Old Virgin*," in *Virgin Territory: Representing Sexual Inexperience in Film*, ed. Tamar Jeffers McDonald (Detroit: Wayne State University Press, 2010), 255–68.

13   J. H. Arnold, "The Labour of Continence: Masculinity and Clerical Virginity," in *Medieval Virginities*, ed. Anke Bernau, Ruth Evans, and Sarah Salih (Toronto: University of Toronto Press, 2003), 103.

14   Boys who belong to the Catholic Pure Love Club are warned under the section "What Does It Mean to Be a Man?" that they compromise their purity "when you lust after a girl or look at pornographic images or passionately kiss, passionately embrace or have sex with a girl who you are not 100% sure is the one to be your future spouse." "The Pure Love Club," http://www.pureloveclub.org/virginity.htm.

15   Northrop Frye, *The Secular Scripture and Other Writings on Critical Theory, 1976–1991*, ed. J. Adamson and J. Wilson (Toronto: University of Toronto Press, 2006), 18: 348.

16   The Pure Love Club, for example, is the project of "a Christian Catholic parent" and "does not represent any Catholic parish and is not associated with any Catholic diocese or organization," yet it provides a clear distinction between virginity and purity: "*Virginity* is about the past and you cannot change that but *Chastity* is about the future and it's in your hand. . . . If you have already lost your virginity that doesn't mean you should keep on sinning. You can regain your purity immediately with one confession. . . . Just go to confession and sincerely repent and confess your sins. God will make you as white as snow. It's the purity and virginity of the heart that counts. "The Pure Love Club," http://www.pureloveclub.org/virginity.htm.

17   This phenomenon is not particular to the United States; Bernau, *Virgins*, 171–74, points to similar tendencies in the United Kingdom.

18   Danielle N. Borgia, "*Twilight*: The Glamorization of Abuse, Codependency, and White Privilege," *Journal of Popular Culture* 47, 1 (2014): 153.

19 Gareth Terry, "'I'm Putting a Lid on That Desire': Celibacy, Choice, and Control," *Sexualities* 15, 7 (2012): 871.

20 Anna Silver, "Twilight Is Not Good for Maidens: Gender, Sexuality, and the Family in Stephenie Meyer's *Twilight* Series," *Studies in the Novel* 42, 1–2 (2010): 127.

21 Victoria E. Collins and Dianne C. Carmody, "Deadly Love: Images of Dating Violence in the 'Twilight Saga,'" *Affilia: Journal of Women and Social Work* 26, 4 (2011): 384–85.

22 Silver, "Twilight Is Not Good for Maidens," 128.

23 Caryss Crossen, "'Would You Please Stop Trying to Take Your Clothes Off?' Abstinence and Impotence of Male Vampires in Contemporary Fiction and Television," in *The Monster Imagined: Humanity's Re-Creation of Monsters and Monstrosity*, ed. Laura K. Davis and Cristina Santos (Oxford: Interdisciplinary Press, 2010), 112; emphasis added.

24 Ann V. Bliss, "Abstinence, American-Style," in *The* Twilight *Mystique: Critical Essays on the Novels and Films*, ed. A. M. Clarke and M. Osborn (Jefferson, NC: McFarland Press, 2010), 107.

25 Eve Kosofsky Sedgwick, *Epistemology of the Closet* (Berkeley: University of California Press, 1990), 67.

26 Stephenie Meyer, *Eclipse* (New York: Little, Brown and Company, 2006), 456.

27 Gayle S. Rubin, "The Traffic in Women: Notes on the 'Political Economy' of Sex," in *Deviations: A Gayle Rubin Reader* (Durham: Duke University Press, 2012), 44.

28 Ibid., 45. For a discussion of the noble savage stereotype with respect to Jacob and the Quileute tribe, see Kristian Jensen, "Noble Werewolves or Native Shape-Shifters?," in *The* Twilight *Mystique: Critical Essays on the Novels and Films*, ed. Amy M. Clarke and Marijane Osborn (Jefferson, NC: McFarland Press, 2010), 92–106.

29 Meyer, *Eclipse*, 608.

30 Ibid., 83.

31 Ibid., 59.

32 Bonnie Mann, "Vampire Love: The Second Sex Negotiates the Twenty-First Century," in *Twilight and Philosophy: Vampires, Vegetarians, and the Pursuit of Immortality*, ed. Rebecca Housel and J. Jeremy Wisnewski (Hoboken, NJ: John Wiley and Sons, 2009), 140.

33 Meyer, *Eclipse*, 273, 324.

34 Ibid., 452.

35 The sociocultural value assigned to Eve in the Church of Jesus Christ of Latter Day Saints is distinct from the Christian tradition. It is believed in the Mormon faith that her choice in the Garden of Eden opened up humanity to mortality, and mortality is central to humanity's growth (as opposed to stasis) and ultimately leads to a "final state of completion and perfection. See Susan Jeffers, "Bella and the Choice Made in Eden," in *The* Twilight *Mystique: Critical Essays on the Novels and Films*, ed. Amy M. Clarke and Marijane Osborn (Jefferson, NC: McFarland Press, 2010), 138.

36 Meyer, *Eclipse*, 448.

37 Ibid., 450.

38 Silver, "Twilight Is Not Good for Maidens," 129.

39 Lois H. Gresh, *The* Twilight *Companion: The Unauthorized Guide to the Series* (New York: St. Martin's Griffin, 2008), 27.

40 Ibid., 42.

41 Stephanie L. Dowdle, "Why We Like Our Vampires Sexy," in *The* Twilight *Mystique: Critical Essays on the Novels and Films*, ed. Amy M. Clarke and Marijane Osborn (Jefferson, NC: McFarland Press, 2010), 179–88, focuses on Edward's chauvinism, yet we find that it can relate to the other interpretations of stalker and abusive partner; see also Rebecca Housel, "The 'Real' Danger: Fact vs. Fiction for the Girl Audience," in Twilight *and Philosophy: Vampires, Vegetarians, and the Pursuit of Immortality*, ed. Rebecca Housel and J. Jeremy Wisnewski (Hoboken, NJ: John Wiley and Sons, 2009), 177–90; and Leah McClimans and J. Jeremy Wisnewski, "Undead Patriarchy and the Possibility of Love," in Twilight *and Philosophy: Vampires, Vegetarians, and the Pursuit of Immortality*, ed. Rebecca Housel and J. Jeremy Wisnewski (Hoboken, NJ: John Wiley and Sons, 2009), 163–75.

42 Stephenie Meyer, *Midnight Sun*, http://stepheniemeyer.com/pdf/midnightsun_partial_draft4.pdf.

43 Stephenie Meyer, *New Moon* (New York: Little, Brown and Company, 2006), 50.

44 Stephenie Meyer, *Breaking Dawn* (New York: Little, Brown and Company, 2008), 25.

45 Jessica Warner, *All or Nothing: A Short History of Abstinence in America* (Toronto: McClelland and Stewart, 2008) 27–28.

46 Meyer, *Eclipse*, 442.

47 Ibid., 443.

48 Ibid., 444.

49 Eve Kosofsky Sedgwick, "Shame, Theatricality, and Performativity: Henry James's *The Art of the Novel*," in *Gay Shame*, ed. David M. Halperin and Valerie Traub (Chicago: University of Chicago Press, 2009), 50.

50 Meyer, *Eclipse*, 446.

51 Quoted in Steven Connor, "The Shame of Being a Man," *Textual Practice* 15, 2 (2001): 212.

52 Michael Kimmel, *Manhood in America: A Cultural History* (Oxford: Oxford University Press, 2012), 5.

53 For a larger discussion of male virginity and popular romance fiction, see Jonathan A. Allan, "Theorising Male Virginity in Popular Romance Novels," *Journal of Popular Romance Studies* 2, 1 (2013), http://jprstudies. org/2011/10/theorising-male-virginity.

54 Indeed, Margaret M. Toscano points out that "most critics have merely connected Meyer's Mormonism to her characters' conservative morality" and then elaborates on how Meyer "is subtly subversive of her church's teachings." Margaret M. Toscano, "Mormon Morality and Immorality in Stephenie Meyer's *Twilight* Series," in *Bitten by* Twilight*: Youth Culture, Media, and the Vampire Franchise*, ed. Melissa A. Click, Jennifer Stevens Aubrey, and Elizabeth Behm-Morawitz, 21–36 (New York: Peter Lang, 2010), 21. For Toscano, then, one cannot merely suggest that since Meyer is a Mormon the book and its characters therefore follow a theological principle.

55 Fields and Hirschman, "Citizenship Lessons in Abstinence-Only Sexuality Education," 4, 6.

56 William A. Fisher and Janice Gray, "Erotophobia-Erotophilia and Sexual Behavior during Pregnancy and Postpartum," *Journal of Sex Research* 25, 3 (1988): 380. See also Kathryn R. Macapagal and Erick Janssen, "The Valence of Sex: Automatic Affective Associations in Erotophilia and Erotophobia," *Personality and Individual Differences* 51 (2011): 701; Marie Helweg-Larsen and Constance Howell, "Effects of Erotophobia on the Persuasiveness of Condom Advertisements Containing Strong or Weak Arguments," *Basic and Applied Social Psychology* 22, 2 (2000): 111; and John Ince, *The Politics of Lust* (Amherst, NY: Pivotal Press, 2005).

57 Although not one of the central concerns of this chapter, abstinence-only education is heterosexist: "Abstinence-only-until-marriage education is part of a broader attempt to reverse recent shifts that threaten to afford sexual nonconformists access to the category of 'good sexual citizen'"; Fields and Hirschman, "Citizenship Lessons in Abstinence-Only Sexuality Education," 4. Likewise, John P. Elia and Mickey J. Eliason observe that "school-based sexuality education in the United States has almost invariably focused on one particular form of heterosexuality and has almost excluded, both in terms of the discourse and pedagogical practice, teaching about sexualities that have been traditionally marginalized or *othered* such as lesbian, gay, bisexual, transgender, and queer (LGBTQ) sexualities"; John P. Elia and Mickey J. Eliason, "Dangerous Omissions: Abstinence-Only-until-Marriage School-Based Sexuality Education and the Betrayal of LGBTQ Youth," *American Journal of Sexuality Education* 5, 1 (2010): 17.

58 Anastasia Powell, *Sex, Power, and Consent: Youth Culture and Unwritten Rules* (Cambridge, UK: Cambridge University Press, 2010), 15.

59 Ibid., 16.

60 Ince, *The Politics of Lust*, 118.

61 Claire Greslé-Favier, *"Raising Sexually Pure Kids": Sexual Abstinence, Conservative Christians, and American Politics* (Amsterdam: Rodopi Press, 2009), x.

62 Elia and Eliason, "Dangerous Omissions," 21.

63 Ibid.

64 Fields and Hirschman, "Citizenship Lessons in Abstinence-Only Sexuality Education," 4.

65 Elia and Eliason, "Dangerous Omissions," 21.

66 Silver, "Twilight Is Not Good for Maidens," 129.

67 Paula A. Treichler, *How to Have Theory in an Epidemic: Cultural Chronicles of* AIDS (Durham: Duke University Press, 1999), 23.

68 See, for example, Batia Boe Stolar's "The Politics of Reproduction in Stephenie Meyer's *Twilight* Saga," in *Images of the Modern Vampire: The Hip and the Atavistic*, ed. Barbara Brodman and James E. Doan (Madison: Fairleigh Dickinson University Press, 2013), 191–207.

69 Meyer, *Eclipse*, 58.

70 Ibid., 59.

71 Ibid.

REFERENCES

Allan, Jonathan A. "Theorising Male Virginity in Popular Romance Novels." *Journal of Popular Romance Studies* 2, 1 (2013), http://jprstudies. org/2011/10/theorising-male-virginity.

Anatol, Giselle Liza, ed. *Bringing Light to* Twilight: *Perspectives on the Pop Culture Phenomenon*. New York: Palgrave Macmillan, 2011.

Arnold, J. H. "The Labour of Continence: Masculinity and Clerical Virginity." In *Medieval Virginities*, edited by Anke Bernau, Ruth Evans, and Sarah Salih, 102–18. Toronto: University of Toronto Press, 2003.

Bernau, Anke. *Virgins: A Cultural History*. London: Granta Books, 2007.

Bernau, Anke, Ruth Evans, and Sarah Salih, eds. *Medieval Virginities*. Toronto: University of Toronto Press, 2003.

Blank, Hanne. *Virgin: The Untouched History*. New York: Bloomsbury, 2007.

Bliss, Ann V. "Abstinence, American-Style." In *The* Twilight *Mystique: Critical Essays on the Novels and Films*, edited by A. M. Clarke and M. Osborn, 107–20. Jefferson, NC: McFarland Press, 2010.

Borgia, Danielle N. "*Twilight*: The Glamorization of Abuse, Codependency, and White Privilege." *Journal of Popular Culture* 47, 1 (2014): 153–73.

Caron, Sandra L., and Sarah P. Hinman. "'I Took His V-Card': An Exploratory Analysis of College Student Stories Involving Male Virginity Loss." *Sexuality and Culture* 17, 4 (2013): 525–39.

Carpenter, Laura M. *Virginity Lost: An Intimate Portrait of First Sexual Experiences*. New York: New York University Press, 2005.

Clarke, Amy M., and Marijane Osborn, eds. *The* Twilight *Mystique: Critical Essays on the Novels and Films*. Jefferson, NC: McFarland Press, 2010.

Click, Melissa A., Jennifer Stevens Aubrey, and Elizabeth Behm-Morawitz, eds. *Bitten by* Twilight: *Youth Culture, Media, and the Vampire Franchise*. New York: Peter Lang, 2010.

Collins, Victoria E., and Dianne C. Carmody. "Deadly Love: Images of Dating Violence in the 'Twilight Saga.'" *Affilia: Journal of Women and Social Work* 26, 4 (2011): 382–94.

Connor, Steven. "The Shame of Being a Man." *Textual Practice* 15, 2 (2001): 211–30.

Crossen, Caryss. "'Would You Please Stop Trying to Take Your Clothes Off?' Abstinence and Impotence of Male Vampires in Contemporary Fiction and Television." In *The Monster Imagined: Humanity's Re-Creation of Monsters and Monstrosity*, edited by Laura K. Davis and Cristina Santos, 111–23. Oxford: Interdisciplinary Press, 2010.

Deleyto, Celestino. "The New Road to Sexual Ecstasy: Virginity and Genre in *The 40-Year-Old Virgin*." In *Virgin Territory: Representing Sexual Inexperience in Film*, edited by Tamar Jeffers McDonald, 255–68. Detroit: Wayne State University Press, 2010.

Dowdle, Stephanie L. "Why We Like Our Vampires Sexy." In *The* Twilight *Mystique: Critical Essays on the Novels and Films*, edited by Amy M. Clarke and Marijane Osborn, 179–88. Jefferson, NC: McFarland Press, 2010.

Elia, John P., and Mickey J. Eliason. "Dangerous Omissions: Abstinence-Only-until-Marriage School-Based Sexuality Education and the Betrayal of LGBTQ Youth." *American Journal of Sexuality Education* 5, 1 (2010): 17–35.

Fields, Jessica, and Celeste Hirschman. "Citizenship Lessons in Abstinence-Only Sexuality Education." *American Journal of Sexuality Education* 2, 2 (2007): 3–25.

Fisher, William A., and Janice Gray. "Erotophobia-Erotophilia and Sexual Behavior during Pregnancy and Postpartum." *Journal of Sex Research* 25, 3 (1988): 379–96.

Frye, Northrop. *The Secular Scripture and Other Writings on Critical Theory, 1976–1991*, edited by J. Adamson and J. Wilson. Toronto: University of Toronto Press, 2006.

Gresh, Lois H. *The* Twilight *Companion: The Unauthorized Guide to the Series*. New York: St. Martin's Griffin, 2008.

Greslé-Favier, Claire. *"Raising Sexually Pure Kids": Sexual Abstinence, Conservative Christians, and American Politics*. Amsterdam: Rodopi Press, 2009.

Helweg-Larsen, Marie, and Constance Howell. "Effects of Erotophobia on the Persuasiveness of Condom Advertisements Containing Strong or Weak Arguments." *Basic and Applied Social Psychology* 22, 2 (2000): 111–17.

Housel, Rebecca. "The 'Real' Danger: Fact vs. Fiction for the Girl Audience." In Twilight *and Philosophy: Vampires, Vegetarians, and the Pursuit of Immortality*, edited by Rebecca Housel and J. Jeremy Wisnewski, 177–90. Hoboken, NJ: John Wiley and Sons, 2009.

Housel, Rebecca, and J. Jeremy Wisnewski, eds. Twilight *and Philosophy: Vampires, Vegetarians, and the Pursuit of Immortality*. Hoboken, NJ: John Wiley and Sons, 2009.

Ince, John. *The Politics of Lust*. Amherst, NY: Pivotal Press, 2005.

Jeffers, Susan. "Bella and the Choice Made in Eden." In *The* Twilight *Mystique: Critical Essays on the Novels and Films*, edited by Amy M. Clarke and Marijane Osborn, 137–51. Jefferson, NC: McFarland Press, 2010.

Jensen, Kristian. "Noble Werewolves or Native Shape-Shifters?" In *The* Twilight *Mystique: Critical Essays on the Novels and Films*, edited by Amy M. Clarke and Marijane Osborn, 92–106. Jefferson, NC: McFarland Press, 2010.

Kimmel, Michael. *Manhood in America: A Cultural History*. Oxford: Oxford University Press, 2012.

Macapagal, Kathryn R., and Erick Janssen. "The Valence of Sex: Automatic Affective Associations in Erotophilia and Erotophobia." *Personality and Individual Differences* 51 (2011): 699–703.

Mann, Bonnie. "Vampire Love: The Second Sex Negotiates the Twenty-First Century." In Twilight *and Philosophy: Vampires, Vegetarians, and the Pur-*

suit of Immortality, edited by Rebecca Housel and J. Jeremy Wisnewski, 131–45. Hoboken, NJ: John Wiley and Sons, 2009.

McClimans, Leah, and J. Jeremy Wisnewski. "Undead Patriarchy and the Possibility of Love." In Twilight *and Philosophy: Vampires, Vegetarians, and the Pursuit of Immortality*, edited by Rebecca Housel and J. Jeremy Wisnewski, 163–75. Hoboken, NJ: John Wiley and Sons, 2009.

Meyer, Stephenie. *Breaking Dawn*. New York: Little, Brown and Company, 2008.

———. *Eclipse*. New York: Little, Brown and Company, 2006.

———. *Midnight Sun*. http://stepheniemeyer.com/pdf/midnightsun_partial_draft4.pdf.

———. *New Moon*. New York: Little, Brown and Company, 2006.

Monro, Kate. *The First Time: True Tales of Virginity Lost and Found (Including My Own)*. London: Icon Books, 2011.

Park, Maggie, and Natalie Wilson, eds. *Theorizing* Twilight: *Critical Essays on What's at Stake in a Post-Vampire World*. Jefferson, NC: McFarland Press, 2011.

Platt, Carrie Anne. "Cullen Family Values: Gender and Sexual Politics in the *Twilight* Series." In *Bitten by* Twilight: *Youth Culture, Media, and the Vampire Franchise*, edited by Melissa A. Click, Jennifer Stevens Aubrey, and Elizabeth Behm-Morawitz, 71–86. New York: Peter Lang, 2010.

Powell, Anastasia. *Sex, Power, and Consent: Youth Culture and Unwritten Rules*. Cambridge, UK: Cambridge University Press, 2010.

"The Pure Love Club." http://www.pureloveclub.org/virginity.htm.

Rubin, Gayle S. "The Traffic in Women: Notes on the 'Political Economy' of Sex." In *Deviations: A Gayle Rubin Reader*, 33–65. Durham: Duke University Press, 2012.

Santtila, Pekka, N. Kenneth Sandnabba, and Patrick Jern. "Prevalence and Determinants of Male Sexual Dysfunctions during First Intercourse." *Journal of Sex and Marital Therapy* 35, 2 (2009): 86–105.

Sedgwick, Eve Kosofsky. *Epistemology of the Closet*. Berkeley: University of California Press, 1990.

———. "Shame, Theatricality, and Queer Performativity: Henry James's *The Art of the Novel*." In *Gay Shame*, edited by David M. Halperin and Valerie Traub, 49–62. Chicago: University of Chicago Press, 2009.

Silver, Anna. "Twilight Is Not Good for Maidens: Gender, Sexuality, and the Family in Stephenie Meyer's *Twilight* Series." *Studies in the Novel* 42, 1–2 (2010): 121–38.

Stolar, Batia Boe. "The Politics of Reproduction in Stephenie Meyer's *Twilight* Saga." In *Images of the Modern Vampire: The Hip and the Atavistic*, edited by Barbara Brodman and James E. Doan, 191–207. Madison: Fairleigh Dickinson University Press, 2013.

Terry, Gareth. "'I'm Putting a Lid on That Desire': Celibacy, Choice, and Control." *Sexualities* 15, 7 (2012): 871–89.

Toscano, Margaret M. "Mormon Morality and Immortality in Stephenie Meyer's *Twilight* Series." In *Bitten by* Twilight*: Youth Culture, Media, and the Vampire Franchise*, edited by Melissa A. Click, Jennifer Stevens Aubrey, and Elizabeth Behm-Morawitz, 21–36. New York: Peter Lang, 2010.

Treichler, Paula A. *How to Have Theory in an Epidemic: Cultural Chronicles of* AIDS. Durham: Duke University Press, 1999.

Warner, Jessica. *All or Nothing: A Short History of Abstinence in America.* Toronto: McClelland and Stewart, 2008.

Wilson, Natalie. *Seduced by* Twilight*: The Allure and Contradictory Messages of the Popular Saga*. Jefferson, NC: McFarland Press, 2011.

Wogan-Browne, Jocelyn. "Virginity Always Comes Twice: Virginity and Profession, Virginity and Romance." In *Maistresse of My Wit: Medieval Women, Modern Scholars*, edited by Louise D. D'Arcens and Juanita Feros Ruys, 335–69. Turnhout: Brepols, 2004.

CHAPTER 4

LADY OF PERPETUAL VIRGINITY: JESSICA'S PRESENCE IN *TRUE BLOOD*

Janice Zehentbauer and Cristina Santos

> In a hymen (out of which flows Dream), tainted with vice yet sacred, between desire and fulfillment, perpetration and remembrance: here anticipating, there recalling, in the future, in the past, under the false appearance of a present. [1]

> Gather ye rosebuds while ye may,
> Old time is still a-flying
> And that same bud that smiles today
> Tomorrow will be dying.[2]

n a keynote address at a conference at the University of Western Ontario in March 2012, Cristina Santos, in her paper "Monstrous Miracle Workers: Powerful Female Virgins," posed this question: is virginity becoming a trend?[3] Certainly, in the past two decades in America, evangelical church groups and the American government have united to encourage youth in general, and young women in particular, to choose abstinence, emphasizing personal choice as the key to sexual agency.[4] Historian and independent scholar Hanne Blank points out that, "of all the developed world, the United States is the only one that has to date created a federal agenda having specifically to do with the virginity of its citizens."[5] At the end of *Virgin: The Untouched History*, she outlines how the

Adolescent Family Life Act, formed in the early 1980s, continues to grant federal money to schools and church groups to promote abstinence education. Such legislation and funding, the proliferation of abstinence groups, the formation of purity clubs, and the wearing of purity rings are visible signs of a phenomenon that, more than a trend, is a whole industry revolving around abstinence groups and purity pledges, from music to summer camps, not to mention merchandise. As Santos notes, part of this industry includes "purity balls" (dances that mimic debutante balls or even weddings in which a daughter pledges to her father to remain a virgin until she is married), a ritual that Jessica Valenti criticizes as pseudo-incestuous (we would also add pedophilic) and placing the young girl (sometimes prepubescent) as a "wife in training."[6] Valenti describes this modern purity/abstinence culture as making "women's worth . . . contingent upon their ability to please men and to shape their sexual identities around what men want,"[7] yet "it's not women's sexuality that we have to watch out for, it's the way men construct it."[8] Jessica Hamby's vampiric blood in the television series *True Blood* is demarcated as doubly diseased within such a context since it "imparts both death and sexual deviance."[9]

Twenty-first-century America's obsession with virginity also emerges in many artifacts of popular culture, especially those of the gothic or supernatural genres. In her influential *Our Vampires, Ourselves*, Nina Auerbach argues that vampires, in the Anglo-American cultural imaginary, embody and signify the sociopolitical concerns of the era that produces them. It is not surprising, then, that HBO's cult show *True Blood* magnifies the vertiginous changes of the twenty-first century. Populated by hybrid figures (including not only vampires but also werewolves, fairies, shapeshifters, and *brujos* [male witches]), *True Blood*'s fast pace and multiple plot lines embrace the multiplicities and complexities of postmodernism. Often the show skewers right-wing political thought and orthodox religion (specifically Christianity) while also problematizing and unsettling socially conservative ideologies, such as female virginity and sexuality. We propose that these numerous concerns coalesce in *True Blood* with the problematic figure of Jessica Hamby.[10]

Her characterization as a perpetual virgin in the television series embodies the obsession with (young) female sexuality and contributes to the fetishization of female virginity in contemporary American culture. The perpetual virgin vampire paradigm as developed by the *True Blood* writers reveals the problem of defining female sexuality as externally imposed by paternalistic and misogynistic ideologies that place women in a position of being "forever children." It also promotes what Sarah Salih, Anke Bernau, and Ruth Evans have identified as "a hierarchy of authoritarian and hegemonic deployment" in which "the virgin can do violence as well as suffer it."[11] Jessica remains in a position that denies a healthy and fair expression of female sexuality apart from the male fantasy of female virginity. Even in her purportedly liberated state as a vampire, Jessica struggles, both physically and emotionally, with what Valenti calls the "virgin/whore strait-jacket."[12] Ultimately, Jessica is enclosed in an externally defined role characterized by a lack of separation among virginity, violence, and patriarchal control over women's bodies that further fetishizes youth and virginity.

What does it mean to be a perpetual virgin in twenty-first-century America? For seventeen-year-old Jessica, perpetual virginity is a curse, another unwelcome surprise that she receives while coping with her newly transformed vampiric body. In her experience, it is not the "first time" but the second sexual encounter that spells disaster: she is mortified to discover that her hymen has grown back. However, the "hymen" is not specifically mentioned, odd for a show that unflinchingly discusses and depicts almost every other taboo.[13] Jessica protests that "*It* grew back!"[14] Hoyt tells her not to worry: "That thing that grows back? It's just a *thing*."[15] But is it? Why this inability or unwillingness to articulate the term "hymen"? Is it because the hymen is fundamentally irreducible and unintelligible? If so, then what does that mean for female sexuality or gender construction and the articulation—or, conversely, the silence—of that construction? How does one approach the construction of Jessica's perpetual virginity in conjunction with her hypersexualized state as a vampire? Is it to be interpreted as the male fetish of converting the resistant virgin to the nymphomaniac, or is it the continued male need to define/make woman?[16] Does this imply a return to a historical moment in which the woman cannot speak for herself and only her body provides the required proof of her virginity because it is set up to exist within a cultural imaginary in which "the man masters his virginity but a woman's virginity is mastered by man"?[17] Or, in other words, does virginity loss not belong to a woman because it happens *to* her?[18]

Jessica's elusive, regenerating hymen reinforces the myth that all women have this membrane, thereby allowing for physical proof of "first blood" so prized within patriarchal cultures. In fact, and especially in Jessica's case, "virginity is a paradoxical condition, both perfect and *monstrous*."[19] Yet history has also upheld in certain cultures the belief of the "power of the virgin" in that sex with a virgin—and by extension the first blood—could cure a venereal disease.[20] In her vampiric form, Jessica can cure with her blood, yet she is monstrous not only because she is a vampire but more so because of her perpetual virginity. Each time she has intercourse her regenerating hymen causes blood to flow, providing the sign of no previous partner while constantly reminding Jessica, as well as the audience, of her transgressive nature in the repetitive and violent tearing of the hymen.[21]

The show's insistence on her virginity simultaneously sexualizes and infantilizes Jessica; although her vampiric body does offer her sexual agency, that agency is undermined by the show's insistence on her role as both a sexual object and a virgin. The elusiveness of the sign "hymen" itself provides moments of possibility and freedom from objectification, but this membrane, this mark, constantly emphasizes her virginity. The unmentionable hymen can be used both to enforce patrimony's anxiety over female sexuality and to set up a situation in which it can be applied to control female sexuality by the patriarchy.[22] The hymen further highlights the patrimonious treatment of female sexuality prevalent in the conservative social codes in the television program's setting of the American Deep South.

Valenti contends that the concept of social purity is a myth, one that damages young women by enforcing a patriarchal ideology that makes a woman's perception of self inextricably linked to her body and her ability to be a "moral" actor entirely dependent on her sexuality.[23] The link between female virginity and female social morality, Valenti argues, intrinsically objectifies and pathologizes the female body, putting female morality at risk.[24] The virginity/ purity movement in the twenty-first century makes definitions of female purity, sexuality, and morality more regressive by emphasizing the ideal of the passive woman by dangerously conflating sexuality and morality.[25] Jessica in *True Blood* plays with the notion of female sexuality as both transgressive and dangerous to society as a whole: after all, she is a vampire. Nonetheless, Ron Hirschbein remarks that "vampire myths are universal because they reflect what's universal in us—*primal instincts* and *defense mechanisms*."[26] Furthermore, the virgin/whore and human/vampire paradigms represented in Jessica further highlight the cultural preoccupation of woman as "dirty," in which "goodness" is more confining than socially perceived "badness."[27] Jessica's perpetual vampiric virginity accentuates the idea of female "goodness" as being predominantly regulated externally, eschewing an authentic expression of a liberated female sexual identity, experience, or desire. Instead, there is a negation of an independent female sexuality in favour of the male fantasy of a "virgin ideal" of woman as docile and submissive and whose body can be "marked" only by the penetration of the male phallus (penis and/or fangs).[28]

Clergy and politicians are not the only ones preoccupied with youth and virginity. The works of psychologists, sociologists, and literary critics reveal that virginity (particularly female virginity) has almost always, almost universally, been fraught with anxiety. A facet of the anxiety is the elusive definition of female virginity, usually framed in terms of *loss*. While talking with patients during psychoanalytical sessions, doctors Deanna Holtzman and Nancy Kulish were struck by the number of patients who framed narratives of their first sexual experiences in language of negation, a haunting "nevermore": "Defloration, like birth and death, is a one-time occurrence that cannot be repeated."[29] Sociologist Laura M. Carpenter's studies further demonstrate that definitions of virginity and its "loss" in the twenty-first century change as concepts of gender and sexuality change. Virginity loss has been identified traditionally as the first time that a person experiences penile-vaginal intercourse;[30] however, this heteronormative definition is being altered by youth who are gay, lesbian, or bisexual.[31] Similarly, Blank observes that "virginity is invariably defined in terms of what it is not, and is believed to be proven most incontrovertibly by whatever signs (blood, pain, etc.) become obvious only in the moment of its obliteration."[32] Blank further emphasizes that virginity has been used historically as an "organizing principle of human cultures" and is a malleable cultural idea.[33]

Within these terms of "loss" and "negation," however, literary critic Kathryn Schwarz contends that the indeterminate nature of virginity allows for some possibility: "Virginity accumulates to something inscrutable. It is in the past, in the future, in the negative, in the subjunctive, an impossibility, a fantasy, a provocation, a performance, a lie."[34] We mentioned above that for some virginity loss is irrecoverable and cannot be recreated or redone. Nonetheless, Jessica experiences all three repeatedly. As a vampiric virgin, she can recoup a loss, and for this reason she is situated within the social dynamics of female virginity as "a provocation, a performance, a lie." Furthermore, within the traditional patriarchal construct of hetero-normative gender power relations, virginity loss is a loss of power for women and a gain of power for men. In losing her virginity, the woman experiences a loss of value within the patriarchal marketplace, for the loss is a devaluation of her as a commodity. Female virginity becomes valued as a social performance of an externally constructed ritual of female transformation from girlhood to womanhood based upon the patriarchal social acknowledgement of this sexual transition.[35] Yet this traditional view of female virginal commodification is questioned and tested by Jessica's perpetual virginity, since her vampiric state allows Jessica to reinstitute her unending value in the social marketplace.[36] She has the advantage of not having to pay for her hymen reconstruction[37] while maintaining her value in this marketplace.

Despite their seeming incongruity, vampires and virgins share several similarities in the Western cultural imaginary. Indeed, virgins are common fodder for horror movies, as critics Andrea Sabbadini and Pete Falconer demonstrate (in their respective essays in *Virgin Territory: Representing Sexual Inexperience in Film*). Virgins are sacrifices for monstrous figures, such as Count Dracula,[38] who prefer to bite virtuous young women in the taking of both their purity and their virginity.[39] Virgins are also positioned as the "Final Girl," the character who not only survives in slasher films but also, according to Falconer, parallels the killer in several ways.[40] True to form, *True Blood* itself is rife with virginity. For example, Jessica's first boyfriend, Hoyt Fortenberry, is himself a virgin; at twenty-eight, he explains his "late life" virginity as his belief in romantic love and his reason for waiting for a "nice" girl like Jessica:

> HOYT: I was gonna wait, you know, till I met the right one. Well, the right one never showed up. By then I had waited so long I figured I couldn't give it away to just anybody. So now I'm twenty-eight . . .Most girls probably think I'm like some kinda bisexual gay or somethin'. Not that I got any kind of problem with them. But I'm not.[41]

His position, then, provides a contrast to that of other male characters in the show (particularly that of his friend Jason Stackhouse). Additionally, *True Blood*'s central heroine, Sookie Stackhouse (herself a version of the Final Girl), also waits until her twenties to experience intercourse for the first time, with vampire Bill Compton. Furthermore, in flashbacks depicted in season 2, a young Sam (a shapeshifter and the owner of Merlotte's tavern) is a virgin when he encounters Marianne for the first time, and because of this she appears years later in Bon Temps to sacrifice Sam to her god Dionysus. In season 3, when Lafayette's boyfriend Jesus excitedly pleas to take "V" again, Lafayette chuckles, "Just *like* a virgin."[42] Despite the candid sexuality of the series—or because of it—virginity plays a prominent role in *True Blood*, yet the show refuses to use the word *hymen* when Jessica loses her virginity. Regardless of its progressive views of sexuality, the hymen still seems to be sufficiently taboo even for *True Blood* and as such remains unmentionable.

The shared characteristics of virgins and vampires embody several cultural taboos, including the intersections of erotic charge, blood, and violence. Sigmund Freud hypothesizes that, "wherever primitive man institutes a taboo, there he fears a danger, and it cannot be disputed that the general principle underlying all these regulations and avoidances is a dread of [the] woman."[43] For Freud, these regulations all revolve around the woman in her "sexual life," such as during menstruation, and in her function as a mother.[44] Furthermore, in *Totem and Taboo*, Freud discusses the fear of the dead: "But originally, says Kleinpaul, *all* of the dead were vampires, all of them had a grudge against the living and sought to injure them and rob them of their lives. It was from corpses that the concept of evil spirits first arose."[45] According to Freud, taboos signal the simultaneous existence of the sacred and the profane. This is the position of Jessica in *True Blood*. She constitutes a double threat to traditional patriarchal values regarding woman; as both virgin and vampire, she embodies the fantasy of sexual purity coupled with the fantasy and/or anxiety of a voracious sexual predator. This double threat is particularly emphasized in the final episode of season 2, in which she initiates sex with a truck driver at a highway stop:

JESSICA: Just before we go any further, I think there's something you ought to know.

TRUCKER: Yeah, what's that, sugar?

JESSICA: I'm a virgin.

TRUCKER: That's okay. In fact, I kinda like it.

JESSICA: Do you?

Trucker nods.

JESSICA: Well, I don't like it one bit![46]

Jessica realizes, in this scene, that her status as a virgin is even more powerful in sexual bartering than her status as a vampire. Her virginity acts as a disguise here, the most effective one in this exchange, and her power as a vampire is realized when she lunges at the trucker (and ultimately drains and kills him, as viewers find out in season 3).

Scholars of popular culture often recognize that vampires function as a sign of sexual excess. Similarly, virginity, as Blank points out, is charged with erotic potential because of the idea of the virgin as a blank slate on which others can project their fantasies as well as "unthinkable thoughts and perverse desires."[47] The vampire and the virgin also insist on the female *body* that needs to be penetrated/conquered by the male.[48] Virginity was (and continues to be) *proven* with the sign of first blood on the bed sheet; blood, of course, authenticates the vampire as well.[49] Regarding the vampiric body, critics such as Nina Auerbach and Christopher Craft argue that vampires transgress gender as well as heteronormative sexual boundaries. In psychoanalytic terms, fangs operate as twin phallic symbols that penetrate the flesh—Auerbach calls them "little penile eruptions popping out of . . . mouths"[50]—and indeed Jessica finds that her fangs "pop out" uncontrollably while kissing Hoyt. She simultaneously carries the signs of the "blank slate" and the phallic fang; as Angela Tumini stipulates, the female vampire, in penetrating her victim with her fangs, embodies not only "the stereotypical masculine trait of aggressiveness" but also the danger of feminizing men and the threat of bisexuality.[51]

The bloody mouth, on the other hand, represents the vagina, the "wound" of psychoanalytic theory; it is wounded (in the male conquest of female virginity with the rupture of the hymen) and itself capable of wounding (Freud's theory of the male fear of castration by the vagina dentata). Let us recall that in Mitchell Lichtenstein's film *Teeth* the heroine, Dawn, possesses vagina dentata attributed to an evolutionary adaptation, the self-protection of her purity promise, or an environmental mutation (her family lives behind a chemical plant).[52] If we were to juxtapose this film example with Valenti's criticism of government-funded abstinence education, what is the current sociopolitical environment doing to women's bodies but making them *monstrous* or, in Jessica's case, forever virginal? However, unlike Jessica, Dawn's "teeth" emerge only when Dawn feels that she is being sexually attacked and/or violated. Regardless, one cannot ignore that in contemporary vampire culture the unveiled fangs not only symbolize "genital contact" but also merge sex and procreation with eating and nutrition[53] and underline male anxiety about being drained of their virility.[54] And, as the adoptive "good" father figure Bill tries to ensure that Jessica does not "eat" her dates, this can be read not only as a paternal desire to control a newborn vampire's bloodlust but also as a young woman's emerging sexual appetite.

Craft particularly points out that vampiric mouths are an especially effective example of gender ambiguity: "With its soft flesh barred by hard bone . . . this mouth compels opposites and contrasts into a frightening unity, and it asks some disturbing questions. Are we male or are we female? Do we have penetrators or orifices? And if both, what does that mean?"[55] Certainly, Jessica embodies the "both" of the duality, this fluidity of gender, yet the insistence on her particularly *female* sign of virginity, the hymen, ultimately works to reduce any gender freedom that she might find in her vampiric state. As a vampire, she is indeed sexually transgressive; part of such "transgression" is the duality of the female "wound" and the phallic fang. However, the hymen (her "blank slate") marks her as specifically, biologically female; its persistent presence insists that she cannot (entirely) cross gender boundaries. This in itself reflects the traditional vampire motif of the human girl "as the virgin victim . . . but the sexual woman [as] automatically a vampire."[56]

Undoubtedly, *True Blood* playfully and pointedly punctures right-wing, conservative anxieties about sexuality. The fact that vampires have "come out of the coffin" demands that viewers and critics alike align vampires' struggles for vampire rights with the struggles of gay, lesbian, and transgender groups for civil liberty in America. In one of the more famous images from the opening credits of the series, a sign in a church parking lot reads "God Hates Fangs," lampooning the infamous slogan "God Hates Fags"[57] of the Westboro Baptist Church in Topeka, Kansas. Jessica's "rehymenization" might also be a further parody of abstinence movements in which her virginity can be seen as an extreme version of imposing the ideal of purity. However, this parody appears at the cost of her ability to "choose"—as a human, Jessica does not *choose* to become a vampire; as a vampire, she does not *choose* to remain a virgin.

Her double status as virgin and vampire also signals the conflation of sex and violence in the discourse of virginity. A number of critics note the violence inherent in the language of virginity loss, as in supposedly innocuous popular slang such as "busting the cherry."[58] Derrida's analysis of Mallarmé's poem "Mimique" not only emphasizes the ephemerality of the hymen but also points to the violence of male control:

> The hymen, the consummation of differends, the continuity and confusion of the coitus, merges with what it seems to be derived from: the hymen as protective screen, the jewel box of virginity, the vaginal partition, the fine, invisible veil which, in front of the hystera, stands *between* the inside and the outside of a woman, and consequently between desire and fulfillment. It is neither desire nor pleasure but in between the two. Neither future nor present, but between the two. It is the hymen that desire dreams of piercing, of bursting, in an act of violence that is (at the same time or somewhere between) love and murder.[59]

Derrida's analysis here positions the hymen and virginity as specifically female (in his analysis here of a poem on heterosexuality). The "in between" state of the virgin can be said to give the female some degree of agency, of sexual choice, but as this analysis makes clear the "between the two" position is aligned with explicitly violent male desire. Jessica might have some degree of power as virgin and vampire, yet the persistence of her virginity, her fetishized youthful body, undercuts any notion of sexual agency. This further underlines the need to enclose women's sexuality within clear parameters: virgin or not. Any in-between space is abnormal and monstrous since it negates the clear participation of the phallus in marking the distinction of a woman's sexual individuality.

Indeed, Jessica is "strait-jacketed" from the moment of her introduction into the series. Her forced transformation from human to vampire is akin to a rape and is constructed as one of the most harrowing scenes of the first season. When she "meets her maker," she is a seventeen-year-old girl with little experience of the "outside world": "a calm, gentle, complacent, and *traditional* girl."[60] We learn later that Jessica has been home-schooled and raised in an orthodox Christian household; her father used the belt when his daughters attempted any sort of rebellion. Fulfilling—unwillingly—the traditional role of the sacrificial virgin, she is kidnapped from her family and "given" to Bill by the vampire tribunal as a punishment: because he has killed one vampire, he must create another one.[61] Jessica prays and pleads for her life in front of the vampire audience, who only react with bloodlust as Bill bites into her—a bloodlust that she inherits as a vampire with a new "rebellious nature."[62] As a female vampire, Jessica enters what has been traditionally a sexually liberated status in which blood imbues her with power rather than marking her as "weak."[63] Yet viewers are also reminded of her sexual innocence from this first scene; any sexual liberation that she might have as a vampire is cancelled by her perpetual virginity.

At first, Jessica revels in her vampiric state, finding in it a liberation: "No more home school. No more belts. Yeehah! I'm a vampire!"[64] Yet she finds that she cannot escape patriarchal rules; Bill restricts her movements ("There will be no hunting in this house") and nurses her on a diet of Tru Blood ("You have to keep your strength. Two-thirds of vampires never survive the first year"[65]), a regime that not even Bill can tolerate.[66] The only character who has any sympathy for Jessica's experience as a new vampire is Sookie:

BILL: When a vampire is as new as Jessica is, she has no humanity. She's in the grips of an overwhelming number of transformations. There will be times when she cannot control even a single impulse. Believe me, she has many.

SOOKIE: How is that any different from being a teenage girl? No humanity, check. In the grips of overwhelming transformations, check. Cannot control impulses, check. Sorry, how is that different?[67]

Sookie underlines here the harshness of Bill's attitude toward his offspring in addition to how Bill controls (or wants to control) Jessica's impulses and desires. This seems to mimic what Naomi Wolf deems a patriarchal society's tendency to link sexually assertive and self-aware women as empowered women—thereby being difficult to "drive to self-destruction, to manipulate and control."[68] That is, Bill's attempt to curb Jessica's experiencing her sexuality to the fullest is a way to suppress her innate power as a woman, and that can ultimately lead to a suppressed rage.[69] Such a rage eventually prompts Jessica to go on a rampage of drinking human blood and culminates in her attempt to kill her biological father in season 2.

Another facet of her blood (and sexual) rage involves another "nevermore"—Jessica will never reach full adulthood. Auerbach, in a discussion of Anne Rice's *Interview with the Vampire*, notes that the little girl Claudia, whom Louis and Lestat turn into a vampire and adopt, will remain forever a "doll"; for Claudia, "vampirism is no release from patriarchy, but a perpetuation of it until the end of time."[70] This is the position in which the teenaged Jessica finds herself. She is simultaneously sexualized and infantilized by both the characters around her and by the show itself—both actions reflect the purity movement's treatment of women and the implicit "rolling back of women's rights."[71] For instance, Pam dresses her up in short plaid skirts and ponytails, like a "schoolgirl" male fantasy, and Bill takes the position of a father figure and forces her to wash off her makeup: "I will not have you looking like a slattern," he tells her when she is returned to his house.[72] Defying his orders to drink only Tru Blood, Jessica curls her hair and dons a bright yellow sundress to hunt for a human jugular at Merlotte's; as she enters the tavern, the song "Sex and Candy" plays while the men admire her. Although the looking is mutual in this scene—plainly, Jessica is stalking the men as much as they are ogling her—the song in the background undercuts her desire by forcing viewers to see her only as the object of the male gaze. The lyrics of the song provide a narrative for Hoyt, who *is* "just hanging 'round" when "there she was."[73]

Similarly, in the last episode of season 4, the background music again undercuts Jessica's sexual agency and desire. The scene is a wonderfully atmospheric one in which Jessica, dressed up as Little Red Riding Hood for Halloween, approaches Jason's house for a sexual encounter. The song is a haunting version of a southern American folk song with roots in African American blues—"Where Did You Sleep Last Night?"—performed by Jim Oblon.[74] Once again her dual status as virgin and vampire is evident: her disguise outwardly links her to the sexually innocent young girl of the Charles

Perrault fairy tale, yet she is clearly also acting the part of the wolf, the predator in the tale associated with transgressive female libido, tempting Jason.[75] Nonetheless, the song's lyrics are positioned as an address, putting Jessica in the position of an object: "Little girl, little girl, don't you lie to me, / Tell me where did you sleep last night?"[76] Her enjoyment in seducing Jason is once more undercut by the "little girl" status, and yet again an outside male voice demands an account of her sexual activity.

Despite undercutting her desire in the above-mentioned scenes, the show does place Jessica and Hoyt on equal ground in season 2; both are virgins and decide together to have intercourse for the first time (though his carefully planned romantic encounter is interrupted by Bill). When Hoyt and Jessica unite again, she says, "I can't believe I waited so long, we're going to do it every single night, whether you want to or not."[77] However, the signs of virginity—pain and blood—become manifest once more:

HOYT: Is that blood again?

JESSICA: Oh, my God. No, no, no. . . .

HOYT: What Jessica? What?

JESSICA: It grew back!

HOYT: It . . . what?

JESSICA: My [indiscernible], it fucking grew back! I should have known it. I mean, everything heals when you're a goddamn vampire.

HOYT: It's gonna be beautiful. Every time will be like our first time.

JESSICA: It'll hurt like hell! I'm a fucking deformity of nature. I'm going to be a virgin forever.[78]

In other words, Jessica sees her everlasting virginal state as another aspect of her "monstrosity."[79] If, as Blank relates, "virginity is a sort of placeholder, something that exists until such time as it is removed or destroyed by man,"[80] then what does Jessica's continual defloration say about the gendered power relationship intrinsic to the heterosexual couple? That is, does each moment of being deflowered allow Hoyt to feel a sense of male superiority when he, as a human, is otherwise powerless in his relationship with vampiric Jessica? The assumed fetish of the conquest of the virgin[81] (or even parthenophilia, a sexual interest in virgins[82]) is later undermined when they end their relationship, she searches for other sexual partners, and he exclaims, "I deserve someone who isn't going to be a fuckin' virgin for all of eternity."[83] Hoyt also conflates her virginity with monstrosity when he labels a box of her possessions "For You, Monster."[84] As season 4 progresses, Jessica's emerging promiscuity is used to undermine the traditional view of the virgin ever "belonging" only to one man and, as a result, undercuts the male construct of sexual power relations.

For all her sexual adventurousness in later seasons, however, Jessica remains physically a virgin. After she finds out, in season 2, that she will be a virgin forever, she expresses the wish to escape her "condition":

JESSICA: Maybe I'll get used to it. Or maybe there's an operation. . . . I can't be the only vampire virgin.

HOYT: Intercourse isn't the only way to have sex.

JESSICA: But I WANT to have intercourse.[85]

Here Jessica expresses the desire to experience "normal" heterosexual intercourse; her perpetual virginity denies her the chance of feeling sexual pleasure without being painfully reminded of her sexual abnormality. After she says that Hoyt should break up with her, he replies, "'Hell, no. That thing that grows back . . . it's just a *thing*.'"[86] As previously noted, neither Jessica nor Hoyt specifically names the "thing" the hymen; this avoidance is a sign not of erasure, but of what Schwarz determined in an earlier quotation: "Virginity accumulates to something inscrutable."[87] However, the hymen is not "just a thing" for Jessica; it maintains her in a bodily containment that supports the heteronormative patriarchal view of female sexuality that preserves not only a male sense of honour by sacrificing the female body but also a male sense of superiority by inscribing female sexual identity with the intervention of the phallus.

A question remains: how far have we come in our treatment of female virginity and sexual agency in the twenty-first century? Our study of Jessica's role in the series *True Blood* reveals that for women—especially young women—the constraints governing their sexuality remain eerily similar to those of 1950s America; "good" girls remain virgins until they are married, and there is social ostracism for those who do not. For all of its celebration of sexual subversion and diversity, *True Blood* adheres in the end to middle-class American "family values." Jessica remains trapped—physically—in the body of a virgin, an emblem of female "purity." Later seasons show her exploring and flaunting her sexuality, yet her promiscuity does not signal any sense of female sexual liberation. Moreover, in the seventh and final season, Hoyt returns to Bon Temps, and he and Jessica are married. This is not a "happily ever after" since it is a marriage based upon the manipulation of his memory—he is glamoured into forgetting his previous relationship with her. This act of erasure has a double function in which the (sexual) past is forgotten and rewritten into the present, in which the marriage actually cancels her previous sexual freedom and returns her sexual history to a clean slate—a virginal reinscription into the patriarchal institution of marriage. Indeed, the marriage of Hoyt and Jessica becomes a stereotypical narrative: two young sweethearts marry their first love and/or sexual partner. Nevertheless, she still embodies the problems and paradoxes of an unfixed and undocumentable female virgin. Sarah Luttfring asserts that "virginity in our contemporary society does not rest solely on a sign of purity by supposing it is inextricably linked to modesty or shame of female sexuality."[88] So far the twenty-first century has seen the rising popularity and accessibility of medical procedures such as hymenoplasty, revirginization, and vaginal rejuvenation that reconstruct and reconfigure female virginity while further fetishizing it. What seems at first to be a new sense of female sexual empowerment—as represented by Jessica as a vampire—is but another commodification and regulation of female sexuality under a new guise. She is not only forever dead as a vampire but also forever reminded of her humanity in her perpetual virginity—forever enclosed within an existence that both empowers and limits her as the vampire virgin.

NOTES

1   Stéphane Mallarmé, quoted in Jacques Derrida, *Dissemination* (1972), trans. Barbara Johnson (Chicago: University of Chicago Press, 1981), 209.

2   Robert Herrick, "To the Virgins, to Make Much of Time," in *Seventeenth Century Prose and Poetry*, ed. Alexander M. Witherspoon and Frank J. Warnke, 2nd ed. (New York: Harcourt Brace Jovanovich, 1982), 813.

3   Cristina Santos, "Monstrous Miracle Workers: Powerful Female Virgins," keynote address at the 14th Annual Graduate Student Conference, Department of Modern Languages and Literatures, University of Western Ontario, London, ON, March 3, 2012.

4   Peter S. Bearman and Hannah Brückner note that abstinence and virginity pledges work primarily through "identity constructions": that is, youth identify with the movement when it seems to be unique and special, but as the movement increases and the groups grow in number the sense of membership in the group, and consequently the teen's identification with the group, diminish. Other factors, such as the amount of religiosity (this study seems to focus on Christian religions) in the home and other outside influences (e.g., the media), also determine whether or not a teen drops out of the movement. See Peter S. Bearman and Hannah Brückner, "Promising the Future: Virginity Pledges and First Intercourse," *American Journal of Sociology* 106, 4 (2001): 859–912, doi: 10.1086/320295.

5   Hanne Blank, *Virgin: The Untouched History* (New York: Bloomsbury, 2007), 238.

6   See Jessica Valenti, *The Purity Myth: How America's Obsession with Virginity Is Hurting Young Women* (Berkeley: Seal Press, 2010), 65–79. In her keynote address, Santos drew a clear parallel between these purity balls and weddings.

7   Valenti, *The Purity Myth*, 91.

8   Ibid., 96.

9   Paul E. H. Davis, "Dracula Anticipated: The 'Undead' in Anglo-Irish Literature," in *The Universal Vampire: Origins and Evolution of a Legend*, ed. Barbara Brodman and James E. Doan (Madison: Fairleigh Dickinson University Press, 2013), 28. Davis discusses the female vampire's "doubly diseased" blood in his analysis of the character of Carmilla, one of the first examples of female vampirism, in Sheridan Le Fanu's *Carmilla* (1872), which predates Bram Stoker's *Dracula* by twenty-five years.

10 We examine here the television series only, not the Sookie Stackhouse novels written by Charlaine Harris, upon which the series is based, since there is a considerable digression in plot development between the two.

11 Sarah Salih, Anke Bernau, and Ruth Evans, "Introduction: Virginities and Virginity Studies," in *Medieval Virginities*, ed. Anke Bernau, Ruth Evans, and Sarah Salih (Toronto: University of Toronto Press, 2003), 6.

12 Valenti, *The Purity Myth*, 4.

13 For a discussion of the liberties provided by televising *True Blood* with HBO, see Brigid Cherry, "Before the Night Is Through: *True Blood* as Cult TV," in True Blood: *Investigating Vampires and Southern Gothic*, ed. Brigid Cherry (New York: I. B. Tauris, 2012), 3–21.

14 "Timebomb," *True Blood*, season 2, episode 8, first broadcast August 9, 2009, by HBO, directed by John Dahl, written by Alexander Woo.

15 "I Will Rise Up," *True Blood*, season 2, episode 9, first broadcast August 16, 2009, by HBO, directed by Scott Winant, written by Nancy Oliver.

16 See Valenti, *The Purity Myth*, 194.

17 Ibid., 195.

18 For a discussion of virginity loss, psychological virginity, and its social indoctrination, see Nancy Friday, *My Mother/My Self: The Daughter's Search for Identity* (1977; reprinted, London: HarperCollins, 1994), 297–305.

19 Salih et al., "Introduction," 2; emphasis added.

20 Blank, *Virgin*, 62, 65.

21 See Jocelyn Wogan-Browne, "Virginity Now and Then: A Response to *Medieval Virginities*," in *Medieval Virginities*, ed. Anke Bernau, Ruth Evans, and Susan Salih (Toronto: University of Toronto Press, 2003), 242. It has been important throughout history to differentiate between "the first blood of defloration" and menstrual blood since the latter had a long tradition of affirming the "venomous nature" of blood emanating

from woman. See Esther Lastique and Helen Rodnite Lemay, "A Medieval Physician's Guide to Virginity," in *Sex in the Middle Ages: A Book of Essays*, ed. Joyce E. Salisbury (New York: Garland Publishing, 1991), 60, 67. See also Aviva Briefel, "Monster Pains: Masochism, Menstruation, and Identification in Horror Film," *Film Quarterly* 58, 3 (2005): 16–27, doi:10.1525/fq.2005.58.3.16, who argues that male monsters perform masochistic acts of self-mutilation before they embark on their killing sprees, whereas female monsters suffer from abuse (sexual, parental) before they start killing. The female's wound is not self-inflicted but the "wound" of psychoanalytical thought—menstruation. For Briefel, male killers' actions create a critical distance for the audience, whereas female killers' actions prompt empathy from the viewer.

22   For further discussion, see Blank, *Virgin*, 23–31.

23   Interestingly, the Born Again Virgins of America movement is focused on restoring moral fibre by encouraging people to "reassert power over their bodies and gain self-respect." Bonnie MacLachlan, "Introduction," in *Virginity Revisited: Configurations of the Unpossessed Body*, ed. Bonnie MacLachlan and Judith Fletcher (Toronto: University of Toronto Press, 2007), 3.

24   Valenti, *The Purity Myth*, 33.

25   Ibid., 23.

26   Ron Hirschbein, "Sookie, Sigmund, and the Edible Complex," in True Blood *and Philosophy: We Wanna Think Bad Things with You*, ed. George A. Dunn and Rebecca Housel (Hoboken, NJ: John Wiley and Sons, 2010), 127.

27   Valenti, *The Purity Myth*, 41, 51.

28   Ibid., 63.

29   Deanna Holtzman and Nancy Kulish, *Nevermore: The Hymen and the Loss of Virginity* (Northvale, NJ: Jason Aronson, 1997), 3.

30   Laura M. Carpenter, "The Ambiguity of 'Having Sex': The Subjective Experience of Virginity Loss in the United States," *Journal of Sex Research* 38, 2 (2001): 127–39, doi: 10.2307/3813703, 346.

31   Ibid., 131.

32   Blank, *Virgin*, 96.

33   Ibid., 7–9, 20.

34   Kathryn Schwarz, "The Wrong Question: Thinking through Virginity," *Differences: A Journal of Feminist Cultural Studies* 13, 2 (2002): 2, http://muse.jhu.edu/journals/dif/summary/v013/13.2schwartz.html.

35   See Blank, *Virgin*, 97–103.

36   For the purposes of this chapter, however, we refer specifically to the traditional heterosexual definition since *True Blood* itself insists on it and particularly since it insists on aligning female physiology as a sign or "proof" of female virginity loss (and male virginity gain/conquest) vis-à-vis the current purity philosophy.

37   Also known as hymenorrhaphy or hymenoplasty, the procedure has increased in popularity in the United States, western Europe, and Japan in plastic surgery clinics. The procedures act as interventions after rape or other trauma and, in some cases, for aesthetic reasons.

38   Andrea Sabbadini, "The Window and the Door," in *Virgin Territory: Representing Sexual Inexperience in Film*, ed. Tamar Jeffers McDonald (Detroit: Wayne State University Press, 2010), 225.

39   Edward O. Keith, "Biomedical Origins of Vampirism," in *The Universal Vampire: Origins and Evolution of a Legend*, ed. Barbara Brodman and James E. Doan (Madison: Fairleigh Dickinson University Press, 2013), 70.

40   Pete Falconer, "Fresh Meat? Dissecting the Horror Movie Virgin," in *Virgin Territory: Representing Sexual Inexperience in Film*, ed. Tamar Jeffers McDonald (Detroit: Wayne State University Press, 2010), 131. Falconer cites Carol Clover's term "Final Girl." In the horror and slasher genres, a young girl is the sole survivor at the end of the film; she outwits the murderer and evades the killing spree. Gender is significant here: girls survive more often than boys in these films. Also, the Final Girl is often the more reserved member of her teenaged social set and usually a virgin or the least promiscuous of her friends (notably, her friends are usually killed after having sex).

41   "Release Me," *True Blood*, season 2, episode 7, first broadcast August 2, 2009, by HBO, directed by Michael Ruscio, written by Raelle Tucker.

42   "Fresh Blood," *True Blood*, season 3, episode 11, first broadcast August 29, 2010, by HBO, directed by Daniel Minahan, written by Nancy Oliver.

43   Sigmund Freud, "The Taboo of Virginity" (1918), in *Sexuality and the Psychology of Love*, ed. Philip Rieff (New York: Touchstone, 1997), 66.

44   Ibid,, 65.

45 Sigmund Freud, *Totem and Taboo* (1913), in *The Standard Edition*, trans. James Strachey, introd. Peter Gay (New York: W. W. Norton, 1989), 74–75.

46 "Beyond Here Lies Nothin'," *True Blood*, season 2, episode 12, first broadcast September 13, 2009, by HBO, directed by Michael Cuesta, written by Alexander Woo.

47 Hirschbein, "Sookie, Sigmund, and the Edible Complex," 129. Hirschbein continues that, "just as we can't vanquish these desires that constitute what we detest in ourselves, [so too] we can't readily kill vampires since they are simply the projection of all those parts of ourselves that we wish to disown." Ibid.

48 Interestingly, the popular romance series *Winning Virgin Blood* (five volumes) by Destiny Blaine insists on the idea of the male vampire's lifemate as virginal.

49 In another popular romance by Kerrelyn Sparks, *The Vampire and the Virgin* (New York: Avon Books, 2010), another trope is highlighted in which the heroine's virginity loss is marked not only by the sign of first blood but also by her vampiric lover's fangs.

50 Nina Auerbach, *Our Vampires, Ourselves* (Chicago: University of Chicago Press, 1995), 129.

51 Angela Tumini, "*Vampiresse*: Embodiment of Sensuality and Erotic Horror in Carl Th. Dreyer's *Vampyr* and Mario Bava's *The Mask of Satan*," in *The Universal Vampire: Origins and Evolution of a Legend*, ed. Barbara Brodman and James E. Doan (Madison: Fairleigh Dickinson University Press, 2013), 124.

52 *Teeth*, dir. Mitchell Lichtenstein (Dimension Extreme, 2008).

53 Bruce A. McClelland, "Un-*True Blood*: The Politics of Artificiality," in True Blood *and Philosophy: We Wanna Think Bad Things with You*, ed. George A. Dunn and Rebecca Housel (Hoboken, NJ: John Wiley and Sons, 2010), 81.

54 Katherine Allocco, "Vampiric Viragoes: Villainizing and Sexualizing Arthurian Women in *Dracula vs. King Arthur* (2005)," in *The Universal Vampire: Origins and Evolution of a Legend*, ed. Barbara Brodman and James E. Doan (Madison: Fairleigh Dickinson University Press, 2013), 156.

55 Christopher Craft, "'Kiss Me with Those Red Lips': Gender and Inversion in Bram Stoker's *Dracula*," *Representations* 8 (1984): 109, doi: 10.2307/2928560.

56 Nancy Schumann, "Women with Bite: Tracing Vampire Women from Lilith to *Twilight*," in *The Universal Vampire: Origins and Evolution of a Legend*, ed. Barbara Brodman and James E. Doan (Madison: Fairleigh Dickinson University Press, 2013), 117.

57 Many of the essays in The Blackwell Philosophy and Popular Culture Series text on *True Blood* draw attention to this sign and this inversion. The Westboro Baptist Church actually uses the slogan as its URL; its "Picket Schedule" page equates atheists and "fags."

58 See Blank; Holtzman and Kulish; Salih et al.; and Naomi Wolf, *Vagina: A New Biography*, 2nd ed. (New York: HarperCollins, 2013).

59 Derrida, *Dissemination*, 212–13.

60 Sarah Grubb, "Vampires, Werewolves, and Shapeshifters: The More They Change, the More They Stay the Same," in True Blood *and Philosophy: We Wanna Think Bad Things with You*, ed. George A. Dunn and Rebecca Housel (Hoboken, NJ: John Wiley and Sons, 2010), 222; emphasis added.

61 "I Don't Wanna Know," *True Blood*, season 1, episode 10, first broadcast November 9, 2008, by HBO, directed by Scott Winant, written by Chris Offutt.

62 Grubb, "Vampires, Werewolves, and Shapeshifters," 222; "Keep This Party Going," *True Blood*, season 2, episode 2, first broadcast June 21, 2009, by HBO, directed by Michael Lehmann, written by Brian Buckner.

63 It is a long-standing patriarchal view that menstrual blood as "unclean" is a sign of woman's physical inferiority to man; see Tumini, "*Vampiresse*," 123.

64 "To Love Is to Bury," *True Blood*, season 1, episode 11, first broadcast November 16, 2008, by HBO, directed and written by Nancy Oliver.

65 "Nothing but the Blood," *True Blood*, season 2, episode 1, first broadcast June 14, 2009, by HBO, directed by Daniel Minahan, written by Alexander Woo.

66 At first, in his obsessive desire to protect Sookie, Bill "unloads" his creation, Jessica, onto Eric and Pam. His actions here as creator are on par with Frankenstein's toward his creature: both men abandon their offspring. As *True Blood* progresses, however, Bill and Jessica develop a relationship of mutual respect.

67 "Keep This Party Going," *True Blood*, season 2, episode 2.

68 Wolf, *Vagina*, 59.

69 Ibid., 121, 123.

70   Auerbach, *Our Vampires, Ourselves*, 154.

71   Valenti, *The Purity Myth*, 39.

72   "Nothing but the Blood," *True Blood*, season 2, episode 1.

73   "Scratches," *True Blood*, season 2, episode 3, first broadcast June 28, 2009, by HBO, directed by Scott Winant, written by Raelle Tucker.

74   The song has been recorded many times, most famously by American blues musician Huddie William "Lead Belly" Ledbetter in 1944 and by American "grunge" band Nirvana in 1993.

75   The classic scholarly work regarding the various permutations and symbolism of the "Little Red Riding Hood" fairy tale is Jack David Zipes, *The Trials and Tribulations of Little Red Riding Hood: Versions of the Tale in Sociocultural Context* (South Hadley, MA: Bergin and Garvey, 1983).

76   "And When I Die," *True Blood*, season 4, episode 12, first broadcast September 11, 2011, by HBO, directed by Scott Winant, written by Raelle Tucker.

77   "Timebomb," *True Blood*, season 2, episode 8.

78   Ibid.

79   It is interesting that, in the inaugural 2013–14 season of the television series *Dracula*, the title character, played by Jonathan Rhys Meyers, makes a link between humanity and monstrosity. When he discovers Lucy's betrayal of Mina's friendship, he goes to Lucy one night and punishes her for her infraction: "Hello, Lucy. If you insist on acting like a monster, I'm going to make you one"—and he proceeds to bite her. "Four Roses," *Dracula*, season 1, episode 9, first broadcast January 17, 2014, directed by Tim Fywell, written by Daniel Knauf.

80   Blank, *Virgin*, 85.

81   Ibid., 106–07.

82   Ibid., 215.

83   "Spellbound," *True Blood*, season 4, episode 8, first broadcast August 14, 2011, by HBO, directed by Daniel Minahan, written by Alan Ball.

84   Ibid.

85   "I Will Rise Up," *True Blood*, season 2, episode 9.

86   Ibid.

87   Schwarz, "The Wrong Question," 2.

88   Sara Luttfring, "Bodily Narratives and the Politics of Virginity in *The Changeling* and the Essex Divorce," *Renaissance Drama* 39 (2011): 102.

REFERENCES

Allocco, Katherine. "Vampiric Viragoes: Villainizing and Sexualizing Arthurian Women in *Dracula vs. King Arthur* (2005)." In *The Universal Vampire: Origins and Evolution of a Legend*, edited by Barbara Brodman and James E. Doan, 149–64. Madison: Fairleigh Dickinson University Press, 2013.

Auerbach, Nina. *Our Vampires, Ourselves.* Chicago: University of Chicago Press, 1995.

Bearman, Peter S., and Hannah Brückner. "Promising the Future: Virginity Pledges and First Intercourse." *American Journal of Sociology* 106, 4 (2001): 859–912.

Blank, Hanne. *Virgin: The Untouched History.* New York: Bloomsbury, 2007.

Briefel, Aviva. "Monster Pains: Masochism, Menstruation, and Identification in the Horror Film." *Film Quarterly* 58 ,3 (2005): 16–27. doi:10.1525/fq.2005.58.3.16.

Carpenter, Laura M. "The Ambiguity of 'Having Sex': The Subjective Experience of Virginity Loss in the United States." *Journal of Sex Research* 38, 2 (2001): 127–39.

Cherry, Brigid. "Before the Night Is Through: *True Blood* as Cult TV." In True Blood: *Investigating Vampires and Southern Gothic*, edited by Brigid Cherry, 3–21. New York: I. B. Tauris, 2012.

Craft, Christopher. "'Kiss Me with Those Red Lips': Gender and Inversion in Bram Stoker's *Dracula*." *Representations* 8 (1984): 107–33.

Davis, Paul E. H. "Dracula Anticipated: The 'Undead' in Anglo-Irish Literature." In *The Universal Vampire: Origins and Evolution of a Legend*, edited by Barbara Brodman and James E. Doan, 17–31. Madison: Fairleigh Dickinson University Press, 2013.

Derrida, Jacques. *Dissemination* (1972). Translated by Barbara Johnson. Chicago: University of Chicago Press, 1981.

Falconer, Pete. "Fresh Meat? Dissecting the Horror Movie Virgin." In *Virgin Territory: Representing Sexual Inexperience in Film*, edited by Tamar Jeffers McDonald, 123–37. Detroit: Wayne State University Press, 2010.

Freud, Sigmund. "The Taboo of Virginity" (1918). In *Sexuality and the Psychology of Love*, edited by Philip Rieff, 60–76. New York: Touchstone, 1997.

———. *Totem and Taboo* (1913). *The Standard Edition.* Translated by James Strachey. Introduction by Peter Gay. New York: W. W. Norton, 1989.

Friday, Nancy. *My Mother/My Self: The Daughter's Search for Identity.* 1977; reprinted, London: HarperCollins, 1994.

Grubb, Sarah. "Vampires, Werewolves, and Shapeshifters: The More They Change, the More They Stay the Same." In True Blood *and Philosophy: We Wanna Think Bad Things with You*, edited by George A. Dunn and Rebecca Housel, 215–27. Hoboken, NJ: John Wiley and Sons, 2010.

Herrick, Robert. "To the Virgins, to Make Much of Time." In *Seventeenth Century Prose and Poetry*, edited by Alexander M. Witherspoon and Frank J. Warnke, 2nd ed., 813. New York: Harcourt Brace Jovanovich, 1982.

Hirschbein, Ron. "Sookie, Sigmund, and the Edible Complex." In *True Blood and Philosophy: We Wanna Think Bad Things with You*, edited by George A. Dunn and Rebecca Housel, 123–35. Hoboken, NJ: John Wiley and Sons, 2010.

Holtzman, Deanna, and Nancy Kulish. *Nevermore: The Hymen and the Loss of Virginity*. Northvale, NJ: Jason Aronson, 1997.

Keith, Edward O. "Biomedical Origins of Vampirism." In *The Universal Vampire: Origins and Evolution of a Legend*, edited by Barbara Brodman and James E. Doan, 61–73. Madison: Fairleigh Dickinson University Press, 2013.

Lastique, Esther, and Helen Rodnite Lemay. "A Medieval Physician's Guide to Virginity." In *Sex in the Middle Ages: A Book of Essays*, edited by Joyce E. Salisbury, 56–79. New York: Garland Publishing, 1991.

Luttfring, Sara. "Bodily Narratives and the Politics of Virginity in *The Changeling* and the Essex Divorce." *Renaissance Drama* 39 (2011): 97–128.

MacLachlan, Bonnie. "Introduction." In *Virginity Revisited: Configurations of the Unpossessed Body*, edited by Bonnie MacLachlan and Judith Fletcher, 3–12. Toronto: University of Toronto Press, 2007.

McClelland, Bruce A. "Un-*True Blood*: The Politics of Artificiality." In *True Blood and Philosophy: We Wanna Think Bad Things with You*, edited by George A. Dunn and Rebecca Housel, 79–90. Hoboken, NJ: John Wiley and Sons, 2010.

Sabbadini, Andrea. "The Window and the Door." In *Virgin Territory: Representing Sexual Inexperience in Film*, edited by Tamar Jeffers McDonald, 223–37. Detroit: Wayne State University Press, 2010.

Salih, Sarah, Anke Bernau, and Ruth Evans. "Introduction: Virginities and Virginity Studies." In *Medieval Virginities*, edited by Anke Bernau, Ruth Evans, and Sarah Salih, 1–13. Toronto: University of Toronto Press, 2003.

Santos, Cristina. "Monstrous Miracle Workers: Powerful Female Virgins." Keynote address at the 14th Annual Graduate Student Conference, Department of Modern Languages and Literatures, University of Western Ontario, London, ON, March 3, 2012.

Schumann, Nancy. "Women with Bite: Tracing Vampire Women from Lilith to *Twilight*." In *The Universal Vampire: Origins and Evolution of a Legend*, edited by Barbara Brodman and James E. Doan, 109–20. Madison: Fairleigh Dickinson University Press, 2013.

Schwarz, Kathryn. "The Wrong Question: Thinking through Virginity." *Differences: A Journal of Feminist Cultural Studies* 13, 2 (2002): 1–34.

Sparks, Kerrelyn. *The Vampire and the Virgin*. New York: Avon Books, 2010.

Tumini, Angela. "*Vampiresse*: Embodiment of Sensuality and Erotic Horror in Carl Th. Dreyer's *Vampyr* and Mario Bava's *The Mask of Satan*." In *The*

Universal Vampire: Origins and Evolution of a Legend, edited by Barbara Brodman and James E. Doan, 121–35. Madison: Fairleigh Dickinson University Press, 2013.

Valenti, Jessica. *The Purity Myth: How America's Obsession with Virginity Is Hurting Young Women*. Berkeley: Seal Press, 2010.

Wogan-Browne, Jocelyn. "Virginity Now and Then: A Response to *Medieval Virginities*." In *Medieval Virginities*, edited by Anke Bernau, Ruth Evans, and Sarah Salih, 234–53. Toronto: University of Toronto Press, 2003.

Wolf, Naomi. *Vagina: A New Biography*. 2nd ed. New York: HarperCollins, 2013.

Zipes, Jack David. *The Trials and Tribulations of Little Red Riding Hood: Versions of the Tale in Sociocultural Context*. South Hadley, MA: Bergin and Garvey, 1983.

FILMS AND TV SERIES

"And When I Die." *True Blood*. Season 4, episode 12, first broadcast September 11, 2011, by HBO. Directed by Scott Winant. Written by Raelle Tucker.

"Beyond Here Lies Nothin'." *True Blood*. Season 2, episode 12, first broadcast September 13, 2009, by HBO. Directed by Michael Cuesta. Written by Alexander Woo.

"Four Roses." *Dracula*. Season 1, episode 9, first broadcast January 17, 2014. Directed by Tim Fywell. Written by Daniel Knauf.

"Fresh Blood." *True Blood*. Season 3, episode 11, first broadcast August 29, 2010, by HBO. Directed by Daniel Minahan. Written by Nancy Oliver.

"I Don't Wanna Know." *True Blood*. Season 1, episode 10, first broadcast November 9, 2008, by HBO. Directed by Scott Winant. Written by Chris Offutt.

"I Will Rise Up." *True Blood*. Season 2, episode 9, first broadcast August 16, 2009, by HBO. Directed by Scott Winant. Written by Nancy Oliver.

"Keep This Party Going." *True Blood*. Season 2, episode 2, first broadcast June 21, 2009, by HBO. Directed by Michael Lehmann. Written by Brian Buckner.

"Nothing but the Blood." *True Blood*. Season 2, episode 1, first broadcast June 14, 2009, by HBO. Directed by Daniel Minahan. Written by Alexander Woo.

"Release Me." *True Blood*. Season 2, episode 7, first broadcast August 2, 2009, by HBO. Directed by Michael Ruscio. Written by Raelle Tucker.

"Scratches." *True Blood*. Season 2, episode 3, first broadcast June 28, 2009, by HBO. Directed by Scott Winant. Written by Raelle Tucker.

"Spellbound." *True Blood*. Season 4, episode 8, first broadcast August 14, 2011, by HBO. Directed by Daniel Minahan. Written by Alan Ball.

Teeth. Directed by Mitchell Lichtenstein. Dimension Extreme, 2008.

"Timebomb." *True Blood*. Season 2, episode 8, first broadcast August 9, 2009, by HBO. Directed by John Dahl. Written by Alexander Woo.

"To Love Is to Bury." *True Blood*. Season 1, episode 11, first broadcast November 16, 2008, by HBO. Directed and written by Nancy Oliver.

PART 3:
MEN BE VIRGINS TOO: QUEERING VIRGINITY

CHAPTER 5

THE QUEER SAINT: MALE VIRGINITY IN DEREK JARMAN'S *SEBASTIANE*

Kevin McGuiness

British film director Derek Jarman (1942–94) ranks among the most celebrated filmmakers of queer cinema. Prior to his untimely demise because of complications from AIDS, he produced a number of provocative and avant-garde works. One of his most challenging and poetic works is his 1976 film *Sebastiane*,[1] a fictional recounting of the final days in the life of the Christian saint executed for his religious convictions. *Sebastiane* functions as a mixture of narrative drama and experimental cinema, and it draws tremendously from the plethora of historical artworks that addresses the saint's martyrdom.

The film depicts Saint Sebastian as a chaste religious zealot within the hedonistic world of the ancient Roman Empire who sublimates his sexual desires and redirects them toward God. His refusal to submit to the sexual solicitations of his male comrades, particularly those of his superior, Severus, indirectly results in his death. Jarman's depiction of the virginal saint's life is fraught with eroticism, and the elaborate execution scene at the conclusion of the film functions as a symbolic gang rape, violently reconciling the sexual tension that persists throughout the film. The homoerotic connotations of Sebastian's death are explored in vivid terms through Jarman's use of cinematography. In this chapter, I reveal the means by which Jarman communicates both Sebastian's virginity and repressed homosexuality through his use of imagery associated with historical images of the saint in both literature and painting.

Numerous art historians and scholarly writers, including Germaine Greer and Richard Kaye, have commented on the erotic undertones present in historical images of the saint. Within renderings of Sebastian, the notion of sexual penetration is manifested through the symbolic arrows that puncture his flesh. Death and sexual intercourse are bound together in this scene, serving to illustrate the analogous notion of orgasm as the *petite mort*. Sebastian moans in agony and pleasure as his flesh is violated in a process akin to sexual penetration. His "beautiful demise" functions as a metaphor for the first bite of forbidden fruit and the shedding of virginal blood, a concept that takes centre stage in Jarman's film.

Employing a methodology of semiotics, I examine in this chapter the visual language used in the film and the implicit relationship that Jarman builds among the themes of male virginity, sexual penetration, and death. I explore these ideas predominantly on a symbolic level, conveyed to the reader through the employment of signs and motifs appropriated from the history of artistic representations of Sebastian. Through the act of sexual transgression, represented by the arrows that penetrate him at the conclusion of the film, his symbolic virginity is lost, and his death occurs. Jarman therefore implicitly communicates the idea that sex and death, embodied in the figure of Sebastian and his chastity, are inextricably tied together.

JARMAN AND *SEBASTIANE*

Sebastiane marks the directorial debut of Jarman, a canonical figure in first-wave European queer cinema. He completed the film, made in 16mm, on a budget of £30,000[2] provided by an anonymous Italian businessman.[3] Jarman began work on *Sebastiane* after graduating from the University of London with a degree in English, history, and art history.[4] Produced on a shoestring budget, the film was shot on the beaches of Sardinia and features a cast of unknown actors.[5] *Sebastiane* is ultimately a thoughtful, introspective, and sexually charged examination of the life of the young martyr.

The film received mixed responses upon its release, dismissed in certain circles as a failed attempt at gay pornography, applauded by others as a progressive addition to queer cinema. It was rejected by Cannes, though it played to record audiences at the Gate Cinema in Notting Hill and was applauded in Italy and Spain.[6] In America, it "was buried in porno houses"[7] and classified as a sex film; the French panned it, and the Germans found it difficult.[8] Among the most vocal opponents of the film was Thomas Waugh, who offered a searing criticism in his text *The Fruit Machine: Twenty Years of Writing on Queer Cinema*, stating that the film "comes across as a second-rate skin flick all dressed up in a costume that doesn't fit."[9] Needless to say, the film was not universally embraced and enjoyed a rather scant release, premiering to befuddled crowds in gay pornographic film theatres across North America.

Despite such harsh reviews, the press did look favourably on certain aspects of the film, particularly the visionary nature of its depiction of homosexuality. The review in *Gay News* indicated that the movie possessed "power and authority" and was "a very special, and indeed, a quite remarkable film that represents a milestone in the history of gay cinema."[10] Likewise, Michael O'Pray in *Derek Jarman: Dreams of England* commended the film for celebrating "the male body from a manifestly homoerotic perspective in a way that had never been done either in mainstream or art cinema,"[11] and therefore the film marked a profound moment in queer cinema. As O'Pray indicated, Jarman fuses queer cinema with Christian subject matter in a manner that is both engaging and erotic.

SEBASTIANE AND THE HISTORICAL SAINT SEBASTIAN

Jarman's rendering of the story of Sebastian is a fascinating mixture of historical and fictional elements, creating a cocktail of sexual imagery interwoven with themes of Christian spirituality. The film charts the story of Sebastian, captain of the palace guards, who falls out of favour with his protector, Emperor Diocletian, as a result of his allegiance to Christianity. He is subsequently relegated to an isolated outpost of the Roman Empire where he is persecuted and eventually executed by his fellow soldiers.[12] This account closely echoes the life of the historical Sebastian, who, according to the *Acta sanctorum*, was "dearly beloved" by Diocletian[13] and thus appointed captain of a company of the praetorian guards.[14] However, once his devotion to Christianity was discovered, Sebastian was impeached, and Diocletian berated his defiant serf and delivered him over to archers from Mauritania.[15]

Reality and fiction diverge at this point, for Jarman excised the fact that Sebastian did not perish from the wounds inflicted by the archers but recovered and accosted Diocletian on a staircase, protesting the cruelty that the emperor had perpetrated against Christians.[16] Diocletian had Sebastian arrested and beaten to death with cudgels, and his body was subsequently thrown into the Roman sewer.[17] Jarman's omission of the saint's recovery from his encounter with the archers functions to maintain the illusion of Sebastian's erotic death, permanently supplanting his later and less dramatic demise.

EARLIER DEPICTIONS OF SAINT SEBASTIAN IN ART

The film also takes advantage of the homoerotic connotation of historical images of Sebastian as it appropriates and draws inspiration from the renderings of artists from the Italian Renaissance. Jarman's implicit references to earlier sensual images of the saint are observed by Maria Wyke: "*Sebastiane* itself is a painterly film that contains numerous references to the martyr's homoerotic iconography."[18] This trend is observed simply through Jarman's characterization of Sebastian, depicted as a brooding, attractive, and vaguely effeminate young man with dark features and a quiet intensity. This vision of him as an androgynous youth is an extension of a tradition that began largely during the early Renaissance.

Previous images of the saint from the medieval period portray Sebastian as a middle-aged man often dressed in soldierly attire. A mosaic from 680 C.E. in San Pietro in Vincoli depicted him with a beard, wearing a Roman habit,[19] and carrying a martyr's crown.[20] He also appeared in an ancient glass window in the Strasbourg Cathedral dressed as a knight and armed with a sword; in both representations, his signature arrows were absent.[21] During the next eight centuries, conventions associated with depictions of Sebastian were altered significantly; specifically, his clothing was removed aside from a small white loincloth, bound at the groin.[22] From the 1600s onward, he was also more commonly envisioned as "an exquisite youth," transformed from a Roman soldier into a "beardless adolescent of Apollonian beauty."[23] This trend of articulating Sebastian as an eroticized youth can be observed in the images of artists such as Guido Reni and Giovanni Antonio Bazzi, a pattern that definitely influenced Jarman's vision of the martyred saint.

Jarman had the opportunity to visit the Catacomb of Saint Sebastian and witness the works by famed Italian artists Bernini and Giorgetti depicting him.[24] Reflecting on these images, Jarman likened the arrows that pierce Sebastian's flesh to caresses,[25] recognizing the sexual undertones of his execution. He also referenced certain Renaissance images of Sebastian in his construction of the execution scene, a tactic noted by Wyke. The composition, gestures, and expressions all echo famous historical paintings of the saint and reference the long lineage of sensuous imagery connected with his death:

> The arrangement of the six executioners around the martyr in the closing sequence of *Sebastiane* recalls that [used] in the painting by the Pollaiuolo brothers. The actor who plays the Roman soldier, Leonardo Treviglio, is posed with both hands tied above his head and with one arrow in his armpit in imitation of the [Guido] Reni Sebastian . . . while . . . his uplifted expression of ecstatic agony . . . [is] suggestive of works by "Il Sodoma" and Perugino.[26]

Much like Renaissance images of the saint, Jarman's Sebastian appears nude throughout much of his time on screen, and the director emphasizes the erotic properties of his youth and beauty through extended slow-motion shots that gradually caress the contours of his body. Sebastian is continually posited as the subject of his comrades' desires, and his persistent rejection of their advances results in sexual frustration that permeates the group. His virginal beauty is therefore a fixture of obsession and mockery for his comrades, and their desire for him eventually culminates in his execution, which functions as a symbolic orgy.

SAINT SEBASTIAN AS A VIRGIN

The relationship between sexuality and spirituality is central to Jarman's film, and Sebastian's chastity becomes the central focus of the narrative by its conclusion. Jarman communicates Sebastian's virginity and sexual purity through the use of elaborate symbolism

Figure 1. Sebastian (Leonardo Treviglio) bathing himself as Severus (Barney James) watches in the background. SOURCE: still from Jarman and Humfress, *Sebastiane*.

and cinematography. Specifically, he juxtaposes extended shots of the young saint with images of the unspoiled Roman landscape, interweaving the two themes until they become synonymous.

Depictions of the untouched bucolic countryside operate as a metaphor to express the celestial beauty and untrammelled purity of Sebastian. As O'Pray points out, "Sebastian's spirituality and otherworldly innocence are depicted through images of pastoral idealism," which appear frequently throughout the film.[27] Sebastian is envisioned as a being who cannot be possessed on a material level; instead, he can reach fulfillment only within the spiritual realm through his release from the bonds of mortal existence. It is through his death at the conclusion of the film that he will remain forever youthful and beautiful; under this light, his execution becomes an act of sacrifice, a means by which he will be united with the God whom he worships with erotic fervour.

Likewise, Sebastian is associated with symbols throughout the film, specifically the lily, that signify his virginal status. Early in the film, the viewer observes him bathing before his commanding officer, Severus (see Figure 1). In the soundtrack, Sebastian can be heard reciting an encomium celebrating both himself and an unnamed deity, presumably the Judeo-Christian God. Within this poem, he states that "the lily gives forth perfume when the young God rises";[28] historically, the lily has been associated with the Virgin Mary and is indicative of sexual purity.[29] As Paul Albert Leitner recounts in *Sebastian: Love, Death, and Paradise*, the lily holds powerful connotations concerning the bloom of youth and conversely the decay of death. Traditionally beautiful yet dangerously enigmatic, "the lily is the symbol of innocence and purity; in the ancient world the lily plant . . . . was seen as the flower of death."[30] This duality associated with the lily makes perfect sense, for it is through the destruction of Sebastian's symbolic virginity that his death becomes inevitable.

SAINT SEBASTIAN IN LITERATURE

In an act of transmedia intertextuality, Jarman also implicitly references the literary work of Yukio Mishima (1925–70), a Japanese author born in Tokyo. An exquisite writer, as well as a director and actor, Mishima was nominated three times for the Nobel Prize for Literature and is one of the most celebrated artists to emerge from Asia. His work reflects a profound preoccupation with the figure of Sebastian, and much of his catalogue of writing highlights the masochistic aspects of Sebastian's martyrdom and the erotic imagery of his demise. Most notably, themes such as narcissism and carnal beauty surface within his texts devoted to the coy saint.

In his 1958 text *Confessions of a Mask*, Mishima describes the experiences of Kochan, a young boy struggling with homosexual desires in imperialist Japan. As Kochan grapples with issues related to his body, he finds within the image of Sebastian something irresistibly compelling and begins to identify with the martyred saint. Exploring Sebastian's homoerotic prowess and ethereal beauty, Mishima (much like Jarman) connects the image of the lily with the saint, using it to epitomize his sexual charisma: "On his helmet he wore a white lily, presented to him each morning by maidens of the town. Drooping downward gracefully along the flow of his manly hair as he rested from fierce tourneying [sic], the lily looked exactly like the nape of a swan's neck."[31] Within Mishima's work, the lily appears to convey both the grace and the fragility of Sebastian. The lily is also invested with a benign sexual meaning, for it functions as a token of the maidens' presumed adoration.

Mishima's and Jarman's characterizations of Sebastian are similar, creating an image of a deified creature with ethereal qualities that, by their very nature, are prone to destruction and thus ephemeral.[32] That Jarman was well aware of the writings of Mishima is apparent in his book *At Your Own Risk*, in which the filmmaker states that "all fags liked a good Sebastian. Mishima tried him [St. Sebastian] on like leather chaps."[33] Mishima's rendering of the saint seems to resonate with Jarman, for the British filmmaker echoes the sensuous tone found in *Confessions of a Mask*. However, his filmic depiction of Sebastian differs from all earlier representations in one regard: namely, his sexuality. Whereas literary and artistic works represented him as provocative and demure, Jarman envisions him as a sexually repressed young man obsessed with the transcendent.

SAINT SEBASTIAN AS A HOMOSEXUAL

Although Sebastian's sexual orientation is never overtly divulged in the film, his proclivity toward homosexuality is implied through his pseudo-sexual worship of God, which borders on obsession. At one point in the film, Sebastian has an ecstatic vision in which he believes that he is visited by God. Sebastian is staked to the ground as punishment for refusing the sexual advances of Severus and under the scorching rays of the sun experiences an epiphany. The deity appears before him as an attractive young male clad in leopard skin. This divinity circles Sebastian, leering at his semi-nude body as the protagonist suffers under the excruciating heat of the Mediterranean sun. Through the use of cross-cuts between point-of-view shots from the perspectives of both God and Sebastian, a kinship is indicated that appears to be fraught with erotic and sensual undertones.

The connection between Sebastian and a homosexual identity fits into a much larger trend in depictions of the saint developed in the early twentieth century. With the dawn of the modern era, Sebastian became representative of "the homosexual as [a] beleaguered, existential hero . . . . and a prototypical portrait of [a] tortured closet case."[34] He functioned as a semi-covert acknowledgement of a repressed homosexual secret, and the act of revealing his Christianity became a "coming out" narrative.[35]

The fact that Jarman envisioned the saint as a repressed homosexual is evident in his writings. In *At Your Own Risk*, he refers to Sebastian as a "Latin closet case" and goes on to state that, though Sebastian "refused a good fuck, [he] gets the arrows he deserved" at the conclusion of the film.[36] Jarman therefore saw the execution scene as a metaphor for transgression, for the arrows that pierce Sebastian's flesh and bring about his demise are symbolic of sexual penetration. As the director stated in production documents from *Sebastiane*, "the arrows which pierce the passive adolescent are as overt a symbol as any Freudian could wish for."[37] Therefore, in the film, the implied homosexuality of Sebastian is fully realized during his death, in which he comes into contact with the divine and reaches an ecstatic state of sexual fulfillment.

ORGASM AND DEATH

The execution scene functions as a symbolic orgy, giving Sebastian's comrades the opportunity to take part in his figurative loss of virginity. In essence, the act of shooting Sebastian with arrows represents consummation of the erotic desire that his peers have harboured for him since the opening of the narrative (see Figure 2). Filmed in slowmotion, this sequence graphically depicts the close relationship between sex and death. As Richard A. Kaye points out, the scene functions as "the symbolic acting out of an erotic penetration" suggestive of "a gang rape."[38] The scene is shot completely devoid of dialogue, the only sound the wind in the distance. Even the cries of Sebastian are muted, and the audience is only permitted to see, though not hear, the agony that he undergoes as the arrows puncture his flesh and rupture his organs.

Figure 2. Sebastian's execution is filmed in slow motion, amplifying the homoerotic connotation of his death by penetration. SOURCE: still from Jarman and Humfress, *Sebastiane*.

This scene also functions as a morbid re-enactment of a mock orgy at the opening of the film. Prior to his expulsion to a remote outpost, Sebastian attends a bacchanal celebration in honour of Diocletian, at which his devotion to Christianity is discovered. During the symposium, a group of Roman performers cavorting in large costume phalluses dance around a central figure painted white. At the climax of the celebration, the dancers ejaculate onto the chorus leader, covering him in semen as he writhes in ecstasy (see Figure 3). This scene alludes to the dynamic between Sebastian and his executioners since the choreography in both scenes is remarkably similar. Sebastian, much like the chorus leader, twists and contorts his body in painful ecstasy as the arrows pierce his flesh during his death scene, relishing the masochistic torment.

The demise of Sebastian also implicitly conveys the relationship between death and orgasm. As artist Matthew Stradling points out,

Figure 3. A performer, painted white, dances for the emperor as a troupe prances around him before ejaculating on him. SOURCE: still from Jarman and Humfress, *Sebastiane*.

the process of "reaching the point of orgasm is like passing over into death," and as a result "the self is annihilated" as the erotic brings us closer to the grave.[39] Through the destruction of his physical self, Sebastian is brought into the realm of the spiritual, and the worlds of the material and the metaphysical are momentarily aligned. He struggles throughout the film to reconcile his sexual and spiritual selves, a dynamic manifested through his acts of asceticism and torment. His desire to reach spiritual fulfillment eventually culminates in his martyrdom, which he pursues with masochistic fervour.

SEBASTIANE, MARTYRDOM, AND MASOCHISM

In Jarman's film, the themes of martyrdom and masochism are fused together in the character of Sebastian, who courts his own death throughout the film. The torture that Severus exacts on his underling appears to satisfy some strange desire for pain that Sebastian harbours. Ultimately, this punishment culminates in the erotic and violent death of the saint. Throughout the film, his close confidant, Justin, attempts to steer his friend away from his tragic fate, but Sebastian seems to be irresistibly drawn to his own demise.

Anita Phillips recognizes the parallel roles of the martyr and the masochist in Sebastian: "Like St. Sebastian, who is the more filled with love the deeper he is pierced with arrows, the masochist saturates the channels created with a renewed capacity for passion."[40] The figure of Sebastian therefore functions as an amalgamation of martyr and masochist, hungering for pain in the name of religious zeal. As Wolfgang Fetz points out, the martyr accepts torture as a fanatical form of tolerance, not as an injustice but as a blessing.[41]

Derived from the Greek word for "witness," a "martyr" is an ancient notion that became popular within the Christian tradition.[42] It was not until the second century that Christian writers adopted the term, and it then took on its deathly connotation.[43] Lacey Baldwin Smith outlines the characteristics of martyrs, stipulating that they must exercise a degree of agency in their own executions.[44] Through such interactions, martyrs consciously reject the prospect of existing in a world that fails to recognize their perspectives.[45] Some theorists have openly dismissed martyrs as self-murderers, obsessed with a death wish.[46] G. W. Bowersock states that martyrs' "enthusiasm for death comes very close to a desire to commit suicide—a suicide to be arranged by an external agent but with the clear complicity of the victim."[47] This facet of the martyr's persona is explicit in the figure of Sebastian as he acts as a complicit agent in his own demise.

It is his conscious participation in his own martyrdom, through his defiance of the ruling elite, that links Sebastian with masochism. The film continually indicates that he views the material world and the spiritual terrain as divided by a schism that can only be bridged through death. Although body and spirit are deeply intertwined, the former functions as a vehicle to sate the latter, privileged in the film. The ecstatic pain that Sebastian undergoes in an attempt to attain religious fulfillment also functions to reconcile the sexual tension that persists throughout the film. His execution therefore brings physical and spiritual realms close to one another and allows the saint to experience material pain and metaphysical joy simultaneously.

CONCLUSION

Sebastiane is a paradoxical film, occupying an arena that encompasses both the sacred and the profane. Drawing on previous artistic depictions of Sebastian, Jarman creates a fascinating and engaging image of a young man trapped between his religious convictions and his mortal obligations. Through the sublimation of his sexual desires, Sebastian redirects his energy into the pursuit of absolute spiritual devotion. The execution functions as the climactic conclusion of the film and resolves the sexual tension between Sebastian and his comrades as well as between the saint and his God. Through elaborate cinematography and iconography, Jarman communicates to the audience the relationship between spiritual and sexual fulfillment.

Exploring themes of male sexuality, homoeroticism, and religious mystery, Jarman invites his audience into a realm in which the disturbing relationship between desire and death is made explicit. Sebastian in essence is an ephemeral creature, one who cannot be confined to the realm of mortality, which will doom him to wither with age. Instead, Jarman envisions him as a beautiful being who transcends the material world of death and decay and moves into a sphere of absolute harmony and bliss. His overwhelming ethereal beauty seems to render his death inevitable, for Sebastian is "a wayfarer soon to be gone."[48]

NOTES

1   *Sebastiane* (1976), dir. Derek Jarman and Paul Humfress (Mongrel Media, DVD, 2004).

2   Michael O'Pray, *Derek Jarman: Dreams of England* (London: British Film Institute, 1996), 80.

3   Chris Lippard, ed., *By Angels Driven: The Films of Derek Jarman* (Wiltshire: Flick Books, 1996), 2.

4   Ibid.

5   Ibid.

6   O'Pray, *Derek Jarman*, 93.

7   Derek Jarman, *At Your Own Risk: A Saint's Testament* (London: Vintage, 1993), 84.

8   O'Pray, *Derek Jarman*, 93.

9   Thomas Waugh, *The Fruit Machine: Twenty Years of Writings on Queer Cinema* (Durham: Duke University Press, 2000), 70.

10 Jarman, *At Your Own Risk*, 73.

11 O'Pray, *Derek Jarman*, 83.

12 Ibid., 86.

13 James M. Saslow, "The Tenderest Lover: Saint Sebastian in Renaissance Painting. A Proposed Homoerotic Iconology for North Italian Art 1450–1550," *Gai Saber: Journal of the Gay Academic Union* 1, 1 (1977): 58–66.

14 Moses Finley, *Aspects of Antiquity: Discoveries and Controversies* (New York: Viking Press, 1968), 146.

15 Ibid., 129.

16 Alban Butler, *Butler's Lives of the Saints* (New York: Viking Press, 1996), 129.

17 Ibid., 130.

18 Maria Wyke, "Playing Roman Soldiers: The Martyred Body, Derek Jarman's *Sebastiane*, and the Representation of Male Homosexuality," in *Parchments of Gender: Deciphering the Bodies of Antiquity*, ed. Maria Wyke (Oxford: Clarendon Press, 1998), 258.

19 Anna Jameson, *Sacred and Legendary Art* (Boston: Houghton Mifflin and Company, 1972), 407.

20 Butler, *Butler's Lives*, 130.

21 Ibid.

22 Germaine Greer, *The Beautiful Boy* (London: Thames and Hudson, 2003), 207.

23 Wyke, "Playing Roman Soldiers," 252.

24 Ibid., 255.

25 In Item 3 of production documents on *Sebastiane* in the British Film Institute's Derek Jarman Collection, quoted in ibid., 247.

26 Ibid., 258.

27 O'Pray, *Derek Jarman*, 92.

28 Steven Dillon, *Derek Jarman and Lyric Film: The Mirror and the Sea* (Austin: University of Texas Press, 2004), 68.

29 George Ferguson, *Signs and Symbols in Christian Art* (Oxford: Oxford University Press, 1961), 33.

30 Paul Albert Leitner, *Sebastian: Love, Death, and Paradise*, trans. Wolfgang Fetz (Wein: Sonderzahl, 1993), 12.

31 Yukio Mishima, *Confessions of a Mask*, trans. Meredith Weatherby (Tokyo: C. E. Tuttle, 1986), 44.

32 Ibid.

33 Jarman, *At Your Own Risk*, 83.

34 Richard A. Kaye, "Losing His Religion: Saint Sebastian as Contemporary Gay Martyr," in *Outlooks: Lesbian and Gay Sexualities and Visual Cultures*, ed. Peter Horne and Reina Lewis (London: Routledge, 1996), 87–89.

35 Richard A. Kaye, "Saint Sebastian: On the Uses of Decadence," in *Saint Sebastian: A Splendid Readiness for Death*, ed. Wolfgang Fetz, Gerald Matt, and Kusthalle Wien (Bielefeld: Kerber, 2003), 11–12.

36 Jarman, *At Your Own Risk*, 83.

37 In Item 2b of production documents on *Sebastiane* in the British Film Institute's Derek Jarman Collection, quoted in Wyke, "Playing Roman Soldiers," 253.

38 Kaye, "Losing His Religion," 98.

39 Matthew Stradling, "The Aura of Timelessness," in *Outlooks: Lesbian and Gay Sexualities and Visual Cultures*, ed. Peter Horne and Reina Lewis (London: Routledge, 1996), 143.

40 Anita Phillips, *A Defense of Masochism* (New York: St. Martin's Press, 1998), 162.

41 Wolfgang Fetz, "Saint Sebastian: Love, Death, and Paradise," in *Saint Sebastian: A Splendid Readiness for Death*, ed. Wolfgang Fetz, Gerald Matt, and Kunsthalle Wein (Bielefeld: Kerber, 2003), 102.

42 G. W. Bowersock, *Martyrdom and Rome* (New York: Cambridge University Press, 1995), 5.

43 Ibid.

44 Lacey Baldwin Smith, *Fools, Martyrs, Traitors: The Story of Martyrdom in the Western World* (New York: Alfred A. Knopf, 1997), 11.

45 Ibid.

46 Ibid., 17.

47 Bowersock, *Martyrdom and Rome*, 61.

48 Mishima, *Confessions of a Mask*, 44.

REFERENCES

Bowersock, G. W. *Martyrdom and Rome*. New York: Cambridge University Press, 1995.

Butler, Alban. *Butler's Lives of the Saints*. New York: Viking Press, 1996.

Dillon, Steven. *Derek Jarman and Lyric Film: The Mirror and the Sea*. Austin: University of Texas Press, 2004.

Ferguson, George. *Signs and Symbols in Christian Art*. Oxford: Oxford University Press, 1961.

Fetz, Wolfgang. "Saint Sebastian: Love, Death, and Paradise." In *Saint Sebastian: A Splendid Readiness for Death*, edited by Wolfgang Fetz, Gerald Matt, and Kunsthalle Wien, 102–04. Bielefeld: Kerber, 2003.

Finley, Moses. *Aspects of Antiquity: Discoveries and Controversies*. New York: Viking Press, 1968.

Greer, Germaine. *The Beautiful Boy*. London: Thames and Hudson, 2003.

Jameson, Anna. *Sacred and Legendary Art*. Boston: Houghton Mifflin and Company, 1972.

Jarman, Derek. *At Your Own Risk: A Saint's Testament*. London: Vintage, 1993.

Jarman, Derek, and Paul Humfress, dirs. *Sebastiane* (1976). Mongrel Media, DVD, 2004.

Kaye, Richard A. "Losing His Religion: Saint Sebastian as Contemporary Gay Martyr." In *Outlooks: Lesbian and Gay Sexualities and Visual Cultures*, edited by Peter Horne and Reina Lewis, 86–105. London: Routledge, 1996.

———. "Saint Sebastian: On the Uses of Decadence." In *Saint Sebastian: A Splendid Readiness for Death*, edited by Wolfgang Fetz, Gerald Matt, and Kunsthalle Wien, 11–18. Bielefeld: Kerber, 2003.

Leitner, Paul Albert. *Sebastian: Love, Death, and Paradise*. Translated by Wolfgang Fetz. Wein: Sonderzahl, 1993.

Lippard, Chris, ed. *By Angels Driven: The Films of Derek Jarman*. Wiltshire: Flick Books, 1996.

Mishima, Yukio. *Confessions of a Mask*. Translated by Meredith Weatherby. Tokyo: C. E. Tuttle, 1986.

O'Pray, Michael. *Derek Jarman: Dreams of England*. London: British Film Institute, 1996.

Phillips, Anita. *A Defense of Masochism*. New York: St. Martin's Press, 1998.

Saslow, James M. "The Tenderest Lover: Saint Sebastian in Renaissance Painting. A Proposed Homoerotic Iconology for North Italian Art 1450–1550." *Gai Saber: Journal of the Gay Academic Union* 1, 1 (1977): 58–66.

Smith, Lacey Baldwin. *Fools, Martyrs, Traitors: The Story of Martyrdom in the Western World*. New York: Alfred A. Knopf, 1997.

Stradling, Matthew. "The Aura of Timelessness." In *Outlooks: Lesbian and Gay Sexualities and Visual Cultures*, edited by Peter Horne and Reina Lewis, 139–47. London: Routledge, 1996.

Waugh, Thomas. *The Fruit Machine: Twenty Years of Writings on Queer Cinema*. Durham: Duke University Press, 2000.

Wyke, Maria. "Playing Roman Soldiers: The Martyred Body, Derek Jarman's *Sebastiane*, and the Representation of Male Homosexuality." In *Parchments of Gender: Deciphering the Bodies of Antiquity*, edited by Maria Wyke, 243–66. Oxford: Clarendon Press, 1998.

CHAPTER 6

TROPING BOYISHNESS, EFFEMINACY, AND MASCULINE QUEER VIRGINITY: ABDELLAH TAÏA AND EYET-CHÉKIB DJAZIRI

Gibson Ncube

> It is an infantile superstition of the human spirit that virginity would be thought a virtue and not the barrier that separates ignorance from knowledge.[1]

> If you scratch a child, you will find a queer, in the sense of someone "gay" or just plain strange.[2]

The "official gay movement has never been quick to attend to issues concerning effeminate boys," laments Eve Kosofsky Sedgwick in her seminal paper "How to Bring Your Kids Up Gay."[3] In her reasoning, "there is a discreditable reason for this in the marginal or stigmatized position to which even adult men who are effeminate have often been relegated in the movement."[4] This stigmatization and marginalization of effeminacy reflects what Carol Mavor terms "effeminophobia,"[5] a pervasive fear or hatred of effeminate boys.

This chapter contributes to the growing discussion of the neglected phenomenon of effeminacy through an analysis of the troping of boyishness, effeminacy, and masculine queer virginity in the novels of two openly gay writers of Maghrebian origin: Abdellah Taïa (Morocco) and Eyet-Chékib Djaziri (Franco-Tunisian). Taïa and Djaziri, alongside writers such as Rachid and Aniss, are part of a burgeoning canon of francophone Maghrebian novelists involved in rehabilitating queerness through their literary works. Born in 1973, Taïa studied in Rabat before moving to Geneva, where he studied for a semester in the mid-1990s. He then moved to study at the Sorbonne in Paris. A highly publicized interview in the literary magazine *Tel Quel* in 2007 marked his official coming out amid a frenzy of mediatized controversy in Morocco. In four of his novels—namely, *Mon Maroc* (My Morocco) (2000), *Le rouge du tarbouche* (The Red of the Fez) (2004), *L'Armée du salut* (The Salvation Army) (2006), and *Une mélancolie arabe* (An Arab Melancholia) (2008)—Taïa confronts the difficulty of assuming one's homosexuality in a homophobic Arab Muslim society deeply entrenched in piety and cultural practices. Djaziri was born in Tunis in 1957 of a Turco-Tunisian father and a French mother. At age sixteen, he followed his mother to France after the divorce of his parents. He cut short his studies, at the age of twenty-two, to join an airline. For sixteen years, he toured the world. After calling it a day with the airline, he devoted himself to writing. His autofictional diptych *Un poisson sur la balançoire* (A Fish on a Swing) (1997) and *Une promesse de douleur et de sang* (A Promise of Pain and Blood) (1998) chronicles the sexual awakening of the protagonist-narrator Sofiène in an Arab Muslim society that, as Eric Levéel states, condemns queer sexuality even though it is obsessed by it.[6] This chapter focuses on *Une mélancolie arabe* by Taïa and *Un poisson sur la balançoire* by Djaziri because in these novels queer virginity is explicitly depicted.

The novels of these two writers reflect an intriguing intermingling of the three concepts in traditionally patriarchal societies of Morocco and Tunisia in the late 1980s and 1990s. They broach stories of gay protagonists who retrospectively consider their childhoods as effeminate boys who have to face both effeminophobia and homophobia as they awaken to their queerness.

There is a cavernous gap in the research on male virginity, in particular masculine queer virginity in the Arab Muslim societies of North Africa, in literature or otherwise. Disproportionate attention to the feminine condition has rendered masculinity and queerness sacrosanct, taboo, and unquestioned (inescapably underquestioned) domains. Stephen O. Murray and Will Roscoe acknowledge that "in Arab and other Islamic societies, everyone successfully avoids public recognition (let alone discussion) of deviations from normative standards—sexual or other."[7] Although sexual and gender deviations exist, they are not openly acknowledged and are thus relegated to marginalized phenomena that seek to impose themselves on the dominant discourses.

This chapter sets out to demystify Arab Muslim masculinity and sexuality through a problematization of the tropes of boyishness, effeminacy, and masculine queer virginity in the autofictional novels of Taïa and Djaziri. By engaging these novels in a conversation, this chapter seeks to analyze the conditions in which masculine queer virginity is constructed as well as the implications of its literary representation on the heteropatriarchal Arab-Muslim societies of the Maghreb.[8] I further argue that masculine queer virginity is a central marker of "a defiant form of deviance," which, as Cristina Santos and Adriana Spahr explain, designates "a state of opposition and a disposition to resist that deviates from the norm."[9] They further clarify that this "defiant deviance" signifies "a person or persons that differ markedly—either in intelligence, social adjustment, and/or sexual behavior—from what is considered to be within acceptable limits of his/her socio-cultural environment."[10]

Mireille Rosello's study "Queer Virginity: Leïla Marouane's *La vie sexuelle d'un Islamiste à Paris*" is groundbreaking in its examination of how Marouane's novel "complicates the construction of virginity and penetration and presents the narrative voice as an inextricable web of male and female threads."[11] Her analysis demonstrates that the novel "refers to . . . and explores the limits of traditional sexual scripts inscribed in a dominant poetics of binary oppositions between genders, between cultures, between norms and dissidence."[12] I will juxtapose Rosello's literary perspective on queer virginity with Renée C. Hoogland's theoretical formulations on the construction of identity and desire. Hoogland points out that "the question of embodied being, because of its inescapable multi-facetedness, must be released from the chains of both liberal humanist and poststructuralist thought, in order to be addressed more productively from a genuinely multidimensional, interdisciplinary perspective, in which any form of mind/body distinction can no longer be legitimately maintained."[13] I will thus use queer, hermeneutic, psychoanalytic, and literary modes of analysis to better understand the construction and literary representation of boyishness, effeminacy, and masculine queer virginity in the works of Taïa and Djaziri.

Before delving into the troping of these concepts, I will theorize the term "queer" (as theory, identity, and critical praxis) as well as the connected notions of the "queer child" and "queer virginity." I take the term "queer" to refer to a repertoire of positions and theoretical perspectives that attempts to challenge all normative representations of sexuality and gender. As such, it sets out to "dislodge systems and structures from their comfortable niches."[14] As a theory, "queer" rejects the perception that sexuality and gender are stable and fixed notions and that heterosexuality is the norm. Insofar as it is an identity, "queer" involves a problematization of hegemonic concepts of gender, sexuality, and desire. This involves an identity that falls outside the ambit of commonly accepted heterosexuality. Although the term was originally derogative and pejorative, in the past twenty years or so it has been reclaimed and given positive connotations by non-heterosexuals to represent their empowerment. Finally, as a critical praxis in literary analysis, "queer" attempts to go beyond the examination of "defiantly deviant" modes of being in that it calls for questions on how texts reveal sexuality, mainly marginalized forms, within a particular literary and/or social setting. It thus examines how literary texts are informed by sexuality and ultimately seeks to consider how traditional forms of gender and sexuality are undermined by the emergence of alternative modes of being.

A consideration of masculine queer virginity as portrayed in the novels of Abdellah Taïa and Eyet-Chékib Djaziri certainly requires an initial examination of the tropes of the effeminate boy and queer child. Stockton posits that a queer child, as in a gay child, does not exist given that such an identity is essentially in the domain of adulthood. She explains that "the proto-gay child has only appeared through an act of retrospection and after a death. For this queer child, whatever its conscious grasp of itself, has not been able to present itself according to the category 'gay' or 'homosexual'—categories culturally deemed too adult, since they are sexual."[15] This resonates with the proto-gay protagonists of Taïa and Djaziri who are not aware of sexual categories. Sofiène, Djaziri's protagonist-narrator, is shocked when he learns for the first time of the term "homosexual": "Je n'ai jamais entendu ce mot, je t'assure. Qu'est-ce que c'est ? . . . Je restai abasourdi. Moi qui m'étais cru unique, voilà que je me découvrais des millions de semblables."[16] It is only through the vantage point of hindsight that these protagonists can qualify their difference as they grow up as effeminate boys. Lucas Hilderbrand in an article entitled "Mediating Queer Boyhood: *Dottie Gets Spanked*" concurs that "queer kids remain nearly unimaginable in our culture, except as the past lives of gay adults—even if the children recognized their difference at the time."[17] He concludes in this line of reasoning that "proto-gay identities are usually only claimed in retrospect, read through the long-term signs of sissy-ness. As such, queer boyhood precariously exists as an unstable identity that remains unarticulated, displaced and deferred during childhood and can only be decoded and remembered from afar in childhood."[18]

Ken Corbett, in his book *Boyhoods: Rethinking Masculinities*, contends that boyhood effeminacy can be considered a transitional period because "for some [boys] the femininity is a mere trace, as they move into adulthood, perhaps they are seen as particularly loving fathers. For some the boyhood femininity may be the harbinger of adult homosexuality. . . . For some the femininity may deepen and develop toward a transgendered subjectivity."[19] An important observation of Corbett's theorization is that it seems to suggest that there is a natural correlation between boyhood and adulthood as well as between boyhood effeminacy and adult male homosexuality. Chung-Hao Ku seems to *queery* such a theorization of boyhood effeminacy when he attests that, "because of the link between effeminacy and homosexuality, a sissy boy is sometimes translated into a proto-gay child. Although the idea of proto-gayness is a back-formation constructed from the perspective of an 'out' gay man, it generates proleptic or preventive readings of queer children."[20] Even if there might be a relationship between boyhood effeminacy and the later homosexuality of the protagonists of Taïa and Djaziri, it is imperative to view effeminacy as an intrinsic part of their makeup and not only as a signifier of future homosexuality.

Taïa, in an op-ed article in the *New York Times* of March 25, 2012, acknowledges that growing up effeminate went together with numerous gender challenges in that, though he considered himself a boy, everyone else saw in him a "little girl":

> I was barely 12, and in my neighborhood they called me 'the little girl.' Even those I persisted in playing soccer with used that nickname, that insult. . . . I was no kid anymore. My body was changing, stretching out, becoming that of a man. But others did not see me as a man. The image of myself they reflected back at me was strange and incomprehensible.[21]

The virginity of the effeminate characters plays an important role in the construction of their "gay" identities. Queer virginity is central to how they perceived themselves and their sexuality. The term "queer virginity" refers to identity, as in gay identity politics, but simultaneously acts on virginity in the sense that queer is a mode of theory for reading or questioning virginity. The term thus surpasses mere reference to gay identity politics in that it calls to attention the unsettling of monolithic conceptions of virginity, gender, and sexual orientation. Such a consideration of queer virginity as an unsettling force reveals "the conceptual need of the gay movement to interrupt a long tradition of viewing gender and sexuality as continuous and collapsible categories—a tradition of assuming that anyone, male or female, who desires a man must by definition be feminine; and that anyone, male or female, who desires a woman must, by the same token, be masculine."[22]

It is important to note that masculine queer virginity in the novels of Taïa and Djaziri, as in Arab Muslim societies of the Maghreb, is constructed alongside female virginity, on which extreme importance is placed. According to Isabelle Charpentier, the sacralization of female virginity is directly linked to sociocultural constructions of gender and sexuality.[23] To protect female virginity (and consequently the integrity of a family's name), there is a strict separation of boys and girls as they grow up. Such a separation is aimed at ensuring that girls are virgins when the time for marriage arrives. This separation minimizes opportunities for premarital heterosexual encounters and consequently creates sexual frustration for both boys and girls. The only possible sexual encounters are therefore between members of the same sex. Mohamed-Ali, a character in Djaziri's *Un poisson sur la balançoire*, graphically explains to Sofiène, the protagonist-narrator, how such a separation of girls from boys compels him to engage in same-sex erotic encounters so as to "quench" his sexual frustration:

> Elles veulent arriver vierges au mariage. Elles allument comme des salopes et au moment de passer à l'acte, il n'y a plus personne. Mais moi je n'en peux plus. J'ai des désirs naturels qui ne demandent qu'à s'exprimer. Mon sang bouillonne dans mes veines, quant à mes couilles, je ne t'en parle pas ! D'ailleurs, ça ne devrait pas te déplaire. Tu crois que je n'ai jamais remarqué la façon dont tu me tournais autour, l'année dernière, comme une chienne en chaleur ? Je suis sûr qu'en t'enlevant simplement le pantalon et en te prenant par derrière, j'arriverais sans problème à me persuader que tu es une fille.[24]

Here Mohamed-Ali reveals two important issues with regard to queer virginities in Arab Muslim societies. First, he articulates the sexual frustration faced by many young Arab Muslim men because of the separation of sexes and the importance placed on female virginity. Second, he expresses how sexually frustrated young men are compelled to resort to the closest substitute for women: effeminate boys such as Sofiène. It is fascinating how female virginity and how it is safeguarded at all costs are directly linked to the apparition of masculine queer sexuality. Lamenting in the op-ed article the anguish and distress faced by effeminate boys in Arab Muslim societies in his homeland, Taïa states that,

> in the Morocco of the 1980s, where homosexuality did not, of course, exist, I was an effeminate little boy, a boy to be

sacrificed, a humiliated body who bore upon himself every hypocrisy, everything left unsaid. By the time I was 10, though no one spoke of it, I knew what happened to boys like me in our impoverished society; they were designated victims, to be used, with everyone's blessing, as easy sexual objects by frustrated men. And I knew that no one would save me—not even my parents, who surely loved me. For them too, I was shame, filth. . . . Like everyone else, they urged me into a terrible, definitive silence, there to die a little more each day.[25]

In its candid deconstruction of the effeminate boy and masculine queer virginity, this article brings to the fore a subject area hitherto neglected, distant, and underresearched. It poses a philosophical challenge to the understanding of gender and identity dynamics in the Maghreb in that it reveals the deep historical, religious, and cultural interconnections of gender construction, patriarchy, and imposed heterosexuality. Concurrently, in its disconsolate representation of the violence of effeminophobia, the article "questions the ontological security of understandings of homosexuality between men in francophone North African countries, and argues that the novel challenges the deafening silence surrounding being gay in Morocco."[26]

In the novels of Taïa and Djaziri, the virginity of the effeminate protagonists plays an important role in mapping and negotiating their queer identities. In the novel *Une mélancolie arabe*, the protagonist-narrator's virginity is directly related to the construction of his queer identity. In one scene, Abdellah, the protagonist-narrator, is almost sexually violated by a group of older boys. During this encounter, the only thing that he keeps thinking of is the need to be treated by his aggressors as an equal and not as an inferior or a woman: "Ce n'était pas parce que j'aimais sincèrement et pour toujours les hommes qu'il pouvait se permettre de me confondre avec l'autre sexe. De détruire ainsi mon identité, mon histoire."[27] He makes it clear that because he is effeminate and attracted to men is no reason for other boys to abuse him sexually. In this scene, in which he is nearly raped, Abdellah acknowledges the power that he wields through his queer virginity:

> Ce cul de Leïla dont je découvrais la force sexuelle ne m'appartenait plus. Son destin était désormais entre les mains de Chouaïb. J'ai voulu un moment lui donner mon vrai prénom, lui dire que j'étais un garçon, un homme comme lui. Lui dire qu'il me plaisait et qu'il n'y avait pas besoin de violence entre nous, que je me donnerais à lui heureux si seulement il arrêtait de me féminiser.[28]

In the face of impending sexual abuse by an older boy named Chouaïb, Abdellah is more preoccupied with the influence of his virginity and the need to be treated as a man. Of particular interest is his acknowledgement of the power of his virginity, which, in spite of possible rape, gives him the confidence to boldly face his aggressors. It is ironic, however, that he refuses to be feminized by his aggressors, though he accepts being referred to as Leïla, a female name. This apparent contradiction should not be viewed as a weakness of the protagonist. On the contrary, it should be considered a "defiantly deviant" way of subverting and questioning binaries that compartmentalize sexual identities. This delicate oscillation between the masculine and the feminine destabilizes the discourses that consider sexuality and identity in monolithic binaries. Moreover, given that the virgin Abdellah is aware of his innate power, it is important to recognize that sexuality is predominantly a question of power relations. As illustrated by Andreas Eppink, the "relation with a sexual object—boy, woman or 'buggered one'—is a relation with an inferior; penetration is felt to be a manifestation of male power. Sex is essentially penetration."[29] In addition to the question of power associated with penetration, it is important to highlight some medical as well as medico-moral ramifications of penetration in male-male contexts. David M. Halperin explains that "the male sexual penetration of a subordinate male certainly represented a perverse act, but it might not in every case signify a perversion of the sexual instinct, a mental illness affecting 'the whole personality': it might indicate a morally vicious character rather than a pathological condition."[30] In such discourses from the nineteenth and twentieth centuries, a man penetrating another man was a sign of perversity, and the penetrated man was usually looked down on and loathed. Halperin further expounds that penetrated boys did not necessarily experience pleasure through their sexual subordination: "In the premodern systems of pederasty and sodomy, boys do not derive much pleasure from the sexual act: they are the more or less willing objects of adult male desire, but they are not conventionally assigned a share of desire equal to that of their senior male partners, nor are they expected to enjoy being penetrated by them."[31] In addition to these moral issues of what constituted "correct" or "normal" sexual behaviour was the medical dimension, brought to the fore with the advent of AIDS, which made penetration, especially unprotected (bareback) penetration, a medical concern regarding the spread of the epidemic. These medico-moral discourses played an important role in constructing binaries such as normal/abnormal, healthy/diseased, clean/dirty, and morality/immorality. Male-male penetration was thus framed as abnormal, diseased, immoral, and dirty in contrast to male-female penetration.

In the case of Abdellah, he attempts to subvert this status quo. Although he is willing to be penetrated by Chouaïb, he nonetheless refuses to be viewed as an inferior. He further states candidly that "j'étais moi-même avec eux. Moi-même et différent. Je les adorais, oui, oui. Je restais avec eux même quand ils m'insultaient, me traitaient d'efféminé, de *zamel*, de pédé passif."[32] The juvenile Abdellah is well aware of two important issues that centre on his queer virginity and sexuality. First, he is conscious that, by accepting to be penetrated, he unwittingly agrees to have the derogatory tag of "*zamel*" (passive homosexual) placed on him. As such, he has to accept the mortifying and debased consideration by his peers, who view him as an inferior, as a woman. Second, Abdellah recognizes that his queer virginity and its loss are important facets in the construction of a homosexual subjectivity and identity. As noted by Smith, "the assertion of exclusive homosexuality, not in terms of the temporary sexual act but rather as a permanent chosen sexual identity, challenges current dominant cultural norms in most, if not all, countries whose populations are predominantly

Muslim."[33] The protagonist is different from his peers in that he rejects the perception that same-sex sexuality is nothing more than a form of substitution and that "passive homosexuality is shameful and signifies automatic emasculation."[34] Smith rightly explains in this context that

> this early episode can therefore be read as a clash of perceptions between a nascent gay identity, which finds itself in violent contradiction with the accepted discourses of Abdellah's world. Nevertheless, the protagonist is not the only one left troubled by this clash of ideologies. The tension experienced by the other participants is highlighted in the short excerpt above by the verbal abuse to which they submit the protagonist. His evident desire for homosexual contact and their categorization of him as *zamel* and *pédé passif* identify Abdellah as a scapegoat, allowing the others to simultaneously engage in the act whilst escaping any blame or dishonour that may come their way as a consequence. This functions as a kind of group-glue, which paradoxically both binds and separates the group at the same time by marginalizing Abdellah for his difference and by establishing a hierarchy within the group—those who are active and hyper-masculine, and he who is passive, weak and abject.[35]

Abdellah's virginity thus becomes the locus of divergent discourses concerning identity, gender, and sexuality. It represents a resolute rejection of subservience to hegemonic and dominant discourses that function to render Abdellah an inferior social being because of his passive homosexuality. By rebuffing anal penetration by Chouaïb, the virginal Abdellah becomes a larger symbol of the subversive refusal to be trapped in a continuum that would reduce him to a non-man.

The situation is similar for Djaziri's Sofiène, who is also fully aware of the power innate in his virginity and uses it seductively from an early age. Although aware of this power cocooned in his virginity and sexuality, he realizes the need to completely control it: "Je me promis d'être plus discret. Je voulais bien être désiré, mais l'expression trop ouverte de ce désir, exprimé par les autres à mon endroit, m'effrayait suffisamment pour tremper mon envie d'allumer de jeunes mâles en mal de femelles."[36] The terms "males" and "females" are interesting here because of how they are used in categorizing genders. These terms incarnate the traditional gender dichotomy. The narrator uses the terms to undermine the traditional gender dichotomy that discounts any gender and sexual expression that falls outside the binary. This queering of the male/female binary allows Sofiène to discern that in his society available gender and sexual roles "are highly masculinized and masculinizing, or if he is penetrated, feminizing."[37] He readily accepts being feminized, stating that "'le quelque chose à enculer', c'était moi."[38] It is fascinating to note that the effeminate protagonist, instead of regarding himself as a person, reduces himself to a "something" to be penetrated by others. As such, Sofiène ceases to view himself as a being and becomes a body that exists for the pleasure of others. He internalizes society's perception of effeminate boys as objects to be used, and willingly accepts the labelling and characterization. Unlike Abdellah, who refuses any such objectification and demands to be viewed as a man and nothing less, Sofiène embraces his feminine side and has no problem being a passive homosexual. With a group of peers, he engages in the exploration of his sexuality through chaste erotic games. He notices and accepts that in the group he is the only one comfortable with being objectified and feminized: "J'avais eu conscience d'être une sorte de garcon objet au sein du groupe."[39] As a fifteen year old cognizant of his embryonic sexuality, Sofiène is equally aware that in his Tunisian society it is the passive homosexual who is despised. Having been caught by his father in a compromising position with another boy, it is striking that his father wants to know only which one of them was the active participant in the erotic act. Sofiène explains thereafter that "Il est vrai que les mentalités ici sont ainsi faites que celui qui a le rôle actif ne perd rien de sa virilité et peut même raconter ses exploits, il n'en sera applaudi, encouragé. L'homme qui aura eu le rôle passif se verra, lui, traité de pédé et sera méprisé."[40] In many instances, he compares himself to girls and competes with them for the attention of boys. Like the girls, he realizes the power of virginity, pausing to reflect that "comme beaucoup de jeunes filles de bonnes familles, elles avaient dû sacrifier leurs arrières au profit d'une virginité qu'elles réservaient pour le grand soir. Nous avions un point commun, finalement. À la différence que le sacrifice de mes arrières avait sonné le glas de ma virginité, n'ayant qu'un nombre restreint d'orifices à offrir."[41] Sofiène acknowledges above that, unlike the girls with whom he competes, by being penetrated from behind his queer virginity is lost forever. The girls who offer their behinds, however, guard their more treasurable vaginal virginity, which they reserve for their future husbands. Be that as it may, the loss of his queer virginity to Khélil, albeit characterized by violent physical passion, is central to the constitution of his "gay" identity: "Il est vrai aussi que j'avais eu très mal. Le sexe de Khélil m'avait paru énorme lorsqu'il l'avait introduit en moi. J'avais eu l'impression qu'il me déchirait. Et il m'avait déchiré en s'installant dans mes entrailles."[42] In spite of the sadomasochistic nature of his first sexual encounter, Sofiène describes it in a relatively lyrical and positive light: "Khélil devenait l'alchimiste de mes sens, le chef d'orchestre de mes frissons, menant avec maestria les instruments de ma chair dont il savait tirer de voluptueuses mélodies, où alternait soupirs lascifs et gémissements furtifs. Jusqu'à présent, le dosage avait été parfait car, loin de me rétracter sous ses tortures qui n'en étaient plus, je m'étais offert plus encore."[43] In spite of the pain inherent to penetration, Sofiène seems to be more concerned with the fact that the sexual act cements his difference and sexual identity. This perception of himself and his sexuality is nevertheless destabilized when, during a visit to his maternal grandparents in France, he makes the acquaintance of Frédéric. Unlike the men whom Sofiène had come to know in Tunisia, Frédéric is interested neither in his posterior virginity nor in feminizing him. On the contrary, he considers Sofiène an equal in the sexual act: "Frédéric m'avait utilisé comme moi-même aimais utiliser les autres hommes. Il n'avait pas exploité mon côté féminin. C'était bel et bien mon attribut masculin qui l'avait attiré. Khélil et les autres garçons du groupe, ou même Abdelwahab, n'avaient jamais prêté la moindre attention à ce que j'avais dans la braguette."[44] Although the verb *use* suggests an objectification and commodification of the protagonist, to some extent this experience allows him to identify diverse ways in which he can explore his queer sexuality. Sofiène acknowledges after this encounter that "il était possible d'aimer et d'être aimé, tout en conservant son intégrité physique."[45] As noted by Andrea Duranti, Frédéric introduces Sofiène "to the Western, 'history-laden' concept of gay identity, i.e. concrete identitary reference and the basis for an equal and mutual relationship, including sexual praxes."[46] It is thus interesting that, in choosing to be a passive homosexual and accepting to be penetrated, Sofiène essentially threatens the status quo in that he steadfastly decides on what the dominant order ignores and refuses to recognize. The protagonist—in emphasizing his passive homosexuality while making it clear that "je ne suis pas fou! Je ne suis pas anormal!"[47]—wants to be accepted as he is without having his queerness pathologized. In so doing, he provides a fundamental shift in the representation of homosexuality in Maghrebian literature written in French because he compellingly discards any attempt by his family and society to disregard his difference.

The examination of the representation of queer virginity above reveals that its loss is the demarcating point between two stages in the development of the sexual identities of the protagonists. In the first instance, the pre-gay period before the loss of virginity is characterized by "pre-sexual realities of gay experience,"[48] given that the gay identity has not yet fully developed. (Homo)sexual intercourse and the subsequent loss of virginity mark the beginning of the second stage, when the queer identity ceases to be a theoretical entity and begins to be a reality. For Abdellah, the loss of his virginity is followed almost directly by the verbalization of his desire in his native dialect: "Une voix, la mienne, a dit, pour la première fois en arabe: 'Je t'aime!'"[49] This verbal declaration of his queer difference takes root from the moment that he engages in (homo)sexual intercourse. It is as if the sexual act is a precondition for him to fully embrace his gay identity: "J'allais décoller, voler, écrire autre chose, aimer au grand jour, dire mon amour, être ce qui ne se dit pas, n'existe pas."[50] He further explains how he is propelled, in this period after the loss of his queer virginity, to openly express and display his difference: "Le monde m'observait. C'est là dans cette rue, ce petit coin écrasé par la morale et la peur, ce coin que j'aimais et détestais à la fois, que j'allais me révéler tout entier aux yeux des autres, les secouer, créer le choc, faire l'événement."[51]

Similarly, Sofiène confesses, after his initial sexual encounters, that, "dans ce monde nouveau, j'avais le sentiment de dominer mes semblables. Je me sentais grandi, invincible. Rien ne me paraissait impossible."[52] Upon the loss of his queer virginity, Sofiène begins to construct and "acquire a definite gay, male self-referentiality as he abandons the indefinite, swappable queer dimension that is performative."[53]

It is pertinent to consider how the two protagonists grapple with the question of being boyish after the "pre-gay" period. This is particularly the case with Abdellah, older in the author's later novels. In this regard, Mavor posits that "our cultural imagination of gay man, even in supposedly gay-affirmative revisionist psychoanalysis, is a boy who . . . does not grow out of his boyishness. . . . In the body of a growing or grown male, 'boyishness' is always already feminine."[54] She explains further that, for an older gay man, boyishness brings about the "notion of the body split"[55] between the thin and slender childhood body and the plump adult body. As an adult, Abdellah has to contend with being eternally boyish and "always already feminine." It is interesting, however, that when his body does become plump he feels that he has lost the boyish innocence of his adolescence:

> Nu, je me voyais. Je me regardais. Je voyais un visage différent de moi, un corps différent de moi, loin, loin de l'image que j'avais dans ma tête, loin d'Abdellah à l'intérieur. Quelque chose avait changé en moi, sur moi, à mon insu. Le temps avait fait son travail. On me disait si jeune. Et pourtant, c'était là, devant mes yeux, une autre vérité: j'avais vieilli et j'étais en train de devenir gros, gras. Perdu, même dans mon corps.[56]

This complex relationship of Abdellah with his own body provokes a certain number of questions. What does it mean when a boy is effeminate? How do we think through the effeminate boy? Is the effeminate gay man boyish? In spite of himself, Abdellah challenges identitarian understandings of the intersection of gender, sexuality, and time. Effeminacy and boyishness in the novels of Taïa and Djaziri demonstrate how the protagonists express their unique and queer subjectivities through their non-normative uses of time. The protagonists disrupt the traditional linear development from childhood to adulthood by adopting a more fluid and often nebulous perception of reality and being. In the case of Abdellah, when others view him as young or boyish when he feels old, the production of a new timeline of experiencing maturation within this discontinuity is created. Furthermore, thinking through the image of the effeminate boy and the boyish gay man, we can see how the protagonists challenge, in spite of themselves, the perception that effeminacy and boyishness are states of halted development. In fact, the proto-gay characters renounce maturity/adulthood, for it would require them to frame their sexuality and desire in ways that replicate the heteropatriarchal status quo, in which adulthood is equated with a litany of rites of passage such as marriage and reproduction.

The effeminacy, boyishness, and virginity of the queer protagonist-narrators in the novels of Djaziri and Taïa are thus important loci in the reimagination and mapping of their adult gay identities. The loss of virginity is intrinsically linked to the development of a sexual identity considered deviant, "unspeakable,"[57] and undesirable in the Arab Muslim world of the protagonists. They have to grapple with the hypothetical question of a diachronic and integrated sense of self that attempts to impose itself on a milieu characterized by hostility, homophobia, and a deep entrenchment in piety and cultural practices. Abdellah and Sofiène attempt to impose their difference in spite of the obvious resentment that they face in doing so. Sofiène notes, for example, that "que je couche avec un autre garçon était un acte qui portait un nom et l'on m'avait appris qu'il y avait des millions d'adeptes de cette pratique. . . . Je sentais confusément que je transgressais plus qu'une règle: une loi, une tradition, un tabou !"[58] Even though Sofiène is fully aware of the existence of millions of people who, like him, are queer, he has to grapple with the reality that such queerness is not only taboo but also inadmissible in his Tunisian Arab Muslim community.

It is relevant to refer as well to Michel Foucault's and Leo Bersani's theorizations of the idea of passive homosexuality. In his second volume of *The History of Sexuality*, Foucault documents the recognition and even exaltation of homosexuality in ancient Greece. Homosexuality was viewed in the active versus the passive dichotomy, and he attests that the more "honorable and valorized" of the two entailed "being active, in dominating, in penetrating, in asserting one's superiority."[59] He also observes that "to bear the marks of inferiority, submission to domination, and acceptance of servitude . . . could only be considered as shameful: a shame that was even greater if he offered himself as the obligating object of another's pleasure."[60] In his discussion of this Foucauldian discourse on the penetrator/penetrated binary, Bersani explains that "the moral taboo on 'passive' anal sex in ancient Athens is primarily formulated as a kind of hygienics of social power" because "to be penetrated is to abdicate power."[61] Regarding his consideration of passive homosexuality, Bersani seems to call for a shift in viewing it as "demeaning" because, for him, "the rectum is the grave in which the masculine ideal (an ideal shared—differently—by men and women) of proud subjectivity is buried."[62] He concludes that passivity should thus be celebrated, "not because of its subversive potential for parodies of machismo, not because it offers a model of genuine pluralism to a society that at once celebrates and punishes pluralism, but rather because it never stops re-presenting the internalized phallic male as an infinitely loved object of sacrifice."[63] These perspectives are particularly relevant in the context of the novels of Taïa and Djaziri because, far from incarnating power dynamics in relation to gender and sexuality, it is through masculine queer virginity that "proud" masculinity is subverted and buried. As a theoretical concept, queer virginity destabilizes the traditional hegemony of heterosexuality by revealing that it is possible to experience and perceive sexuality and gender in "other" ways.

Beyond their innovativeness and boldness in broaching a taboo subject, the open depiction of queer virginity and sexuality by Taïa and Djaziri is entangled with, and a metaphor for, the destabilization of monolithic conceptualizations of gender and sexual identity. This open narrativization of queerness can play an important role in effecting change in the perception of queerness in the Arab Muslim societies of the Maghreb. To begin with, this is achieved through an "outing" of the "specter of queerness"[64] that continues to haunt the Maghreb. By making visible queer virginity and sexuality and making them the centre of the literary universe, Abdellah Taïa and Eyet-Chékib Djaziri move these phenomena from the margins to the mainstream of literary space. This visibility of queerness both unshackles and exposes bodies that had been pushed to the sidelines, and Shani D'Cruze and Anupama Rao rightly explain in this vein that "the stigmatized bodies, bodies burdened by their proximity to the material circumstances of daily life, queer bodies—embodiments of alterity, in brief—have been subject to targeted violations even as their exceptional status has provoked discussion, debate and more simply, fascinated attention."[65] By offering a candid and unassuming picture of queer virginity and sexuality in the contexts of Arab Muslim societies of North Africa, the novels of the two writers show that "the world can be seen through other signs, interpreted through other figures, or opened up to different possibilities if the mechanics of sexual reproduction are not given transcendental cultural meaning."[66] Furthermore, through such candid literary depictions of effeminacy and masculine queer virginity, it is possible to recognize that "les romans apparaissent ainsi comme un espace de résistance où se déploie une voie / une voix 'homosexuelle' qui met à mal l'hétérosexisme en déplaçant les limites du dicible et du visible et en conférant ainsi une légitimité à des expériences et des subjectivités 'abjectées.'"[67]

In conclusion, it is worth pointing out that a more comprehensive understanding of queer virginity, in North Africa as in other places, is not only necessary but also well overdue. Although the work of Bersani, Foucault, Sedgwick, and Stockton remains seminal in this respect, it does not adequately address the question of queer virginity and sexuality in Arab Muslim North Africa. As such, there is a need for an original appraisal of the construction of queer sexuality, particularly masculine queer virginity, in literary works emanating from North Africa.

NOTES

1   Voltaire, *Treatise on Tolerance and Other Writings*, ed. Simon Harvey (Cambridge, UK: Cambridge University Press, 2000), 132.

2   Kathryn Bond Stockton, *The Queer Child: Or Growing Sideways in the Twentieth Century* (Durham: Duke University Press, 2009), 1.

3   Eve Kosofsky Sedgwick, "How to Bring Your Kids Up Gay," *Social Text* 29 (1991): 18–27.

4   Ibid., 20.

5   Carol Mavor, *Reading Boyishly: Roland Barthes, J. M. Barrie, Jacques Henri Lartigue, Marcel Proust, and D. W. Winnicott* (Durham: Duke University Press, 2007), 72.

6   Eric Levéel, "Eyet-Chékib Djaziri: Transcription subjective d'une entrevue objective," *International Journal of Francophone Studies* 8, 1 (2005): 88.

7   Stephen O. Murray and Will Roscoe, *Islamic Homosexualities: Culture, History, and Literature* (New York: New York University Press, 1997), 15.

8   The postcolonial context of the novels of Taïa and Djaziri includes the problem of competing cultural constructs of virginity and the various subtleties involved. More than just implying sexual chastity, virginity is constructed and perceived in different ways within the Arab Muslim societies of North Africa. Competing cultural and religious traditions certainly have influences on how virginity is regarded. Anne McClintock analyzes virginity vis-à-vis the postcolonial context and affirms that the myth of the virgin land is also the myth of the empty land, involving both a gender and a racial dispossession. Within patriarchal narratives, to be a virgin is to be empty of desire and void of sexual agency, passively awaiting the thrusting male insemination of history, language, and reason. Anne McClintock, *Imperial Leather: Race, Gender, and Sexuality in the Colonial Contest* (New York: Routledge, 1995), 30. Sanya Osha also argues that "African" sexuality "right from its encounters with Euromodernity had a number of barriers with which to contend." Sanya Osha, *African Postcolonial Modernity: Informal Subjectivities and the Democratic Consensus* (New York: Palgrave Macmillan, 2014), 157. This rightly points to the manner in which a concept such as virginity in a postcolonial setting cannot have a monolithic definition and construction.

9   Cristina Santos and Adriana Spahr, "Introduction," in *Defiant Deviance: The Irreality of Reality in the Cultural Imaginary*, ed. Cristina Santos and Adriana Spahr (New York: Peter Lang, 2006), 1.

10   Ibid., 1–2.

11   Mireille Rosello, "Queer Virginity: Leïla Marouane's *La vie sexuelle d'un Islamiste à Paris*," *Modern and Contemporary France* 21, 2 (2013): 167.

12   Ibid., 181.

13   Renée C. Hoogland, "Fact and Fantasy: The Body of Desire in the Age of Posthumanism," *Journal of Gender Studies* 11, 3 (2002): 215.

14   Lawrence R. Schehr, *The Shock of Men: Homosexual Hermeneutics in French Writing* (Stanford: Stanford University Press, 1995), 30.

15   Stockton, *The Queer Child*, 6.

16   Eyet-Chékib Djaziri, *Un poisson sur la balançoire* (Paris: CyLibris, 1997), 43. Translation: I have never heard that word, I assure you. What is it? . . . I remained stunned. I who had believed myself to be unique, here I was discovering millions similar to me. (All translations in this chapter are mine.)

17   Lucas Hilderbrand, "Mediating Queer Boyhood: *Dottie Gets Spanked*," in *The Cinema of Todd Haynes: All that Heaven Allows*, ed. James Morrison (London: Wallflower Press, 2007), 43.

18   Ibid.

19   Ken Corbett, *Boyhoods: Rethinking Masculinities* (New Haven: Yale University Press, 2009), 124.

20   Chung-Hao Ku, "Boyish Narratives: The Art of Not Acting Your Age" (PhD diss., University of Michigan, 2013), 57.

21   Abdellah Taïa, "A Boy to Be Sacrificed," *New York Times*, April 12, 2012, http://www.nytimes.com/2012/03/25/opinion/sunday/a-boy-to-be-sacrificed.html?_r=0.

22   Sedgwick, "How to Bring Your Kids Up Gay," 20.

23   Isabelle Charpentier, "Vierges blessées: Représentations de la virginité féminine dans les œuvres et témoignages d'écrivaines (franco)algériennes et (franco)marocaines depuis 2000," *International Journal of Francophone Studies* 15, 2 (2012): 298.

24   Djaziri, *Un poisson sur la balançoire*, 155–56. Translation: They (girls) want to be virgins when they get married. Like sluts they turn you on, and when it's time to move on to the act they are no longer present. I cannot take that anymore. I have natural desires which simply have to

be expressed. My blood seethes in my veins; as for my balls, I will not speak about that! Besides, that should not put you off. Do you believe that I didn't notice the way you hung around me, last year, like a bitch in heat? I am sure that, by simply removing your trousers and taking you from behind, I would easily convince myself that you are a girl.

25 Taïa, "A Boy to Be Sacrificed."

26 Sophie C. Smith, "'*Être ce qui ne se dit pas*': Negotiating a Gay Identity in Abdellah Taïa's *Une mélancolie arabe*," *International Journal of Francophone Studies* 15, 1 (2012): 36.

27 Abdellah Taïa, *Une mélancolie arabe* (Paris: Seuil, 2008), 22. Translation: It is not because I sincerely and exclusively loved men that he could allow himself to confuse me to the other sex. To destroy as such my identity, my history.

28 Ibid., 21. Translation: This arse of a Leïla, of which I was discovering the sexual prowess, was no longer my own. Its fate now lay in the hands of Chouaïb. I wanted a moment to tell him my real name, tell him I was a boy, a man like him. Tell him that I liked him and that there was no need for violence between us, that I would happily give myself to him if he just stopped feminizing me.

29 Andreas Eppink, "Moroccan Boys and Sex," in *Sexuality and Eroticism among Males in Moslem Societies*, ed. Arno Schmitt and Jehoeda A. Sofer (New York: Haworth Press, 1992), 36–37.

30 David M. Halperin, "How to Do the History of Male Homosexuality," *GLQ: A Journal of Lesbian and Gay Studies* 6, 1 (2000): 95.

31 Ibid., 102.

32 Taïa, *Une mélancolie arabe*, 14. Translation: I remained myself with them. Myself and different. I loved them, of course. I stayed with them even when they insulted me, called me an effeminate, a *zamel*, a passive homosexual.

33 Smith, "'*Être ce qui ne se dit pas*,'" 35–36.

34 Ibid., 42.

35 Ibid., 42–43.

36 Djaziri, *Un poisson sur la balançoire*, 11. Translation: I made a promise to myself to be more discreet. I wanted to be desired, but an all too open expression of this desire, conveyed by others about me, scared me enough to quench my desire to turn on young males who were desperate for females.

37   Smith, "'*Être ce qui ne se dit pas*,'" 45.

38   Djaziri, *Un poisson sur la balançoire*, 15. Translation: "the something to bugger" was me.

39   Ibid., 57. Translation: I realized that I was a kind of objectified boy within the group.

40   Ibid., 70. Translation: It is true that attitudes here are such that he who has the active role does not lose his virility, and he can even tell others of his exploits, he will be applauded and encouraged. The man who has had the passive role will be treated as a fag and will be despised.

41   Ibid., 181. Translation: Like many young girls from good families, they had to sacrifice their behinds so as to retain a virginity they reserved for the big night. We had something in common after all. The only difference was that the sacrifice of my behind had sounded the death knell for my virginity, given the limited number of orifices that I had to offer.

42   Ibid., 29. Translation: It is also true that I felt a lot of pain. Khélil's penis seemed enormous to me when he inserted it into me. I had the feeling that he was tearing me apart. And he did rip me open as he slithered into my bowels.

43   Ibid., 141. Translation: Khélil became the alchemist of my senses, the orchestrator of my thrills, masterfully leading instruments of my flesh of which he could draw voluptuous melodies, alternating lascivious sighs and surreptitious groans. Hitherto, the dosage was perfect because, far from backing down under his tortures, I offered myself even more.

44   Ibid., 41–42. Translation: Frédéric had used me as I had liked using other men. He had not taken advantage of my feminine side. It was indeed my masculine attribute that had attracted him. Khélil and the other boys in the group, or even Abdelwahab, had never paid attention to what lay behind the fly of my trousers.

45   Ibid., 43. Translation: it was possible to love and be loved, while conserving one's physical integrity.

46   Andrea Duranti, "Gay but Not Queer: Defining Liminal Post-Queer Identities in Maghrebian Literature," *Contemporary French and Francophone Studies* 12, 1 (2008): 84.

47   Djaziri, *Un poisson sur la balançoire*, 119. Translation: I am not mad! I am not abnormal!

48   David M. Halperin, "Homosexuality's Closet," *Michigan Quarterly Review* 41, 1 (2002): 23.

49 Taïa, *Une mélancolie arabe*, 31. Translation: A voice, my own, said, for the first time in Arabic: "I love you."

50 Ibid., 31–32. Translation: I was going to take off, fly away, write something else, love in the broad daylight, be that which is unspeakable, does not exist.

51 Ibid., 31. Translation: Everyone was observing me. It is in this road, this small place overburdened by morality and fear, this place that I loved and hated at the same time, where I was going to reveal myself completely in the eyes of others, ruffle them up, create shock, be the major news.

52 Djaziri, *Un poisson sur la balançoire*, 27. Translation: in this new world, I felt I could dominate my peers. I felt grown up, invincible. Everything seemed possible in my eyes.

53 Duranti, "Gay but Not Queer," 85.

54 Mavor, *Reading Boyishly*, 72.

55 Ibid., 6.

56 Taïa, *Une mélancolie arabe*, 70. Translation: Naked, I was seeing myself. I was looking at myself. I was seeing a face different from mine, a body different from mine, far, far from the image that I had in my head, far from the inner Abdellah. Something had changed in me, on me, unwittingly. Time had done its work. People told me I was so young. But however, there, in front of my eyes, was a different truth: I had grown old, and I was becoming bigger, fatter. Lost, even in my own body.

57 Brian Whitaker, *Unspeakable Love: Gay and Lesbian Life in the Middle East* (London: Saqi Books, 2006), 3.

58 Djaziri, *Un poisson sur la balançoire*, 109. Translation: sleeping with another boy was an act that had a name, and I was taught that there were millions of followers of this practice. . . . I, however, felt vaguely that I was transgressing more than a rule: a law, a tradition, a taboo!

59 Michel Foucault, *The Use of Pleasure*, vol. 2 of *The History of Sexuality* (New York: Vintage Books, 1985), 215.

60 Ibid., 216.

61 Leo Bersani, *Is the Rectum a Grave? And Other Essays* (Chicago: University of Chicago Press, 2010), 19.

62 Ibid., 29.

63 Ibid., 30.

64 Jarrod Hayes, *Queer Nations: Marginal Sexualities in the Maghreb* (Chicago: University of Chicago Press, 2000), 17.

65 Shani D'Cruze and Anupama Rao, *Violence, Vulnerability, and Embodiment: Gender and History* (Oxford: Blackwell, 2005), 9.
66 Schehr, *The Shock of Men*, viii.
67 Renaud Lagabrielle, "Le pouvoir de l'homosexualité dans la littérature maghrébine de langue française: À propos d'Eyet-Chékib Djaziri," *Stichproben: Wiener Zeitschrift für kritische Afrikastudien* 11 (2006): 63. Translation: The novels [that openly depict deviant sexuality] appear as a space of resistance in which a "homosexual" slant/voice is unfurled which undermines heterosexuality by moving the boundaries of the expressible and visible and thus conferring legitimacy on "abjected" experiences and subjectivities.

REFERENCES

Bersani, Leo. *Is the Rectum a Grave? And Other Essays.* Chicago: University of Chicago Press, 2010.
Charpentier, Isabelle. "Vierges blessées: Représentations de la virginité féminine dans les œuvres et témoignages d'écrivaines (franco)algériennes et (franco)marocaines depuis 2000." *International Journal of Francophone Studies* 15, 2 (2012): 297–318.
Corbett, Ken. *Boyhoods: Rethinking Masculinities.* New Haven: Yale University Press, 2009.
D'Cruze, Shani, and Anupama Rao. *Violence, Vulnerability, and Embodiment: Gender and History.* Oxford: Blackwell, 2005.
Djaziri, Eyet-Chékib. *Un poisson sur la balançoire.* Paris: CyLibris, 1997.
Duranti, Andrea. "Gay but Not Queer: Defining Liminal Post-Queer Identities in Maghrebian Literature." *Contemporary French and Francophone Studies* 12, 1 (2008): 79–87.
Eppink, Andreas. "Moroccan Boys and Sex." In *Sexuality and Eroticism among Males in Moslem Societies*, edited by Arno Schmitt and Jehoeda A. Sofer, 33–42. New York: Haworth Press, 1992.
Foucault, Michel. *The Use of Pleasure.* Vol. 2 of *The History of Sexuality.* New York: Vintage Books, 1985.
Halperin, David M. "Homosexuality's Closet." *Michigan Quarterly Review* 41, 1 (2002): 21–54.
———. "How to Do the History of Male Homosexuality." *GLQ: A Journal of Lesbian and Gay Studies* 6, 1 (2000): 87–124.
Hayes, Jarrod. *Queer Nations: Marginal Sexualities in the Maghreb.* Chicago: University of Chicago Press, 2000.

Hilderbrand, Lucas. "Mediating Queer Boyhood: *Dottie Gets Spanked*." In *The Cinema of Todd Haynes: All that Heaven Allows*, edited by James Morrison, 42–56. London: Wallflower Press, 2007.

Hoogland, Renée C. "Fact and Fantasy: The Body of Desire in the Age of Posthumanism." *Journal of Gender Studies* 11, 3 (2002): 213–31.

Ku, Chung-Hao. "Boyish Narratives: The Art of Not Acting Your Age." PhD diss., University of Michigan, 2013.

Lagabrielle, Renaud. "Le pouvoir de l'homosexualité dans la littérature maghrébine de langue française: À propos d'Eyet-Chékib Djaziri." *Stichproben: Wiener Zeitschrift für kritische Afrikastudien* 11 (2006): 63–80.

Levéel, Eric. "Eyet-Chékib Djaziri: Transcription subjective d'une entrevue objective." *International Journal of Francophone Studies* 8, 1 (2005): 85–92.

Mavor, Carol. *Reading Boyishly: Roland Barthes, J. M. Barrie, Jacques Henri Lartigue, Marcel Proust, and D. W. Winnicott*. Durham: Duke University Press, 2007.

McClintock, Anne. *Imperial Leather: Race, Gender, and Sexuality in the Colonial Contest*. New York: Routledge, 1995.

Murray, Stephen O., and Will Roscoe. *Islamic Homosexualities: Culture, History, and Literature*. New York: New York University Press, 1997.

Osha, Sanya. *African Postcolonial Modernity: Informal Subjectivities and the Democratic Consensus*. New York: Palgrave Macmillan, 2014.

Rosello, Mireille. "Queer Virginity: Leïla Marouane's *La vie sexuelle d'un Islamiste à Paris*." *Modern and Contemporary France* 21, 2 (2013): 167–82.

Santos, Cristina, and Adriana Spahr. "Introduction." In *Defiant Deviance: The Irreality of Reality in the Cultural Imaginary*, edited by Cristina Santos and Adriana Spahr. New York: Peter Lang, 2006.

Schehr, Lawrence R. *The Shock of Men: Homosexual Hermeneutics in French Writing*. Stanford: Stanford University Press, 1995.

Sedgwick, Eve Kosofsky. "How to Bring Your Kids Up Gay." *Social Text* 29 (1991): 18–27.

Smith, Sophie C. "'*Être ce qui ne se dit pas*': Negotiating a Gay Identity in Abdellah Taïa's *Une mélancolie arabe*." *International Journal of Francophone Studies* 15, 1 (2012): 35–51.

Stockton, Kathryn Bond. *The Queer Child: Or Growing Sideways in the Twentieth Century*. Durham: Duke University Press, 2009.

Taïa, Abdellah. "A Boy to Be Sacrificed." *New York Times*, April 12, 2012, http://www.nytimes.com/2012/03/25/opinion/sunday/a-boy-to-be-sacrificed.html?_r=0.

———. *Une mélancolie arabe*. Paris: Seuil, 2008.

Whitaker, Brian. *Unspeakable Love: Gay and Lesbian Life in the Middle East*. London: Saqi Books, 2006.

PART 4

F*CK: THEY ENTRAPPED US IN SOCIAL ISSUES AND POLITICS

CHAPTER 7

BOLLYWOOD VIRGINS: DIACHRONIC FLIRTATIONS WITH INDIAN WOMANHOOD

Asma Sayed

Virginity and chastity in Bollywood cinema are represented as religious and moral issues.[1] Female virginity remains an important Indian value, a cornerstone of popular culture in India, both reflected in and perpetuated by the Indian film industry—including the Hindi-language film industry, commonly referred to as Bollywood.[2] India is a diverse and multi-cultural country, and the standards for purity vary dramatically for women living in urban or rural areas; issues of class play significant roles in levels of education and degrees of autonomy and freedom of social movement that women enjoy; and, of course, there is a wide range of cultural and religious expectations that affect gender expectations in India. However, generally speaking, Indian girls and women are largely expected to be reserved in their interactions with men outside the family, and the expectation is that all women must remain virgins until marriage. After marriage, women are expected to become sacrificial mothers and dedicated wives who abdicate their own desires and needs for the good of their families, particularly their husbands, and the nation. As in the West with

Hollywood cinema and the associated mainstream press, gender expectations in India are reinforced through the mainstream Bollywood film industry. By the same token, a diachronic study of the representation of virginity in Indian cinema from the late 1960s through to the early 2010s provides an archive of the sometimes subtle, sometimes dramatic changes to female gender expectations in Indian culture.

Starting in the early twentieth century, Bollywood films have largely upheld Indian social ideals of female purity and chastity. Even in the present, Bollywood films play a significant role in maintaining these patriarchal, nationalist, and populist views that normalize the marginalization of women and condone traditional attitudes toward female sexuality. Until the twenty-first century, it was rare to see on-screen displays of physical intimacy. Kissing scenes were often left to the imagination, represented via the synecdoche of birds or flowers. Moreover, female film characters have been represented through clear dichotomies of good woman versus bad woman. Leading female characters, almost always good and triumphant, typically conform to the traditional Indian cultural values: a good woman is a pure virgin, a sacrificial mother, a dedicated wife; she is submissive, confined to the domestic sphere, and willing to sacrifice her own needs for the good of her family, particularly her husband. Conversely, a villainous woman is represented as a vamp, commonly working as a prostitute or bar dancer or as an upper-class woman who has been corrupted by Western influences and therefore forgotten her Indian values. In this configuration, representations of virginity can be read as political commentaries; Bollywood cinema's representation of female virginity, by extension, becomes symbolic of the purity and sanctity of the nation-state.

To provide an overview of Bollywood representations of virginity as part of female identity politics, this chapter focuses on six particularly significant films from the post-independence era in India: *Aradhana* (Prayer, 1969), *Purab aur Paschim* (East and West, 1970), *Dilwale Dulhania le Jayenge* (The Braveheart Will Take the Bride, 1996), *Pardes* (Foreign Land, 1997), *Band Baaja Baaraat* (Wedding Planners, 2010), and *Shuddh Desi Romance* (A Random Desi Romance, 2013). *Aradhana* and *Purab aur Paschim* are representative of 1970s film. *Aradhana*, while showing some boldness in its representations of premarital sex, also displays the social reality of such an encounter. *Purab aur Paschim* is particularly popular for its portrayal of the East/West dichotomy through the body of a woman, emphasizing the good woman/bad woman binary. The 1990s brought in a new wave of liberalization in India, especially following the country's new economic policies. Liberalization led to a change in sociocultural life, affecting women's role and understanding of their identity, sexuality being one of the tropes of identity, and a reflection of the same in cinema. During this time, Hindi cinema saw a dual trend: given that the films were now also targeting the Indian diaspora in the West, there was an attempt to show India as a nation of values (at times represented through the purity and chastity of women), a nation better than the decadent West. *Dilwale Dulhania le Jayenge* and *Pardes*, discussed in this chapter, are exemplary of this trend of the 1990s. On the other hand, some post-1990s films, wanting to showcase the changing country, one that is embracing modern, liberal values of the West, have made superficial attempts to present strong female characters. Although these films from the past two decades have showcased seemingly liberated female characters trying to make independent life choices, most end with these characters concluding that they love the men to whom they lost their virginity. Thus, these films typically end with the female protagonist marrying her first lover—a perpetuation of the patriarchal status quo that historically has restricted women's opportunities. *Band Baaja Baaraat* is an example. I further argue that, though the broader representations of women's virginity remain stereotypical, there have been tentative steps to disrupt the typical gender roles in some recent films, such as *Shuddh Desi Romance*. This film shows modern, liberated, working women who are not completely invested in marriage, consider the loss of virginity as inconsequential, and engage in romantic and sexual relationships irrespective of society's norms. It is important to study these recent trends since they are indicative of changes in Indian society.

INDIAN VIRGINITY AND PATRIARCHY

India is a multicultural society composed of people in various religious, ethnic, and linguistic groups. In spite of this diversity, all cultural subgroups in India remain largely patriarchal; likewise, virginity—a concept rooted in patriarchal concepts of male owner-ship of women's bodies—is sustained as a desirable trait even in the twenty-first century. Virginity has been upheld as a social-cultural value in Indian culture; in fact, as Hanne Blank reminds us in her book tracing the history of virginity, it has been a cornerstone of most societies:

> Virginity has been used as an organizing principle of human cultures for millennia. In the present as well as the past, any woman who trespasses against what her era, religion, community, or family holds as constituting virginity might be teased, harassed, shamed, ostracized, prohibited from marrying, or disowned. In some places and at some times her family might have been fined or punished because of it, or the woman herself might have been sold into slavery. She could be imprisoned, maimed, mutilated, flogged, raped, or even killed as punishment for losing her virginity . . . or even if it was merely believed that she had done so.[3]

Indian culture is influenced in particular by Hindu religious texts such as the *Manusmriti*, the *Ramayana*, and the *Mahabharata*, which have profound influences on people's sensibilities and perceptions of sexuality. After the arrival of Muslim empires in the Indian subcontinent from the tenth century onward, Indian society was further influenced by Islamic sanctions on premarital sex. The British, starting in the seventeenth century, brought with them Christian ideals and certainly by the Victorian period rigid cultural notions of female sexuality. Islamic and Christian influences, particularly the Virgin Mary as the ideal woman, have been strong among women of the subcontinent. As Jyotika Virdi argues, the "Indian woman in popular Hindi cinema is very much the product of this Victorian-Brahminic axis, especially during the first two decades of

[the] independent era."[4] Both the *Mahabharata* and the *Ramayana*, in various situations in the texts, emphasize women's virginity and chastity. Kunti, a single but royal woman in the *Mahabharata*, gives birth to a son by Lord Surya, the solar god, as a result of invoking a boon granted to her by a sage. Kunti, as an unmarried mother, has to give up the child and leaves him in a basket to float in the river and be found and raised by a commoner; the son, Karna, suffers the consequences of her decision for the rest of his life. Kunti also agonizes since she is unable to claim her son as her own throughout her life. Similarly, Sita, the mythical figure from the *Ramayana*, is portrayed as the ideal woman; she walks on fire and comes out unscratched, proving to her husband her chastity and fidelity to him, called into question because she was abducted and held captive by the demon Ravana. The figures of Sita, Kunti, and other literary/mythical/religious women remain popular in India. Stories of their sacrifice, purity, and virtue are recounted on a daily basis as part of both cultural and religious education as well as via popular culture.

The cinematic representation of women and popular imagination are thus overshadowed by these roles of an ideal virginal woman, devoted wife, and sacrificial mother who not only is chaste and pure but also advocates social values rooted in patriarchy and maintains family honour. Thus, historically, Bollywood films have cast women in stereotypical roles, and, apart from some films that have emphasized their liberation, most films lack any progressive representation. Virginity becomes a symbol of traditional values, and modernity is equated with the sexual liberation of women and the blurring of boundaries—often represented as undesirable—between the private female sphere and the public male domain. However, in the twenty-first century, these representations are unrealistic, and traditional roles are unattainable for most women because changing cultural and economic factors mean that many women work outside the home and operate in what have been conceptualized historically as male spheres.[5] In today's India, attitudes toward virginity are complicated by the clash of traditional and modern values. Increased economic freedom also allows more Indian women to live independently outside traditional marital arrangements and extended family situations—ultimately outside what has been considered a fulcrum of the Indian value system. Surveys show that the present young generation is open to premarital sex, whereas Indian cultural representations still emphasize women's premarital virginity and the role of the non-sexual, dutiful wife. In India, as in the West, these unrealistic and conflated ideas of sexy virginal girls and virginal mothers produced not only by Bollywood but also on a much larger cultural scale inevitably set all girls and women up for playing into the hands of the patriarchal system.

VIRGINITY IN INDIAN AND WESTERN CINEMAS

Films, as popular cultural texts, offer ideologies about the world that both shape and reflect a society and can thus be read as political texts. Theorizing virginity in Western cinema, Tamar Jeffers McDonald writes that representations of virginity in popular culture are relationally bound to "femininity and masculinity; identity; the body; sexual agency and control; stardom and performance; the individual and society; and hysteria, trauma and psychosis."[6] Discussing the social obsession with virginity, and arguing that virginity remains an important social issue, she points out that it "was already an important social trope during the early decades of [the] twentieth century as well as during the years of the Second World War, and it remains so today."[7] McDonald adds that,

> indeed, virginity has had a long and vexed history and has never been a simple matter of an ontological either/or. It most often has a chronological, medical, legal, religious, or moral dimension to its loss; frequently its maintenance is seen as being as problematic as its relinquishment. While virginity may seem an "old-fashioned object," it nevertheless remains one of perpetual currency within popular culture and the various cinemas that serve it.[8]

Yet the subject of virginity in cinema, even in the West, is understudied. The reasons for the lack of attention to this issue in the context of Indian cinema are many. In India, there is little discussion about sexuality in general given the cultural silencing of all sexual subjects. The attitude in the past 100 years of Indian cinema has usually been that of following the prescribed norms of chastity. Only in the past decade of Indian film has the conflict between traditional and modern conceptions of femininity—as they link to virginity—been brought to the forefront in a comparatively open manner. However, filmmakers have characterized virginity, its upholding, and its loss, both legitimate and otherwise, in a variety of ways.

For instance, one of the most popular cinematic images is that of the wedding night and the ritualistic nature of the loss of virginity. Writing about virginity and ritual, Blank argues that, "throughout history, losing one's virginity has been viewed as a ritual transformation. Not merely the transformation from being one of the people who hasn't slept with anybody to being one of [those] who has, but a ritual that transforms a boy into a man, a girl into a woman, a child into an adult."[9] This is true of Indian society as well, and thus the ritual of the loss of virginity after marriage is usually glamorized in Hindi films. The on-screen representation of the first night after marriage is typically ornate. The bride, usually dressed in red (again a symbol of sexuality), waits for her husband on a bed elaborately decorated with rose garland canopies and rose petals on the sheets. She sits in the middle of the bed with her skirt spread decoratively around her, and often she draws a veil over her face. Her body language suggests the ritualistic nature of the loss of virginity: the blush, the tremble, the fear, the excitement. This oft-invoked scene is symbolic of the legitimate and expected post-marriage loss of virginity.[10] Most scenes of first-night intimacy show the bridegroom getting closer to the bride, implying their sexual union, and the camera then quickly switches away from the bed.

Likewise, many Hindi-film songs metaphorically represent the young female protagonist as a blooming flower, a bud, a red rose, and the lyrics hint at her youth and virginity. In older Hindi cinema of the 1940s–70s, the sexual advances of male characters are usually rejected by the female lead through a variety of standard physical gestures and dance moves. In many films, women's desires are represented through song and dance numbers that are parts of dream sequences. In the dream world, the heroine gives herself to her lover, if at all. In these sequences, the heroine is often dressed in modern clothing and is in a Western locale such as Switzerland or the United States. However, the on-screen presentation of physical intimacy remains suggestive and discreet—never explicit. The heroine either turns or runs away if the hero tries to kiss her or puts her hands on his mouth to stop him from kissing her. While she does so, she shows signs of excitement and fear, sometimes with trembling lips and other times through lowered eyes. All of these gestures indicate her chastity, her desire to wait till marriage, and her status as a good woman from a respectable family background. On rare occasions when intercourse is implied, the camera usually shifts quickly from the couple to two birds or two roses or at times a fire.

In fact, sexual purity in the form of abstinence dominates Bollywood films. In more rare instances when the female protagonist has premarital sex,[11] the film becomes a warning story, and she is either usually married to an older man or a good Samaritan (her lover's brother or friend) or lives a life of seclusion and sacrifice. For example, in *Aradhana*, Vandana (Sharmila Tagore) has to give up her son for adoption after her lover and the father of her child, Arun (Rajesh Khanna), dies before they "officially" get married. *Aradhana* takes a bold approach for the time by representing premarital sexual intimacy. There is a scene with the two unwed lead characters in which they are stranded in a cottage in the middle of the night after they have been drenched by rain. As they put out their clothes to dry, the background soundtrack plays a song: "Roop tera mastana, pyaar mera deewana, bhool koi hamse na ho jaaye!"[12] Vandana becomes pregnant, and Arun dies in a plane crash. She gives up her son for adoption to a couple, in whose house she continues to work as a nanny so that she can be close to her son. As the film takes different melodramatic twists and turns, which include her taking the blame for a murder in order to save her son, Vandana is presented as a woman who suffers throughout her life because of one "mistake." She also becomes an ideal, dedicated, self-sacrificing mother, which can be read as an act of repentance for her "sin." Thus, a woman's premarital sexual activity is a matter of shame and social taboo, and the woman has to correct the "mistake" that she has made in a variety of redemptive measures.

Virdi argues that, "while popular films absorbed principles of female chastity, *Aradhana* was the first to explicitly associate romantic love with sexual desire. Yet harking back to chastity principles, it also shows the ruinous consequences of extramarital sex for women."[13] Vandana's self-inflicted punishment is rewarded in the end as her grown son recognizes his mother, accepts her, and credits her for the award for gallantry that he has won.

THE VIRGINAL NATION

Virginity in cinema can serve "as a metaphor for the coherence of the nation-state and to refer to a literal state of sexual inexperience."[14] Women in cinema, but also in literature and other cultural texts, have long been represented "as emblematic of the nation itself: hence fears of their bodily penetration can be seen as revealing a fundamental uneasiness about [a nation's] safety and inviolability. Yet the [teen] girl is finally shown as the nation's ultimate hope for the future. She can be the ideal citizen, as long as her passions are directed patriotically rather than personally."[15] Similarly, in the Indian context, in Hindi films, the Indian woman's body becomes a medium through which the nation's political ambitions are displayed. The nation-state's sanctity and harmony are represented through the female body. A woman's Hindu self is represented through her Indianized body wrapped in a sari and marked with a bindi and *sindoor*[16] as signs of her marital status. In contrast, a female self transformed by Western influences is represented through Western clothes, short hair, drinking, dancing, partying—all signs of Western decadence. This modern, Westernized woman is not worthy of an Indian man's attention until she changes her ways.

Post-independence popular Indian cinema conveyed the Hindu nationalist position, triggered by the Partition. In the early postcolonial era (i.e., after 1947), "much of Hindi cinema . . . remained anchored to Nehruvian India" and displayed "a bourgeois colonialism with its caste, regional, and religious bias."[17] In the 1970s, postcolonial cinema moved toward presenting nationalist agendas and pride in independent India; it was also focused on telling stories of the rise of an Indian middle class. In the 1990s, the earlier Nehru-era cinema that illustrated Indian patriotism through shows of anger and frustration toward the British Empire continued in a new direction by incorporating economically successful but culturally Indian NRI (non-resident Indian) characters. These NRIs—who have lived in the West but managed to remain untouched by its *decadence*, largely represented in film by women wearing short, Western clothes, drinking, smoking, dancing, and generally disdaining India and its traditional ways—are idealized.[18] Western-influenced characters, both men and women, are shown as engaging in promiscuous behaviour.

Released in 1970, the film *Purab aur Paschim*, directed by Manoj Kumar, plays on the binary of good woman/bad woman and situates traditional Indian virginal womanhood as desirable. The plot begins in colonial India. Harnam (Pran) kills a freedom fighter. Years pass, and the freedom fighter's son, Bharat (Manoj Kumar), goes to university in London. Bharat maintains Indian values and morals while living in England and is affronted by the decadence of diasporic Indians who adopt Western ways. Western decadence is particularly emphasized through the character of Preeti (Saira Banu), who has dyed blonde hair, wears Western clothing, drinks alcohol, and smokes cigarettes. Despite himself, Bharat falls in love with Preeti, and once she visits India with him she realizes the failings of her Western lifestyle. She discovers the beauty and spirituality of Indian life. Thus, the film clearly plays on an East/West dichotomy, attributing to the East purity and love and associating the West with materialism and lust. Preeti, as a liberated woman from the West, is reinstated through her incorporation into India's postcolonial, nationalistic, and patriarchal society; this Indian notion of liberation distances itself from the "misguided" feminist movements of the 1960s West.[19] In fact, as film critic Neepa Majumdar reminds us, the 1960s emergence of "the Westernized woman as the specific incarnation of bad womanhood coincides with the post-Independence imperative to posit a pan-Indian identity to both the world of diegesis and the ideal audience of these films."[20] When the Westernized Indian woman reverts to Indian ways, as in

Purab aur Paschim, she is rewarded with marriage to the patriotic Hindu man and gets to spend her life in sacred India.

Moving into the 1990s, Bollywood gender politics transformed. In this period, films not only addressed an Indian audience but also attempted to attract diasporic viewers. Films were now being set in the West, and the protagonists were sometimes either first- or second-generation Indians living abroad. Nonetheless, the films were mostly critical of Western values. For example, *Dilwale Dulhania le Jayenge* is a blockbuster film hailed as the first Hindi film specifically targeting the Indian diaspora.[21] The two leading characters, Simran (Kajol) and Raj (Shah Rukh Khan), are raised in the West, live a comfortable consumerist life, and abide by Indian values. At the outset of the film, Simran has been engaged through an arranged marriage to Kulwant, who lives in India. Simran and her family go to India for the wedding. But first she goes on a trip and meets and falls in love with Raj, a diasporic Indian man. Raj follows her to India and tries to get her father, Baldev (Amrish Puri), to agree to allow him to marry Simran. Her mother suggests that Raj elope with Simran since she thinks that Baldev will never agree to the alliance, but Raj refuses to compromise his Indian mores and argues that he will marry Simran legitimately only after Baldev agrees. Thus, Raj and Simran, though raised in the West, become classic examples of Indian ideals of purity and chastity. They uphold the Indian value of duty to the family and the traditional expectation of legitimate marriage at all costs. In many ways, the film follows the discourse of *Purab aur Paschim* since it valorizes the Indianness of diasporic characters through an emphasis on sexual purity. Virdi argues that "the figure of the diasporic Indian is metonymic of this anxiety of the invasion of the west and disappearance of an 'Indian Identity,' which it cleverly manipulates to reimagine the nation in response to changing conditions."[22]

A couple of years after the release of *Dilwale Dulhania le Jayenge*, *Pardes* took the nation-gender binary to a new level.[23] It tells the story of diasporic characters negotiating their Indian and American identities. The film acts as a contemporary parable of appropriate "Indianness." Kishorilal, an Indian expatriate who has lived in America for thirty-five years, returns to India and rediscovers that it is the best place in the world. He has always believed that India, above all, promotes love and generosity, as opposed to America, which he perceives to be based upon the concept of "give and take." He visits his long-time Indian friend, whose daughter Ganga, named after the Ganges River, and representing Mother India, is a synecdoche of Indian virtue and femininity. Ganga, as her mythological name suggests, is pure (virginal) and adheres to traditional Indian values. Her many appearances on screen are in white and red outfits, signifying her purity and virginity, mostly against a backdrop of green fields, signifying Indian abundance, both its values and its material wealth. Kishorilal approves of Ganga and wants his son Rajiv to marry her. Rajiv was born and raised in the United States. He is hesitant about marrying her, and thus Arjun, an Indian-born orphan raised by Kishorilal in America, is tasked with convincing him to do so. Arjun is the antithesis of Rajiv: that is, he values Indian culture and tradition while also being a singer in a band, therefore representing a transnational Indian diasporic identity. Arjun and Rajiv visit India to meet with Ganga. Rajiv likes Ganga and admires her for what she represents to him as a Western man: filial piety and devout Indian femininity. He agrees to the marriage. Ganga is sent to the United States with Rajiv for the wedding. Once there, she determines that the Indo-American Rajiv drinks, parties, and is promiscuous, representing Western immorality through her Indian gaze. In one scene, Rajiv, in a drunken stupor, attempts to rape Ganga. Arjun, the good Indo-American guy because he has maintained traditional Indian values, saves her and ultimately marries her. Ganga's virginity is symbolic of India's purity and Hindu past. Even when attacked, Ganga remains pure, and she finally ends up with the affluent, virginal, loving, and caring Arjun, his name invoking the Hindu warrior from the epic *Mahabharata*. Rajiv, in contrast, has been corrupted by Western influences and is therefore portrayed as villainous and undeserving of the virginal Indian woman. Arjun represents what can be preserved in diasporic communities in the right circumstances, a continuity that will ensure enduring love for India, across time and space, according to the ideal that an Indian, no matter where he is, loves India.[24]

THE LIBERATED WOMAN?

Female sexuality is a medium through which patriarchy exerts social and cultural control. The films discussed above represent female purity and male guardianship of that purity as the gender ideals for female and male Indianness. In fact, any behaviour counter to this is read as corrupt and an influence of the West. However, in the twenty-first century, Hindi cinema has witnessed a shift from its emphasis on female virginity to a more sexually liberated woman. Female protagonists in this period are represented as ambitious go-getters. They do not necessarily want to invest their lives in marriage. Both *Band Baaja Baaraat* and *Shuddh Desi Romance* provide novel portrayals of women who have their own work lives and are determined to live on their own terms.[25] The films resist previous representations by focusing on women who do not adhere to expectations of sexual purity and destabilize traditional patriarchal gender hierarchies.

Band Baaja Baaraat, a romantic comedy, is the story of Bittoo (Ranbir Kapoor) and Shruti (Anushka Sharma)—a young man and woman—who start a wedding-planning business together. All is good until one night they get drunk, which leads to a sexual encounter between them. The next morning Shruti is not too concerned, but Bittoo is worried that she, like other Indian girls, might read one-night sex as his love for her and ask him to marry her. This is where the twist comes in: Shruti says that there is no need to get worked up over a one-night stand. She tells Bittoo that she enjoyed their evening together and is unphased by the loss of her virginity. This upends the stereotypical representation of women and their expectations after having sex. Shruti is a woman who understands and accepts her sexual desire. She is not upset about this alcohol-inspired event. Rather, one could argue, alcohol simply becomes the medium through which the film excuses her premarital loss of virginity. However, as the film progresses, Shruti increasingly realizes that she loves Bittoo, but she does not demand anything from him. In fact, tensions between them result in dissolution of the business partnership. Bittoo realizes more slowly that he also loves Shruti; after a few twists and turns, the film ends with the two getting married. Thus, though the film does not take issue with premarital sex and loss of virginity for Shruti (Bittoo, the audience is told, is not a virgin), it does ensure that the loss of virginity is compensated for through marriage. The film shows Shruti as a young woman with confidence, out to conquer the world by being a successful, hardworking businesswoman, but to appeal to mainstream Indian audience expectations her relationship with Bittoo ultimately ends in marriage. In a culture where a woman is expected to remain a virgin until marriage, Shruti has broken the rules and done so willingly. However, this rejection of patriarchal expectations is later neutralized and recuperated through her marriage to the guy to whom she lost her virginity; her transgression is therefore erased.[26]

Shuddh Desi Romance, another romantic comedy, moves further from traditional expectations and takes marriage completely out of the relationship equation. The lead actor, Raghu (Sushant Singh Rajput), works for a wedding planner as a hired guest. When the film opens, he is about to get married to Tara (Vani Kapoor), but on the way to the wedding he meets another hired guest, Gayatri (Parineeti Chopra). After meeting her, Raghu has second thoughts about his marriage and runs away from the wedding. He then starts a romantic relationship with Gayatri, and they begin living together. Eventually, they decide to get married, but this time she is the one who has cold feet at the last moment and runs away from the wedding. Later Raghu has a brief affair with Tara, and just before he decides to propose to her Gayatri reappears, reminding him that she was the one whom he wanted to be with. The melodramatic comedy ends with Raghu and Gayatri deciding to live together out of wedlock. Neither is ready to make a long-term commitment. During the film, it is clear that Gayatri was in relationships before Raghu came into her life, because it is revealed that she had an abortion. Moving away from the stereotype of a god-fearing, husband-worshipping Indian woman, Gayatri smokes, has boyfriends, lives independently, and is not keen to be tied to a marriage. It is not the ultimate goal of this middle-class girl living her own urban life. Tara also does not shy away from non-marital sexual relationships. Thus, the women in this film are presented as non-stereotypical, sexually independent, and having agency over their own bodies and lives.

Although the characters in *Shuddh Desi Romance* opt to live together out of wedlock, they are aware that society doesn't necessarily consider it acceptable. Thus, when one of the neighbours asks Raghu about his identity, he says that he is Gayatri's brother. When Gayatri suggests that this answer is embarrassing, he asks her, "then what should I say? That I am your live-in boyfriend?" The dialogue clearly implies that, though they are in a consensual relationship, they cannot publicly declare it in a society that does not view premarital sex as acceptable. Nonetheless, these social taboos do not deter the characters from pursuing their dreams on their own terms. There is also none of the drama of the old films in which, when a girl's marriage alliance breaks, the girl and her family are stigmatized. In this film, Tara is not shown as heartbroken after her would-be groom leaves her a few minutes before the wedding; she understands his hesitation and moves on with her life. *Shuddh Desi Romance*, in many ways, has paved a path for bolder Bollywood cinema that can showcase gender relations in a newer light and move away from the older emphasis on female virginity.

CONCLUSION

As the above discussion demonstrates, the earlier rhetoric of chastity has been upheld in Hindi cinema throughout historical and cultural shifts in India. The films analyzed here reflect a larger trend in Bollywood that produces and reproduces women's roles in society. But as women in India become economically independent, self-reliant, and less interested in long-term commitments, especially arranged marriages, without being sure of the consequences, cinematic representations are shifting. Contrary to older Hindi cinema, in which a modern, liberated woman is usually punished for her perceived "antisocial" behaviour, either through death or through social rejection and shame, women in contemporary films are not always reprimanded for their sexual transgressions. Nonetheless, even these liberated female characters function within a restrictive social system. Although expectations are slowly and steadily changing, there is still not open acceptance of women's desires for autonomy and selfhood outside the dominant normative behaviours. Thus, the protagonists in these films, while living lives that resist traditional restrictions, cannot publicly declare their non-marital relationships in order to continue to be accepted and lead functional lives within existing social constraints. As Indian society and women continue to push the definitions of acceptable gender norms and behaviours, Indian cinema provides both a site for increasing experimentation and a cultural archive of the incremental shifts taking place.

NOTES

1   I use the terms "virginity" and "chastity" interchangeably; however, in a specific context, virginity refers to sexual inexperience, whereas chastity can denote a married woman expected to be a faithful, dedicated wife and a doting mother.

2   India has the world's largest film industry, releasing approximately 1,200 films a year in a plethora of Indian languages. Hindi-language films, commonly referred to as Bollywood films, have the largest market share. These films target audiences in both India and throughout the global Indian diaspora. Hindi films are usually divided into popular cinema and parallel or art cinema. This chapter focuses only on popular cinema.

3   Hanne Blank, *Virgin: The Untouched History* (New York: Bloomsbury, 2007), 90.

4   Jyotika Virdi, *The Cinematic ImagiNation: Indian Popular Film as Social History* (New Brunswick, NJ: Rutgers University Press, 2003), 63.

5   I focus on virginity in the context of heterosexual relationships; there is very little to no discussion in India on the subject of same-sex relationships, and the loss of virginity through such relationships is a non-issue, though this dynamic is quickly changing.

6   Tamar Jeffers McDonald, "Introduction" in *Virgin Territory: Representing Sexual Inexperience in Film*, ed. Tamar Jeffers McDonald (Detroit: Wayne State University Press, 2010), 3.

7   Ibid., 1.

8   Ibid.

9   Blank, *The Untouched History*, 97.

10   Although not a focus of this chapter, the woman is held responsible even when she loses her virginity as a result of rape. The films usually show such a woman living a life of misery, further abused by society, or committing suicide. Occasionally, she is married to the rapist; at times, such an act is justified by showing the assaulted woman as being secretly in love with the rapist. The 1954 film *Amar* is an example.

11   Premarital sex is usually not presented as an issue for a man. In fact, many recent surveys show that the vast majority of men in India have their first sexual experiences with prostitutes.

12   *Aradhana*, dir. Shakti Samanta, 1969. Translation: Your irresistible beauty, my crazy love; may we not make any mistake!

13   Virdi, *The Cinematic ImagiNation*, 148–49.

14   McDonald, *Virgin Territory*, 3.

15   Ibid., 7.

16   Red powder applied to a woman's forehead as well as in the hair part is a sign of her Hindu marital status.

17   Anirudh Deshpande, "Indian Cinema and the Bourgeois Nation State," *Economic and Political Weekly* 42, 50 (2007): 96.

18   Asma Sayed, "Bollywood in Diaspora: Cherishing Occidentalist Nostalgia," in *Diasporic Choices*, ed. Renata Seredyńska-Abou Eid (Oxford: Inter-Disciplinary Press, 2013), 15.

19   Ibid., 16.

20   Neepa Majumdar, *Wanted Cultured Ladies Only! Female Stardom and Cinema in India 1930s–1950s* (Urbana: University of Illinois Press, 2009), 169.

21   *Dilwale Dulhania le Jayenge*, dir. Aditya Chopra, 1995.

22   Virdi, *The Cinematic ImagiNation*, 197.

23   *Pardes*, dir. Subhash Ghai, 1997.

24   Sayed, "Bollywood in Diaspora," 16.

25   *Band Baaja Baaraat*, dir. Maneesh Sharma, 2013; *Shuddh Desi Romance*, dir. Maneesh Sharma, 2013.

26   In continuation of the so-called liberal female portrayal, Bollywood films showcase many bar or club dances, which have now typically come to be known as "item songs." They are inserted into the film simply to titillate the audience as a scantily clad dancer sings and dances to the tunes of double-meaning songs among a group of drunken men. Although these songs have become immensely popular among audiences, they also further

trivialize the female role. The dancer becomes an object of the male gaze, and many scholars argue that they are having an undesirable influence on youth in Indian society.

REFERENCES

Aradhana. Directed by Shakti Samanta, 1969.

Band Baaja Baaraat. Directed by Maneesh Sharma, 2013.

Blank, Hanne. *Virgin: The Untouched History*. New York: Bloomsbury, 2007.

Deshpande, Anirudh. "Indian Cinema and the Bourgeois Nation State." *Economic and Political Weekly* 42, 50 (2007): 95–101, 103.

Dilwale Dulhania le Jayenge. Directed by Aditya Chopra, 1995.

Majumdar, Neepa. *Wanted Cultured Ladies Only! Female Stardom and Cinema in India, 1930s–1950s*. Urbana: University of Illinois Press, 2009.

McDonald, Tamar Jeffers. "Introduction." In *Virgin Territory: Representing Sexual Inexperience in Film*, edited by Tamar Jeffers McDonald, 1–14. Detroit: Wayne State University Press, 2010.

Pardes. Directed by Subhash Ghai, 1997.

Purab aur Paschim. Directed by Manoj Kumar, 1970.

Sayed, Asma. "Bollywood in Diaspora: Cherishing Occidentalist Nostalgia." In *Diasporic Choices*, edited by Renata Seredyńska-Abou Eid, 11–20. Oxford: Inter-Disciplinary Press, 2013.

Shuddh Desi Romance. Directed by Maneesh Sharma, 2013.

Virdi, Jyotika. *The Cinematic ImagiNation: Indian Popular Films as Social History*. New Brunswick, NJ: Rutgers University Press, 2003.

CHAPTER 8

THE POLICING OF *VIRAGOS* AND OTHER "FUCKABLE" BODIES: VIRGINITY AS PERFORMANCE IN LATIN AMERICA

Tracy Crowe Morey and Adriana Spahr

> Substituting one orifice for the other, as Margo Glantz would say, the mouth was and continues to be the most threatening opening of the feminine body: it can eventually express what shouldn't be expressed, reveal the hidden desire, unleash the menacing differences which upset the core of the phallogocentric, paternalistic discourse.[1]

> To be rapable, a position that is social not biological, defines what a woman is.[2]

In *Versions of Virginity in Late Medieval England*, Sarah Salih discusses the notion of female virginity as performance rather than physical condition: "One is not born, but rather one becomes, a virgin."[3] She argues thereafter, alongside Anke Bernau and Ruth Evans, that "virginity has no ontological security."[4] This becomes evident not only by the enigmatic nature of the hymen and the widely used testing measures of such a physical condition but also by the number of early modern and modern cases of reconstructed virginity that might or might not rely on the physical "intactness" of the vagina.[5] Even in early modern cases of male virginity, scholars who have begun to investigate the question of the male virgin in recent years have pointed to the notion that male virginity is performative but "can be made intelligible only by reference to an elaborate feminized and feminizing signifying system."[6] It is our position that, rather than consider virginity as possibly a third gender separate from the dominant social constructions of either masculinity or femininity,[7] virginity must be read within these social formations in order to unpack the gender politics and gender oppressions of the historical periods examined in this chapter. As such, in beginning with the epistemological (or performed) rather than the ontological (or essentialized) question of virginity, we ask to what degree are gender performances as behaviour or conduct permitted before social regulation and control are instituted? In other words, when does virginity become perceived and necessitated as an "ontological security"? Particularly in reference to female virginity, when does the intact vagina really matter?

We focus on Latin America in this chapter to consider a range of ideological discourses and controls surrounding "female" sexuality and performance as they relate to particular cases of "unruly" or politically active Latin American women historically defined as *viragos*[8]. These women create a space centred not on virginity or the lack of it but on the capacity to perform as a "male"[9] in the public sphere. As we will demonstrate, not all cases of female masculinity are subjugated and/or "rehabilitated" in virginal roles as defined by the heteronormative confines of their society. The differing historical contexts will provide a forum in which to compare how far the feminization of the "dominant" masculine sphere—and hence masculine performance—is tolerated before the question of ontological security is enforced. Our analysis includes Catalina de Erauso (1592–1650), *soldaderas* or female soldiers of the Mexican Revolution (1910–17), and guerrilla women from Argentina and military women from Chile during the military dictatorships of the 1970s and 1980s.

THE EARLY MODERN *VIRAGO*

The historical case of Catalina de Erauso, the famous lieutenant nun of colonial Latin America, is an early modern illustration of the *virago*. Although modern use of the term is rather limited— "unruly" or "masculinized" are used instead—these terms and their meanings are part of the oft-conflated politics of female sexuality.[10] The original definition of *virago* "takes its root from the Latin *vir*, meaning man. Therefore, the virago was specifically construed as a 'woman' who had assumed 'male' traits and transgressed popularly accepted gender roles."[11] The term has encapsulated the notion of women acting as "honorary male[s], aspiring to the unisex ideal,"[12] or the notion of women as unnatural, dangerous, and monstrous, as with the case of the fictional female warriors or Amazons.[13] These monstrous *viragos* were known for their political defiance of male rule as well as for the physical mutilations of their "female" body parts.[14] *Viragos* provoked anxiety for their supposed "freedom" outside the sphere of patriarchal control: that is, outside the economic and social domain as man's property.[15] Constituted as a "free vagina"[16] or a "liberated vagina,"[17] *virago* was used in the eighteenth century to label "public women" as female deviants. The term was also used to address how typically middle-class, white, and heterosexual women had erroneously stepped outside the private sphere of patriarchy, forgetting the "bourgeois" virtues of their sex.[18] Either the *virago* is described in a way that suggests a perversion of the "naturalized" female sex[19] or the *virago* (represented as an aggressive and grotesque anti-woman—"big, coarse, ugly, and often stronger than a man"[20]) reflects a perversion of the male sex—in other words, an "ideal" (read as dominant) form of masculinity gone wrong.

Within the Christian tradition, descriptions of the *virago* inevitably evoked its archetypal figure, the *virgo*, whose most exemplary representative was the Virgin Mary. The antithesis of the *virgo* was Eve, "the original 'virago,' as she is named in the second Vulgate creation account,"[21] because of her birth from man. For early Christian theologians, such a notion gave rise to contrary interpretations regarding the status of woman's place before man. In *One Flesh: Paradisal Marriage and Sexual Relations in the Age of Milton,*

James Gratham Turner demonstrates how Eve is inferior, equal, or superior to Adam.[22] Within the theological debates, Saint Jerome (347–420) offers an intermediary interpretation. Influential in the Western tradition with respect to virginity, sexuality, and marriage, he states that, "as long as woman serves for birth and children, she has difference from man, as body from soul but, if she wishes to serve Christ more than the world, then she will cease to be woman (*mulier*) and will be called man (*vir*)."[23]

In the early Christian church, virgins were admired for their condition of vir*ago*: that is, acting as a man or non-woman.[24] Yet it is important to recognize that, in many instances, these *viragos* were protected within the private sphere of the monastery and did not precipitate "a masculine identity crisis"—*Herrenfrage*, as dubbed by Jo Ann McNamara[25]—as long as religious masculinity continued to show signs of virtue and virility. For example, celibate clerics and friars could be called on as soldiers of Christ, as in the case of early modern Mexico,[26] or, during the Gregorian reforms of the eleventh century, clergy could compete with lay men over degrees of masculinity.[27] Moreover, virginity testing for religious men proved to be ontologically indeterminable (referring back to Kelly's facetious question of "do men have a hymen?") and could only be read on the body through various performance tests such as reported acts of virile military prowess or spiritual chastity, among others.[28]

The case of Catalina de Erauso in colonial Latin America proved to be an exception rather than the norm for *viragos* at that time. Contrasted with another well-known early modern *virago*—Joan of Arc (1412–31) in medieval Europe—Catalina stands as a curious "wonder" of the New World. Both women participated in military activities, dressed as men, were "legally" proven virgins, and were ultimately judged for their social transgressions of behaving and performing like men. Yet their legal verdicts were very different: Joan was burned at the stake by the Inquisition, whereas Catalina was allowed to live out her days dressed as a man. Their fates depended on their differing political and economic circumstances but more importantly on the degree to which their performances disrupted the "essentialized" and binary gender norms of the patriarchal structures of their time. As we will argue, Catalina's success as a *virago* stemmed, in large part, from her validation of Iberian "manliness" while adhering to ideal social norms established by her "condition" of virginity. Joan, in contrast, became the epitome of the "unruly female" whose virginal and "transgendered" body ultimately threatened the sexual and class politics of her time.[29]

Joan the Maid (*La Pucelle*) meets all the requirements of a *virago* or the third position as defined by Saint Jerome—a woman acting as a man in the public sphere is no longer valued economically for her vagina but religiously for her dedication to serving God. Joan of Arc always claimed that all of her actions were ordered by God. With some differences, like Catalina de Erauso, Joan penetrated the exclusivity of a male-dominated political and military arena, reaching an unprecedented position (for a woman at least). However, we contend that it was her virginity as a sign of warrior (in)vulnerability or (im)penetrability that was "tested," and subsequently failed, thus validating the political and class interests of the day.

Joan of Arc was betrayed by her own people, the church, and captured by her allies, the Burgundians, and by Charles VII, who might have freed her had he offered to pay a ransom, a common procedure at the time. Although he did not "bid" for her release, the king of England offered payment to the Burgundians, who refused his offer. The king then persuaded the bishop of Beauvais to accuse Joan of heresy. The captors, pressured by the threat of embargo, turned her over to the Inquisition after receiving a decent sum of money for her exchange.[30] Even though Joan obtained her political power in the most unorthodox of ways, her cross-dressing was the determining factor for punishment in her criminal proceedings. However, it was the idolized status of her virginity in the public sphere that threatened the religious rule of the church.[31] The secularization of her virginity and her military honours ultimately proved to be unequivocal signs of chaos and weakness to those who ruled—and the new king of France was no exception.[32] As a *virago*, Joan was a problem for everyone: she was not a "controllable" woman[33] who sought to comply with the traditional social and secular norms required of her sex; nor did she obey or recognize any sacred authority over her, except for that of God.

At the time of her last trial, the virginity of Joan of Arc had been corroborated at the request of the king by the church, theologians, and scholars. However, by maintaining her independence from any masculine tutelage (father, husband, church) while remaining a virgin, Joan became the quintessential icon of a commodified "free sexual agent." She was held in a civilian prison, guarded by English soldiers in the same cell. According to some versions, she was placed in chains in an iron cage so small that she could not stand upright, whereas others maintain that, in a cage, Joan was upright but chained by her neck, hands, and ankles.[34] The punishment of repeated rape, closely related to denigration and power still current, has been suggested in her case. It has been argued that her rape might have something to do with the popular renderings disseminated at that time of her "invincibility." That is, given her political power, Joan was equally marked by a sexual power, as Dworkin argues:

> There was an aura of magic created by the gossip and legend around the persona of Joan herself, a deviant virgin in that she was a soldier and a deviant soldier in that she was a woman. Virgin and soldier: she was dangerous in both regards. A man who wanted to fuck her might be killed: whether by magic or by combat.[35]

With the suggestion of consecutive rapes committed by the soldiers, Joan went from active subject/independent to passive object/whore. As A. Nicholas Groth and H. Jean Birnbaum argue, whores become "legitimate targets for abuse and mistreatment. They are to be punished for their sexuality, and sex becomes the punishment."[36] Because the woman is violated in each rape, the rapist can continue the violation, for the abused woman is now denigrated as a whore. Thus, rape, as a form of patriarchal policing or discipline, authorizes the disappearance of the *virago* from the public sphere.

If rape was a common treatment of political prisoners, then in Joan of Arc's case, we argue, it was also necessary for her conviction before the Inquisition. That is, because Joan was a virgin, she was not a witch, since the belief at the time was that the devil could not make a pact with a virgin. Therefore, loss of her virginal status would make her a witch, thus validating her sentence to be burned at the stake. In the end, Joan was given the choice of reducing her sentence from death to life imprisonment. But she would have to agree to dress as a woman. She ultimately refused.[37] Feminine clothing represented female subjugation and submission; masculine attire represented equality with men. Such a refusal only served to confirm her heresy once again, and the sentence of death was carried out in Rouen in 1431.

Unlike Joan of Arc, the entrance of the lieutenant nun Catalina de Erauso into the public sphere confirmed rather than defied the patriarchal constructs of the period. Catalina performed the ideal traits for both women and men: virginity for women (read as an intact vagina) and aggression and sexual assertiveness for men, traits highly regarded in medieval Christian (rather than Muslim) Iberia.[38] Recounted in first-person memoirs, *Vida i sucesos de la Monja Alférez* (c. 1625), Catalina's exploits of cross-dressing and military and sexual bravado garnered unprecedented notoriety during Spain's colonization of the New World and thereafter. Dressed as a man and using a man's name, Catalina worked as a page in Spain and then set sail for Spanish America, where she remained for twenty years (1603–23). During that time, she carried out different jobs: in Lima, Catalina joined the *entradas* as a mercenary soldier to fight against the Mapuches (Indians from Chile). As a *virago*, she explored all of the advantages belonging to the male sex. Through the memoirs, we learn that she duelled over women and gambling. She toyed with a proposal of marriage to a woman, killed various men, among them her brother, and served for three years in the struggle against "fierce indigenous tribes."[39] Catalina was wounded in a battle against the Mapuches and received the rank of lieutenant on account of her bravery when reclaiming the Spanish flag. After being accused of murder, she fled to Potosí and then La Paz, where she was finally arrested by a magistrate of the Peruvian viceroyalty and condemned to death. She escaped and fled to Cuzco but was pursued by magistrates for the government, who continued to call for her capture and execution. Catalina finally confessed to being a woman before the bishop of Guamanga, Fray Augustín de Carvajal, in 1622. She revealed her life story and how she came to the Americas after escaping from a Dominican convent when she was about to take her religious vows. Fray Augustín de Carvajal persuaded her to return to the convent and to write her memoirs. These stories reached among others the church and the nobility in Europe, where she went from being anonymous to being a hero.[40]

Catalina was transferred to a convent in Lima under the supervision of the archbishop, and she remained there for seven years. In her narrative, she performs as a submissive, obedient woman, willing to obey the church. This attitude, combined with the need of the viceroys of Peru and Chile to promote female saints in the colony as symbols of a mystical conquest,[41] the social class of the Erauso family, and the need for the Spanish colony and the church to promote local heroes contributed to the success of her case, which in turn allowed her transgressions to go without punishments. As a member of the nobility, Catalina had the resources to solve and/or manipulate any problems that might arise, as she did, since she had access to the heads of the political and Catholic institutions in power (bishop, viceroy, king, and pope). The absence of punishment for her transgressions has been a point of interest in a number of scholarly works dedicated to transgenderism in the early modern period.[42] Kathleen Ann Myers argues that the reason might be how "Catalina (and others) could 're-present' her life in legal petitions"[43] to "conform" to societal norms of gender during this period. Catalina combined contacts from her well-to-do family with a deep knowledge of institutions, the church in particular.[44] The sudden change from outlaw transvestite to nun under the protection of the church allowed her to negotiate her sexuality as performance through the writing of memoirs,[45] which as a consequence allowed her to attract an official audience. In these memoirs, Catalina highlights both her obedience and her exemplarity to church and king—loyalties highlighted in the self-appointed title lieutenant nun. In her petitions, she emphasizes courage on the battlefield in fifteen years of service of "Your Majesty in the wars of the Kingdom of Chile."[46]

The notoriety of her virginity[47] enabled Catalina de Erauso to slip between the secular and ecclesiastical frameworks regulating sexual conduct and identity.[48] Moreover, proof of an intact hymen guaranteed a position of superiority and virtuous integrity, and

Catalina knew how to inscribe these values onto the "political" body. Even gender and clothing did not become an issue for her. Pope Urban VIII authorized her to dress as a man, and she lived the rest of her life as such.[49] Because of her twofold status as *virago* and nun, together with her adherence to (rather than perversion of) the patriarchal models of male behaviour, Catalina presented minimal disruption to the status quo. Indeed, in her memoirs, she goes so far as to underscore her interest in and relations with women. Scholars have questioned why she would be so open to sharing her lesbian encounters when she knew that her life depended on what she wrote. Yet, as Myers, Velasco, and other critics have argued, the concept of lesbianism is relevant in our modern times. Within the cultural imaginary of the early modern period, sexual relations between women were not taken seriously since they were "less sinful than extramarital heterosexual relations" and viewed as "an innocent way to satisfy sexual needs" of widows and virgins, especially if lesbianism was "nothing more than women trying to 'imitate men.'"[50] In the case of Catalina, these relationships with other women did not present a threat to patriarchal society; in fact, as many scholars have noted, part of her legal success was "dependent on her masculinist/macho rhetoric and her recapitulation of patriarchal society."[51] That is, unlike Joan of Arc, her virginal performance advertised impenetrability of the Spanish "body" in the Americas. In the end, Catalina's negotiation of her status as a virgin allowed for slippage and fluidity among gender, genre, and political/social identities; her storied memoirs of her life as a *virago* ultimately made for an exceptional, unique, but non-threatening case of female masculinity.

"UNRULY" WOMEN OF TWENTIETH-CENTURY LATIN AMERICA

There are a number of comparisons to be made between the performative nature of the early modern *virago* and twentieth-century Latin American women deemed "unruly" given their entrance into the public sphere. In the context of modern Latin America, scholars, writers, and activists have paid close attention to the naturalizing and legitimizing discourse of gender regulation shared across a range of social classes and ethnicities. The paradigm of sexual femininity most well known in Latin America is heavily influenced by Marian devotion (*marianismo*) as rooted in western European Christian traditions. Such an opposition has created cultural images that have either glorified women as virgins, martyrs, or self-sacrificing mothers (*mater dolorosa*) or demonized them as whores, witches, or deviant mothers.[52]

Outside Latin America, scholars of virginity have examined the Virgin Mary and her polar opposite as examples of the theorization and legislation of female sexuality within canon and secular law.[53] Although Marian devotion, most popular during the medieval period, idealized Mary's status as virgin and mother,[54] as mother Mary could not be sexually determined without a counterpart.[55] Therefore, as Marina Warner contends, "another figure consequently developed to fill this important lacuna, that of St. Mary Magdalene, who together with the Virgin . . . typifies Christian society's attitudes to women and to sex. Both female figures are perceived in sexual terms: Mary as a virgin and Mary Magdalene as a whore—until her repentance."[56] Moreover, since, as Bernau notes, "virginity and marriage—representative of the 'spiritual' and the 'worldly' respectively—were defined in relation to one another," the legislated and regulated ideals of secular feminine conduct underlined virtues reminiscent of the virgin-mother: that is, asexuality and chastity.[57] As Jocelyn Wogan-Browne argues, "the great penitent Mary Magdalene is as important a mediator of virgin status for wives and mothers—women who have become biologically reproductive—as she is of fallen women in the sense of prostitutes."[58] For this reason, standard tropes of virginity, past and present, allow for discussions such as the "virginity of cronehood"[59] or "chaste matrons."[60]

The cultural female scripts offered through the dichotomy of the two Marys also served a fitting-in-between assignment of secular women within the patriarchal order: namely, the triad of virgin, wife/mother, and whore.[61] In colonial Spanish America, the ideal of femininity rested not so much on the question of virginity as on the role of motherhood, as Ann Twinam notes: "Sexual intimacy did not damage a woman's honor if there were promise of an eventual ceremony. . . . If a couple were social equals and exchanged the promise of matrimony, an elite woman might lose her virginity and engage in a sexual relationship without immediate loss of her honor."[62] That is, virginity in this context rested not on the first sexual intercourse of a virginal bride but on the virtue of her conduct and promise to enter the heteronormative "private" domain as a wife/mother.

Throughout the twentieth century in many Latin American countries, this in-between state also allowed for unmarried women to enter the public sphere long enough for them to procure a marriage partner, and given that they would return to the home once they were married.[63] If women entered the public arena, then there were strict controls and regulations in place. In Chile, for example, during the authoritarian dictatorship (1973–90) of Augusto Pinochet (1915–2006), women could choose service in the army, where surveillance and education were heavily regulated by a patriarchal stand-in for female guardianship. Many of the oral histories and testimonies from women who participated in the state military have been collected and recently published by Cherie Zalaquett in *Chilenas en armas: Testimonios e historia de mujeres militares y guerrilleras subversivas* (Chileans in Arms: Testimonies and History of Military Women and Guerrilla Subversives).[64] In a number of oral interviews, many of the militarized women disclosed the fears of their families when they chose to participate in a "masculinized space." There was also clear disdain for what was understood as "female masculinity" given the perceived risk of losing one's "femininity" while taking part in a decidedly "masculine" space: "When she communicated her decision to join the military, her mother expressed fear: 'This frightens me a little because you're going to become a man.'"[65] Other women discussed the strict gender controls and regulations for women in the military. Those given parental permission to enter the academy had to abide by military regulations that kept them in a state of perpetual girlhood, as Zalaquett reveals:

> They demanded that they take with them stuffed animals, bears, Mickey Mouse toys, or dolls to be put in their rooms as symbols of the continuity of childhood and the home.

They had to put up a picture of their parents, the size of a postcard, on the inside of their closets and situate them at a certain height that would allow them to see it upon opening the locker. Parts of their body, like the length of their hair, their nails, were subject to inspection and guidance from the instructors, who also verified that they were only wearing white underwear, as it is stipulated even today in the rules and regulations.[66]

By keeping female participants childlike, the state was able to control and fashion a passive model of womanhood.[67] Another participant explained that the ideologies of the Women's Military School enforced the feminization of new recruits through clothing and makeup: "Women were considered infant-like subjects who needed to be taken care of, protected, and confined to the private sphere of the home."[68] In many ways, the military replaced the role of the patriarch in the home to educate girls and regulate their behaviour/performance. Many of these women were given administrative duties only: "The army maintained a rigid separation of roles according to traditional stereotypes. Men held positions of power, control, and military combat assignments, while women carried out administrative duties, support roles, reproducing the division of work of the patriarchal home."[69] One of the many desired goals was for women to leave the academy for reputable reasons such as marriage and then motherhood: "The internal regulations of the army counselled to their personnel a 'moral duty' of contracting marriage and having a traditional nuclear family."[70] In this way, the highly dichotomized and gendered performances of masculinity and femininity "officially" remained intact in the public sphere, thereby nullifying any potential threat or contamination of one domain to the other.[71]

Contrasted to the "virginal" ideals perpetuated for "conservative" Chilean women in the state military during the 1970s and 1980s, prescriptions of femininity found in predominantly lower-class and Indigenous revolutionary women in the first part of twentieth-century Mexico underscored female "passivity" through hyper-sexualization. Official and popular renditions recast the Mexican female soldier (*soldadera*[72]) through the virgin/whore paradigm as an *adelita*—an invented character for the real *soldadera* famous in the *corridos*, not to mention Hollywood stories and films.[73] During the revolutionary years, such descriptions and illustrations of these militant women went back and forth between submissive victim to sexualized vixen. The most common image of the *adelita*—including present-day films such as *Desperado* and *Bandidas*—is the promiscuous fighter, dressed provocatively (or scantily) but always with a bandolier and gun.[74] However, why these women became *soldaderas* demonstrates the actual heterogeneity of this group.[75] For example, many of these women held different military positions, including some distinguished and high-level positions of command,[76] yet their representation and official history for the most part have emphasized only the socially accepted—that is, domestic—roles, including "procuring food, curing injuries and satisfying all other needs of the male soldiers."[77]

This newly accepted role in the public sphere potentially provided the *soldadera* with some independence and agency. However, similar to the military activities of their *virago* counterparts, these women were denied political agency through a reconfiguration of their sexuality. Such representations cast the real-life female soldiers as *adelitas* and therefore "objects of desire, rather than equals on the battlefield."[78] In this way, popular and official histories "downplayed the accomplishments of *soldaderas* on the battlefield and instead emphasized their beauty and loyalty to the men in their lives. By rendering female soldiers in a romanticized manner, men effectively neutralized the threat these women posed to their masculinity."[79] In such a state, the now "docile" female militant can no longer provoke fears of emasculation, feminization or metaphoric castration, as illustrated by her earlier *virago* counterpart.

The romanticized rendition of female soldiers illustrates the psychological developments still current regarding gender-based categories that insist on keeping the boundaries between the sexes "unambiguous and impermeable."[80] The imagined threat that *viragos* posed to the sexual identity of men goes back to the archaic notion of the *vagina dentata*[81] or the phallic castrating woman made influential by Freud in the twentieth century.[82] This partially explains why violence has been historically and continuously targeted at the vagina. As we will demonstrate in the case of the *guerrillera* in Argentina, the sexual torture of systematic rape and humiliation of prisoners[83] implemented by the military regime in the second half of the twentieth century was achieved in part as a form of "macho ritual,"[84] which can be understood as one method of legitimization of the military's hegemonic masculinity in the public space. This ritual included the rape of male prisoners—a topic of which survivors have found difficult to speak.[85] For male prisoners immersed in the macho culture, rape represents a double torture: the psychological loss of their sexual identity and masculinity because they have been penetrated in the same way as a woman and the physical torture of having been placed in a sexually dominated position negatively associated within the *machista* culture with the homosexual male. If the rape of a woman shows the sadistic tendency of male perpetrators, then the rape of men by men emphasizes the homosexual inclinations of perpetrators within the sexual politics of humiliation propagated against men.[86] As we argue here, this legitimization occurred through the state-sponsored "fuckability" of the female and "leftist" male militant body, exposed in many female testimonies and silenced in those of their male companions.[87]

Twentieth-century Latin America had an abhorrent history of state-sponsored violence against politically active leftist women and men. After a military coup overthrew the democratic government of President Isabel Perón (1974–76) in Argentina, the armed forces launched a great campaign of repression, not only against leftist groups, but also against their affiliates and relatives, who came to be identified as "the disappeared."[88] This period came to be known as the "dirty war," a term used by the armed forces to justify their policy of extermination of segments of the Argentinean population. Human rights organizations in Argentina refuse to use the term since it does not reflect the reality of what happened in the country.

As noted by many who have examined the evidence from this period, "sexual torture was an integral part of the repressive regimes of the mid 1970s through early 1980s in Argentina; both men and women received electroshock to the genitals; women were raped and verbally humiliated,"[89] with some female prisoners raped "in front of the image of the Virgin Mary."[90] In *Political Violence and Trauma in Argentina*, Antonius Robben offers a brief summary of the sexual torture and traumatization of both male and female militants: "Sexual torture consisted generally of either forcing captives into humiliating sexual relations or genital torture making the captives associate pain, panic, and sexuality. In Argentina, men and women were also frequently raped and sodomized, and forced to perform fellatio on their torturers. Objects would be thrust into the vagina and anus, and at times charged with electric current."[91] For female prisoners, their sexual torture was part of the transformation that would ultimately see them eliminated from the public sphere and reinstated in the "traditional" private domain.[92] For male prisoners, their torturers performed a ritualistic emasculation, "*turning the feared enemy into passive, castrated beings* . . . [and creating] a society of ruling *machos* and obedient, harmless *mansos* [tamed], castrated beings, that would not question orders but would just obey."[93] State-sanctioned sexual violence on the body of the criminalized other signified an invulnerability and ultimately "demonstrated the regime's omnipotence."[94]

Latin America has always been a place of constant struggle, especially throughout the twentieth century, when the middle classes of the population entered the political arena to dispute the oligarchies. From that moment on, democratic governments have alternated with military coups, representative of the interests of the oligarchies. In these occurrences, as we saw in the case of the *soldaderas*, women were present alongside men or occupied places reserved for them. Their participation became more noticeable in the guerrilla movements of the 1960s–80s. These movements, of a Marxist and nationalist nature, were inspired by, among other things, the French May (the uprisings of May 1968), the triumph of the Cuban Revolution (1959), and the independence of African countries (e.g., Algeria in 1962 and Angola in 1975), which had a great impact in the world[95] and Latin America.[96] In all of these cases, the active participation of women in the political arena, as members of either social organizations or guerrilla movements, automatically entailed the accusation of whore, so that, according to the severity of her transgression, a woman would be denigrated to the point of dehumanization through torture and rape, as we saw in the case of Joan of Arc. Let us compare her to the Argentinian female guerrilla. The comparison demonstrates our erroneous perception of moral advancement when we compare ourselves to those in biblical times, since the most inhumane methods are still being used to punish women who dare to challenge the patriarchal system.[97]

Argentinian women made up one-third of citizens targeted by the military junta. The Argentinian female guerrillas belonged to various left-wing organizations during the 1970s, the principal ones being the Marxist-Leninist ERP (Ejército Revolucionario de Pueblo/ People's Revolutionary Party) and Montoneros, which basically represented the left of the Peronist Movement and the Marxist-Leninist FAR (Fuerzas Armadas Revolucionarias/Revolutionary Armed Forces).[98] It is important to note that there was no difference between the guerrillas and the members of various political and social organizations or student and union organizations throughout the country. Guerrilla groups were part of a social movement, and many members of the movement were integrated with different degrees of participation into the structures of these organizations. Unlike in other parts of Latin America and the world, in Argentina there was no war, at least no direct confrontation of the establishment, as in Nicaragua, El Salvador, Algeria, and Vietnam, to name a few. The guerrilla movements in Argentina were urban, and their main work was focused on social and political issues and not military questions.[99] Their social structures were mostly represented by small factions of the wealthy petite bourgeoisie and urban workers with superior qualifications and higher levels of education.[100] The average age of those in the guerrilla movement at the time of their disappearance was under thirty, and a third of them were women.[101]

These organizations, like all the revolutionary organizations of the time, expressed the need for change to create a world free from social and political inequalities and injustices. Women were essential to these movements and as such were prepared to give their lives to bring about a better world for all. All of them challenged the power of the patriarchal system from the political-military standpoint, an area designated exclusively for certain classed Argentinian men. In the case of Argentina, women participated in these movements from the start, as with the example of Esther Norma Arrostito (1940–78). She began her political affiliation at the age of twenty-four. In 1970, she was one of the founders of the guerrilla organization Montoneros, which would raise as its emblem the figure of Evita (Eva Perón), recognized as the indefatigable champion of the rights of the poor.[102] On December 2, 1976, official sources reported the death of Arrostito in a clash with a military patrol. However, she had been arrested and imprisoned illegally at the Navy School of Mechanical Engineering (Escuela Mecánica de la Armada or ESMA).[103] On January 15, 1978, she was put to death by a lethal injection of pentothal.[104] ESMA differed from other clandestine detention centres (centro clandestino de detención or CCD) in its use of prisoners in maintenance work and sociological and political research[105] that would help Lieutenant Commander Jorge Eduardo Acosta (1941–),[106] and especially Admiral Emilio Massera (1925–2010), commander-in-chief of the army, in their political ambitions.[107]

ESMA was defined as "hell" by its survivors.[108] The term is not arbitrary, just as it is not arbitrary to compare it to Auschwitz. Viktor E. Frankl (1905–97), a Holocaust survivor, like the survivors of ESMA, expressed his experiences: "The abnormal becomes normal within a context of arbitrariness and madness where everything was uncertain . . . [except] the guarantee of dying (death)."[109] Life in both places depended on the wish (whim) of those whom they were supposed to obey,[110] and "all [the] energy was channelled into basic survival":[111] that is, to "stay alive."[112] So, regarding what happened in other places in Argentina, no survivor can state exactly why she or he survived; survivors of Auschwitz too could only say "by the aid of many lucky chances or miracles."[113] In both places, being useful to their captors could prolong their lives.[114]

ESMA implemented a program of "reintegration," which implied the possibility of repentance and thus reintegration into the values of an elite patriarchal society.[115] As we observed in the cases of Joan of Arc and Catalina de Erauso, some of the *guerrilleras* in ESMA agreed to be part of the program to save their lives,[116] whereas others did not. The leader of Montoneros, Norma Arrostito, and Joan of Arc did not accept reintegration and thus paid with their lives. If for Joan it was the belief that her actions served God alone, for

Arrostito it was a revolutionary plan that did not place the interests of individuals before those of her political group or comrades. Gabi, as she was commonly known, was brutally tortured, presumably raped, and ill treated by her torturers: "Torture and humiliation were the initiation ritual for the prisoners."[117] Like Joan, Arrostito was held in chains and shackled while in ESMA.[118] However, in the hands of her torturers, she showed the courage of her convictions to the highest revolutionary ideal; she chose death, toward which she turned on more than one occasion rather than collaborate with an enemy whom she considered culpable of acts of injustice against her people.[119]

Ramus, one of the prisoners at ESMA, said in her testimony that Arrostito during her captivity in ESMA was exhibited as a "trophy of war" by her captors, not only before the members of her organization in ESMA, but also to members of the armed forces.[120] As a trophy, Arrostito represented to Massera, the leader of the army, a fuckable body—a prerogative often employed by the enemy during periods of war. As such, she became an object by which he showed his superiority, not only to the devastated enemy, the guerrillas,[121] but also to his political opponents, among whom were the other two armed divisions that comprised the military forces of the country. In fact, these were prebiblical tactics used when women were employed to resolve questions of power among men in order to demoralize or take revenge on an opponent. Furthermore, it shows, yet again, that the act of fucking is a political and social act.[122] In the case of the Argentinian guerrillas, supremacy of the military was shown in the notion of "teaching": that is, disciplining and eradicating a female masculinity from the public sphere through the "rehabilitation or reintegration" of virginity as performance projected onto the female body.[123]

In ESMA, aberration and perversity lived together. The apparent normal functioning of the establishment allowed for operation of the CCDs,[124] where women were killed immediately after giving birth to their children, who then became the property of their captors. Torture was carried out while other prisoners were watching movies.[125] Other testimonies reveal that torturers and their shackled prisoners celebrated national holidays and prisoners' birthdays together; disappeared women were allowed, under strict supervision, to work in legal places with non-prisoners; disappeared women who talked with their friends outside ESMA[126] went shopping, visited the hairdresser, spent a weekend with their children and relatives, and returned to the CCD on Mondays,[127] and they even went to restaurants or clubs for dancing accompanied by marines.[128] The disappeared were able to see and talk to people in the street but not to tell them that they were prisoners.[129] Because of the peculiar way in which ESMA functioned, the coexistence of torturer and torturee was a constant feature,[130] to the point that the formation of couples occurred, not only between prisoners but also between torturer and torturee.[131] Within this framework arose the possibility of survival, but it was necessary to show signs of being or appearing to be a "recovered" person.[132] The recovery process meant being "decent,"[133] not "a whore Montonera," tortured for being such.[134] That is, the woman was expected to return to the image of "saint/mother," a submissive and obedient woman within the framework of patriarchal society. Male reintegration meant leaving behind leftist ideology. For both men and women, though, being part of these programs did not necessarily guarantee their survival.

For example, to counteract the masculine "negativity" of the guerrilla woman, proper clothing and makeup were required: "One had to get dressed up, and, if you were to put on makeup, all the better. The thicker the makeup, the more *recuperada*/reintegrated you were. No more jeans, suede, or moccasins. Lots of earrings and chains, like a Christmas tree."[135] Other survivors recalled similar treatment: "Try to ask for beautiful clothes, we women shall lend you some, we are going to give you makeup so that they, the marine officers, can see that you are better."[136] On another occasion, the military addressed the prisoners in this way: "Either you get dressed and we'll go dancing, or it means that you are not recoverable; I'll inject a lethal injection of pentothal and send you off away, shitty Montonera!"[137] Such was the expected conduct of the *recuperada* ("recuperated") woman; to reject it meant death in ESMA.

In such remaking of gender politics during this period in Argentina, it is not unfathomable to equate the rehabilitation of female and male prisoners with the ontological fantasies of securing and making sex. As Hanne Blank argues in *Virgin: The Untouched History*, virginity is literally rendered a "blank screen upon which to project one's fantasies of sex and of virginity itself."[138] Moreover, as MacKinnon points out, if "women's sexuality is, socially, a thing to be stolen, sold, bought, bartered, or exchanged by others,"[139] then the argument could be made that this sexuality can also be replaced, found, and given back. We also have to wonder if the "reprogramming" of the *virago* as *guerrillera* came from the psychosocial needs of military men to prove themselves as powerful patriarchs of the nation, with godlike potency and righteousness—ultimately understood as performative signs of their "legitimized" masculinity in the public sphere but demonstrable only through and on an ontologically violated but now epistemologically secured body.

When we observe in a critical light the advances in our societies in past centuries, we see that the subjugation of female "masculinity" is not only achieved through violent ends against a "vagina" but also manifest in other forms that can be quite refined and subtle. In terms of the figure of the *virago*, the reaction of heteronormative patriarchal systems is still the same whether referring to Joan of Arc or the *guerrillera*. The reality in many instances is that, after being defeated, these "unruly" women have been modified by official, state-sanctioned "histories" to preserve the status quo of dichotomized gender spaces and oppressions. The Mexican *soldadera* and the Chilean female soldier have been either silenced and represented as sex objects or given limited access to the public sphere with strict supervision and regulation. At least with the examples of Chile and Argentina, military women are testifying to the subtly insidious forms of gender ideology and control in Latin America. If, as scholars have noted, the archaic technologies of the sexual control of women were needed to police both the labia and the lips, in devices such as the chastity belt and the scold's bridle (a torturous muzzle that silenced a woman's other lips),[140] then women's writing of these stories, as Valenzuela points out, can "upset the core of the phallogocentric, paternalistic discourse"[141] found in a definitively masculine public domain.

NOTES

1   Luisa Valenzuela, "Dirty Words," *Review of Contemporary Fiction* 6, 3 (1986): 9.

2   Catherine A. MacKinnon, "Rape: On Coercion and Consent," in *Writing on the Body: Female Embodiment and Feminist Theory*, ed. Katie Conboy, Nadia Medina, and Sarah Stanbury (New York: Columbia University Press, 1997), 53.

3   Sarah Salih, *Versions of Virginity in Late Medieval England* (Cambridge, UK: D. S. Brewer, 2001), 1.

4   Sarah Salih, Anke Bernau, and Ruth Evans, "Introduction: Virginities and Virginity Studies," in *Medieval Virginities*, ed. Anke Bernau, Ruth Evans, and Sarah Salih (Toronto: University of Toronto Press, 2003), 5.

5   Jessica Valenti, *The Purity Myth: How America's Obsession with Virginity Is Hurting Young Women* (Berkeley: Seal Press, 2010), examines the popularity and commodification of vaginal rejuvenation procedures, virginity clubs, abstinence education, and national movements and groups such as Born Again Virgins of America. Such physical and performative "reconstructions" are by no means twentieth-century occurrences. Many of them resemble similar cases in the early modern period, with examples from the Nun of Whatton (b. 1146) and Margery Kempe (b. 1373), to name a couple. Maeve B. Callan, "Of Vanishing Fetuses and Maidens Made-Again: Abortion, Restored Virginity, and Similar Scenarios in Medieval Irish Hagiography and Penitentials," *Journal of the History of Sexuality* 21, 2 (2012): 282–96; Salih, *Versions of Virginity*.

6   Kathleen Coyne Kelly, *Performing Virginity and Testing Chastity in the Middle Ages* (New York: Routledge, 2000), 93. Her tongue-in-cheek question "do men have a hymen?" is pertinent to her study of virginity performance and testing in the Middle Ages given that, for far too long, the "overdetermined" and "naturalized" concept of virginity has pertained to women only. It is our position that female virginity cannot be analyzed in isolation but must take a gender-centred and intersectional focus.

7   For a similar counter to the argument posited by scholars of the medieval period that virginity constituted a third gender that was neither masculine nor feminine, see Cassandra Rhodes, "'What, after All, Is a Male Virgin?' Multiple Performances of Male Virginity in Anglo-Saxon Saints' Lives," in *Representing Medieval Genders and Sexualities in Europe: Construction,*

Transformation, and Subversion, 600–1530, ed. Elizabeth L'Estrange and Alison More (Burlington, VT: Ashgate, 2011), 15–32.

8   One need not look only at historical cases of unruly women and disciplinary control in Latin America. The recent case of virginity testing on politically active women in Tahrir Square in 2011 is one such example. As Naomi Wolf explains in *Vagina: A New Biography* (New York: HarperCollins, 2012), 202, "Samira Ibrahim, twenty-five, a young Egyptian protester, brought suit against that country's military in 2011, asserting that after the army had arrested her in Tahrir Square during a protest, she was forced to undergo a vaginal examination against her will. . . . An army spokesman defended the forced vaginal 'exams': 'We didn't want them to say we had sexually assaulted or raped them, so we wanted to prove they weren't virgins in the first place,' a military source explained to the news site Al Jazeera.'"

9   On use of the terms "male" and "masculinity," we defer to Judith Halberstam, *Female Masculinity* (Durham: Duke University Press, 1998), whose discussions of alternative masculinities found in tomboys, drag queens, and lesbian stone butches, among others, try to expose hegemonic operations of dominant "male" masculinity.

10   One could even include the modern term "tomboy" here, though with less political value than the earlier manifestation of *virago*. Whereas "post-structural and queer theorists deploy the concept of tomboy as a discursive and performative category with multiple meanings," like the *virago*, the tomboy might serve only to valorize hegemonic masculinities rather than promote gender equality. Alex Moore, *Teaching and Learning: Pedagogy, Curriculum, and Culture* (New York: Routledge, 2012), 98. As Halberstam, *Female Masculinity*, 6, reveals, "tomboyism tends to be associated with a 'natural' desire for the greater freedoms and mobilities by boys. Very often it is read as a sign of independence and self-motivation, and tomboyism may even be encouraged to the extent that it remains comfortably linked to a stable sense of a girl identity. Tomboyism is punished, however, when it appears to be the sign of extreme male identification (taking a boy's name or refusing girl clothing of any type) and when it threatens to extend beyond childhood and into adolescence."

11   Katherine Allocco, "Vampiric Viragoes: Villainizing and Sexualizing Arthurian Women in *Dracula vs. King Arthur* (2005)," in *The Universal Vampire: Origins and Evolution of a Legend*, ed. Barbara Brodman and

James E. Doan (Madison: Fairleigh Dickinson University Press, 2013), 152.

12 Catherine S. Cox, "'An Excellent Thing in Woman': Virgo and Viragos in *King Lear*," *Modern Philology* 96, 2 (1988): 145.

13 Allocco, "Vampiric Viragoes."

14 Joan Curbet, "Repressing the Amazon: Cross-Dressing and Militarism in Edmund Spenser's *The Faerie Queene*," in *Dressing Up for War: Transformations of Gender and Genre in the Discourse and Literature of War*, ed. Aránzazu Usandizaga and Andrew Monnickendam (New York: Rodopi, 2001), 157–72.

15 The social and economic value of the vagina goes back to antiquity. For example, the Code of Hammurabi and the Bible state that a virgin's vagina was worth fifty silver coins. See Susan Brownmiller, *Against Our Will: Men, Women, and Rape* (New York: Simon and Schuster, 1975). In modern times, a vagina could be worth up to £930,000. See Lee Moran, "Brazilian Student Who Auctioned Her Virginity for £485,000 Hopes to Sell It AGAIN after Claiming the Last Buyer Did Not Have Sex with Her," *Daily Mail* online, November 20, 2013, http://www.dailymail.co.uk/news/article-2510425/Brazilian-student-auctioned-virginity-hopes-sell-AGAIN.html.

16 Sara D. Luttfring, "Bodily Narratives and the Politics of Virginity in *The Changeling* and the Essex Divorce," *Renaissance Drama* 39 (2011): 105.

17 Wolf, *Vagina*, 160.

18 Lisa Beckstrand, *Deviant Women of the French Revolution and the Rise of Feminism* (Madison: Fairleigh Dickinson University Press, 2009), 12. Many of the Parisian women whose writings and activism during the revolution challenged prevailing norms of their sex were labelled deviant and a corrupting source for the patriarchal society of this period. The following excerpt from *La feuille de salut public, 1793* is demonstrative of public opinion about these active and "unruly" women: "Rappelez-vous cette virago, cette femme-homme, l'impudente Olympe de Gouges, qui abondonna tous les soins de son ménage, voulut politiquer et commit des crimes. . . . Cet oubli de son sexe l'a conduite à l'échafaud." Translation: Never forget that virago, that woman-man, the impudent Olympe de Gouges, who abandoned the cares of her household, to get mixed up in politics and commit crimes. Forgetting the virtues of her sex led her to the guillotine. Cited and translated in ibid., 15.

19   Even into the nineteenth century, "female education . . . was cast as af-
      fecting women's sexual nervous system, rendering 'New Women' who
      insisted on a masculine education, infertile, in the views of some 'experts,'
      or sexually insatiable, in the words of others, and in either case, hairy
      and unmarriageable." Wolf, *Vagina*, 148.

20   Dorrit Einersen and Ingeborg Nixon, "Virago and Lamia: Woman as
      Monster," *Angles on the English-Speaking World* 2 (1987): 4.

21   Cox, "'An Excellent Thing in Woman,'" 144.

22   James Gratham Turner, *One Flesh: Paradisal Marriage and Sexual Rela-
      tions in the Age of Milton* (Oxford: Oxford University Press, 1987), 99, 96,
      107–08.

23   Cited in Cox, "'An Excellent Thing in Woman,'" 144.

24   Anke Bernau, *Virgins: A Cultural History* (London: Granta, 2007); Joc-
      elyn Wogan-Browne, "Virginity Always Comes Twice: Virginity and
      Profession, Virginity and Romance," in *Maistresse of My Wit: Medieval
      Women, Modern Scholars*, ed. Louise D. D'Arcens and Juanita Feros Ruys
      (Turnhout: Brepols, 2004), 335–69.

25   Jo Ann McNamara, "The *Herrenfrage*: The Restructuring of the Gender
      System, 1050–1150," in *Medieval Masculinities: Regarding Men in the
      Middle Ages*, ed. Clare A. Lees (Minneapolis: University of Minnesota
      Press, 1994), 3.

26   Asunción Lavrin, "Masculine and Feminine: The Construction of Gender
      Roles in the Regular Orders in Early Modern Mexico," *Explorations in
      Renaissance Culture* 34, 1 (2008): 3–26.

27   Maureen C. Miller, "Masculinity, Reform, and Clerical Culture: Nar-
      ratives of the Episcopal Holiness in the Gregorian Era," *Church History:
      Studies in Christianity and Culture* 72, 1 (2003): 25–52.

28   Cassandra Rhodes, "'What, after All, Is a Male Virgin?'," 17.

29   Joan of Arc was an illiterate and poor peasant with a social power that did
      not typically belong to either her class or her gender. See Leslie Feinberg,
      Transgender Warriors: Making History from Joan of Arc to RuPaul (Boston:
      Beacon Press, 1996), 34, who states that "Joan's cross-dressing was a power
      class bias. It was an affront to nobility for a peasant to wear armor and
      ride a fine horse."

30   Andrea Dworkin, *Intercourse* (New York: Basic Books, 2007), 109–10.

31   Feinberg, *Transgender Warriors*, 35.

32 Another case in point from the early modern period can be found in the court proceedings of the divorce trial of Robert Devereux, Earl of Essex, and Frances Howard, Countess of Essex, from 1613. Sara D. Luttfring examines the political implications of this divorce for the rule and administration of King James because of the claims of virginity of the Countess during the proceedings. Howard claimed that her marriage to Devereux had never been consummated; as such, she was still a virgin. Her virginity could never be proven or disproven. The problem that arose during the divorce proceedings pertained to the fact that Howard was no longer under the control of either her father or her husband and was thus deemed a "free sexual agent." Howard obtained her divorce, only to marry almost immediately the court favourite, Robert Carr. This marriage linked the powerful Howard family to King James, who supported the divorce of the countess. Luttfring, "Bodily Narratives and the Politics of Virginity in *The Changeling* and the Essex Divorce," 105. The re-entry of the countess into the institution of marriage assuaged the controversy to a degree, but the divorce became a sign of weakness and chaos for the administration of King James.

33 At an earlier age, Joan of Arc defied the secular law of her father when she refused to marry; as a consequence, she was taken to court for not complying with her matrimonial contract. She won the court case, but she did not return to the tutelage of her father, nor did she choose to become a nun, which would have been expected of her; instead, she fled from home to follow her vision of liberating France, demonstrating her courage and valour on the battlefield while maintaining her virginal integrity and independence. Dworkin, *Intercourse*, 109.

34 Ibid., 111, 113.

35 Ibid., 121.

36 A. Nicholas Groth and H. Jean Birnbaum, *Men Who Rape: The Psychology of the Offender* (New York: Plenum Press, 1979), 114.

37 According to some accounts, Joan of Arc did agree to resume wearing female clothing but soon returned to male clothing while in prison. Feinberg, *Transgender Warriors*, 35, notes that her cross-dressing became the "core of the charges," equating her return to male clothing with a relapse, similar to a heretic's relapse of faith.

38 For an examination of the literary representations of Christian orthodoxy read on and through the masculine body in contrast to that of the Mus-

lim enemy in medieval Spain, see Louise Mirrer, "Representing 'Other' Men: Muslims, Jews, and Masculine Ideals in Medieval Castilian Epic and Ballad," in *Medieval Masculinities: Regarding Men in the Middle Ages*, ed. Clare A. Lees (Minneapolis: University of Minnesota Press, 1994), 169–86.

39 Since Indigenous peoples of the Americas were not considered human by Europeans, Catalina did not include in her memoirs the murder of these peoples as crimes under secular/sacred law.

40 Kathleen Ann Myers, *Neither Saints nor Sinners: Writing the Lives of Women in Spanish America* (Oxford: Oxford University Press, 2003), 140–44.

41 Ibid., 4, 143, 146.

42 See, especially, Sherry Velasco, *The Lieutenant Nun: Transgenderism, Lesbian Desire, and Catalina de Erauso* (Austin: University of Texas Press, 2000).

43 Myers, *Neither Saints nor Sinners*, 143.

44 If we can believe her memoirs, Catalina was able to live as a man for more than twenty years, travel to the Americas in a boat belonging to her uncle's company, become educated in a convent where she had lived from the age of four, and obtain work thanks to her contacts; one of her brothers was the minister of war, though according to her she had never let this be known. Her family belonged to the nobility. Her grandfather, Miguel de Erauso, was wealthy and owned land and ships and had a history of commercial success. See Eva Mendieta, *In Search of Catalina de Erauso: The National and Sexual Identity of the Lieutenant Nun*, trans. Angeles Prado (Reno: Center for Basque Studies, 2009), 170.

45 Religious memoirs or autobiographies were popular during the sixteenth and seventeenth centuries in both Spain (the Spanish metropolis) and the colonies, as noted in Myers, *Neither Saints nor Sinners*, 3. During the Counter-Reformation, religious people, nuns, and religious women in particular were judged by the church through these writings, which complemented the act of confession (8). It was through these writings that the bishop or priest would endorse the life of the writer, expected to show "evidence of heroic retreat from the world, penitential practices, obedience to the Church, and personal knowledge of God that had not been learned from books" (14). If not, then they were censored and had severe limitations: "The confession of sins became a didactic confirma-

tion of God's grace and goodness in the subject's life and a story of her doctrinally pure response to those divine gifts" (11).

46   As cited in ibid., 147.

47   The lieutenant nun underwent physical testing to determine an intact hymen.

48   Many recent critics "suggest that the Monja Alférez' life and texts capitalized on loopholes in what has largely been perceived by twentieth-century scholars as a rigid gender and moral code. Perry convincingly argues that Catalina's case slipped through the legal system because civic law reflected society's assumption that people would be prosecuted according to his or her biological sex, either as a man or a woman. Both ecclesiastic and secular frameworks only allowed for two categories for adult whites' sexual identity. Catalina could not be prosecuted as a man for her misdeeds because she had been a nun; but neither could they process her as a woman because she had lived as a loyal soldier." Ibid., 148.

49   Ibid., 146.

50   Mendieta, *In Search of Catalina de Erauso*, 178.

51   Myers, *Neither Saints nor Sinners*, 153.

52   This is evident in women organizations such as Relatives of the Disappeared and Detained for Political Reasons and Mothers of the Plaza de Mayo, who were searching for their children "disappeared" by the Argentine military during the "dirty war" (1976–83). While the mothers modelled their human rights activism on *marianismo*—"good, Catholic Argentine women . . . constructed as pious, self-sacrificing, obedient, and devoted to their families"; Meghan Gibbons, "Political Motherhood in the United States and Argentina," in *Mothers Who Deliver: Feminist Interventions in Public and Interpersonal Discourse*, ed. Jocelyn Fenton-Stitt and Pegeen Reichert Powell (Albany: SUNY Press, 2010), 255—the military junta, fearful of the international attention being gained by these mothers, dismissed them as "madwomen"; Diana Taylor, *Disappearing Acts: Spectacles of Gender and Nationalism in Argentina's "Dirty War"* (Durham: Duke University Press, 1997), 188.

53   Bernau, *Virgins*.

54   Ibid.; Marina Warner, *Alone of All Her Sex: The Myth and the Cult of the Virgin Mary* (London: Weidenfeld and Nicolson, 1976); Wogan-Browne, "Virginity Always Comes Twice."

55   "Biblical scholars generally agree that the ideology of Mary's sacred virginity was as much a belated construct of the church, and that it could not be confirmed in the original texts of the New Testament, which suggest that Mary had several children." Wolf, *Vagina*, 134.

56   Warner, *Alone of All Her Sex*, 229.

57   Bernau, *Virgins*, 40–41, 144.

58   Wogan-Browne, "Virginity Always Comes Twice," 344.

59   Wogan-Browne explains "the virginity of cronehood" as "the regained virginity of the menopause in which decoupling from the politics of biological reproduction becomes possible." Ibid., 345.

60   Ibid., 349. Wogan-Browne makes special reference to the virginal prestige and chaste matron identity enacted on Diana, Princess of Wales.

61   Gloria Anzaldúa comments in *Borderlands/La frontera: The New Mestiza* (San Francisco: Aunt Lute Books, 1999), 17, that in the Latina/Chicana context "women had only three directions to which they could turn: to the Church as a nun, to the streets as a prostitute, or to the home as a mother." If women's sexual experiences deviate from the sanctioned patriarchal categories of *virgin* and then *wife/mother*, then the women are labelled whores and looked on with scorn (22).

62   Ann Twinam, *Public Lives, Private Secrets: Gender, Honor, Sexuality, and Illegitimacy in Colonial Spanish America* (Stanford: Stanford University Press, 1999), 39.

63   For example, Chile legislated and allowed only "virginal" unmarried women to work in the mines and factories, whereas married or single mothers were assigned passive roles in the home while idealized for their obedience, dedication, and self-sacrifice to the family. Cheryl E. Martin and Mark Wasserman, *Latin America and Its People*, 2nd ed. (Toronto: Pearson, 2008), 2: 407.

64   Cherie Zalaquett, *Chilenas en armas: Testimonios e historia de mujeres militares y guerrilleras subversivas* (Santiago: Catalonia, 2009). Unfortunately, Zalaquett does not distinguish in many of the interviews the different social classes and/or racial ethnicities of the interviewees. Only in some cases, such as that of Carmen Castillo, is class mentioned.

65   Ibid., 20. Original: Cuando comunicó su decisión de ser militar, su madre expresó temor: "Esto me asusta un poco porque te vas a convertir en un hombre." Unless otherwise noted, all translations into English are our own.

66 Ibid., 20–21. Original: Les exigieron llevar mascotas de peluche, osos, ratones de Mickey o muñecas para ponerlos en el dormitorio como símbolos de la continuidad con la infancia y el hogar. Debían pegar una fotografía de sus padres, tamaño postal al interior de sus armarios, y situarla a una altura determinada que les permitiera verla apenas abrieron el locker. Partes de su cuerpo como el largo del pelo, y las uñas eran objetos de revisiones e intervenciones de las instructoras, quienes, además, verificaban que usaran solamente ropa interior de color blanco, como lo estipula (hasta hoy) el reglamento.

67 Such controls are very similar to what Valenti, *The Purity Myth*, 68, describes of the virginity movement in the United States: "In the world of the virginity movement, 'femininity' is synonymous with submissiveness and girlishness."

68 Zalaquett, *Chilenas en armas*, 49. Original: La mujer se consideraba un sujeto infantil que debía ser cuidado, protegido, y confinado a la esfera privada del hogar.

69 Ibid., 49–50. Original: El Ejército mantuvo una inflexible separación de roles de acuerdo a los estereotipos tradicionales. Los hombres detentaban el poder, el mando y las tareas de combate propiamente militares, mientras que las mujeres realizaban labores administrativas, auxiliares y de apoyo, reproduciendo la división del trabajo en el hogar patriarcal.

70 Ibid., 51. Original: Las disposiciones internas del Ejército exhortan al personal a un 'deber ser' de contraer matrimonio y constituir una familia nuclear tradicional.

71 The same argument that allowed a public sphere to sustain and legitimize masculine predominance cannot be made for the case of the militarized *miristas*—the leftist revolutionaries fighting Pinochet's dictatorship during the 1970s and 1980s. Written testimonies bear witness to a female masculinity that sought gender equality through, among other ways, aggressive sexual behaviour only assumed and "validated" in males. See, especially, Carmen Castillo's testimony transcribed in ibid., 138–53.

72 "The word *soldadera* has its origins in the Spanish conquest. The soldaderas were responsible for aiding the army by finding food and caring for injured soldiers. The term has also been applied to Spanish women who fought during the Conquest. As Spanish became Mexico's language after the conquest, the term *soldadera* was used to describe all women who fought and aided in the Mexican conflicts." Delia Fernández, "From

Soldadera to Adelita: The Depiction of Women in the Mexican Revolution," *NcNair Scholars Journal* 13, 1 (2009): 53.

73 As Tabea Alexa Linhard describes, "adelita is the quintessential *soldadera*; she is [a] camp follower, a love object, a picaresque character, a whore, a brave woman warrior, a nurse, and always the woman the revolution is worth fighting for." Tabea Alexa Linhard, "Adelita's Radical Act of Counter-Writing," in *Dressing Up for War. Transformations of Gender and Genre in the Discourse and Literature of War*, ed. Aránzazu Usandizaga and Andrew Monnickendam (New York: Rodopi, 2001), 127.

74 Fernández, "From Soldadera to Adelita," 53.

75 Elizabeth Salas, *Soldaderas in the Mexican Military: Myth and History* (Austin: University of Texas Press, 1990).

76 Fernández, "From Soldadera to Adelita"; Jocelyn Olcott, Mary Kay Vaughan, and Gabriela Cano, eds., *Sex in Revolution: Gender, Politics, and Power in Modern Mexico* (Durham: Duke University Press, 2006); Salas, *Soldaderas in the Mexican Military*.

77 Linhard, "Adelita's Radical Act of Counter-Writing," 131.

78 Fernández, "From Soldadera to Adelita," 59. Many of these real-life *soldaderas*, through their active participation in the war, were able to "reject the societal norms imposed on them. Women were able to engage in open relationships with men at this time. Liberated from the Catholic Church, many women chose to have sexual relationships with men they were not married to and had no plans to marry. They could behave like the men who had controlled them for so many years." Ibid., 57.

79 Ibid., 54.

80 Stephen J. Ducat, *The Wimp Factor: Gender Gaps, Holy Wars, and the Politics of Anxious Masculinity* (Boston: Beacon Press, 2004), 5.

81 "Many cultures have a version of what anthropologists call the 'vagina dentata.' This means, literally, 'the vagina with teeth.' . . . The archetypal and universal association (usually by men) of the vagina with the mouth makes the vagina dentata a universal and timeless symbol of male anxiety about engulfment and annihilation by a threatening Mother." Wolf, *Vagina*, 130–31.

82 Ibid., 158.

83 Rape was not limited to a woman's vagina; any orifice suggestive of penetrability was targeted on men as well.

84 Jean Franco, *Critical Passions: Selected Essays*, ed. Mary Louise Pratt and Kathleen Newman (Durham: Duke University Press, 1999).

85 For example, in the case of Osvaldo R., a detainee in the province of Córdoba, he was the first to admit to having been raped by the military. The judicial proceedings against the military began in 2008, and his revelation just appeared on May 10, 2015, in the Argentine newspaper *Página 12*. See Marta Platía, "La peor herida: Terribles testimonios sobre los crímenes sexuales en la megacausa de Córdoba," *Página 12*, May 10, 2015, http://www.pagina12.com.ar/diario/elpais/1-272367-2015-05-10.html.

86 In an interview with Berta Horen, a professor of sociology at the University of Buenos Aires and a political prisoner during the last dictatorship in Argentina, she revealed the following: "The instruction given to the military forces emphasized their unique role of the institution as the saviour of the country. Without knowing exactly how they had to achieve this aim, they acquired a unique sense of entitlement which unified them and maintained their separation from the rest of society without exposing them to a different mindset. However, the long hours they had to remain amongst themselves in the military institutions without specific activities took many to an empty idleness, which opened the door to homosexuality. Unfortunately, this kind of life is also permissible to alcohol, gambling, and drugs. This life without barriers contrasted with the image of 'correct and perfect behaviour' that they claimed to have when they were out of their barracks with their own families or any other member of society." Interview with Berta Horen, Buenos Aires, May 20, 2015.

87 See, especially, María del Carmen Sillato, *Huellas: Memorias de resistencia* (San Luis, Argentina: Nueva Editorial Universitaria, 2008), for a testimonial collection of female and male survivors of the Argentinian concentration camps in which a clear distinction is demonstrated between how female militants speak of their tortured bodies (i.e., rape) and how male militants either use humour or speak of their experiences of heroic resistance as revolutionary masculinity. For an analysis and definition of "revolutionary masculinity," see Florencia E. Mallon, "*Barbudos*, Warriors, and *Rotos*: The MIR, Masculinity, and Power in the Chilean Agrarian Reform, 1965–74," in *Changing Men and Masculinities in Latin America*, ed. Matthew C. Gutmann (Durham: Duke University Press, 2003), 179–215.

88 The *desaparecido* ("the disappeared") was a person detained (in his or her house, workplace, public place, at night, or at daylight) by military forces and taken to *centros clandestinos de detención*, also called concentration camps. The whereabouts of these people were denied to their relatives. In these places, such as ESMA (Escuela Superior de Mecánica de la Armada/ Higher School of Mechanics of the Navy), the disappeared suffered dreadful tortures and finally were murdered. As Pilar Calviero states, with the political repression sporadically appearing after the *coup d'état* of 1966, the figure of the disappeared was institutionalized in the last period of the democratic government of Isabel Perón (1974–76). However, "the coup of 76 represented a substantial change [since] the disappearance and the extermination camp ceased to be one of the methods of repression to become 'the' repressive form of power, executed directly from the military." Pilar Calviero, *Poder y desaparición: Los campos de concentración en Argentina* (Buenos Aires: Colihue, 1998), 26–27.

89 Rosemary Geisdorfer Feal, "The Politics of 'Wargasm': Sexuality, Domination, and Female Subversion in Luisa Valenzuela's *Cambio de Armas*," in *Structures of Power: Essays on Twentieth-Century Spanish-American Fiction*, ed. Terry J. Peavler and Peter Standish (Albany: SUNY Press, 1996), 168.

90 Taylor, *Disappearing Acts*, 84. Taylor goes on to describe how "women were annihilated through a metonymic reduction to their sexual 'parts': wombs, vaginas, breasts. . . . Pregnant women, who made up 3 percent of the disappeared, were often abducted, raped, and tortured simply because they were pregnant." Ibid.

91 Antonius C. G. M. Robben, *Political Violence and Trauma in Argentina* (Philadelphia: University of Pennsylvania Press, 2005), 218.

92 Feal, "The Politics of 'Wargasm,'" 168, also examines the short stories by Argentinean writer Luisa Valenzuela, one in particular, titled "Unlimited Rapes United, Argentina," that chronicles how the "division of the URU is failing to carry out its civic duty of producing the minimum number of rapes to ensure that social and domestic order remain[s] intact."

93 Marcelo M. Suarez-Orozco, "The Treatment of Children in the 'Dirty War': Ideology, State Terrorism, and the Abuse of Children in Argentina," in *Child Survival: Anthropological Perspectives on the Treatment and Maltreatment of Children*, ed. Nancy Scheper-Hughes (Dordrecht: D. Reidel, 1987), 241–42.

94 Robben, *Political Violence and Trauma in Argentina*, 223.

95   Similar movements appeared in Canada (Front de Libération du Québec, 1963–72), the United States (Black Panther Party, 1966–82, and Black Liberation Party, 1970–81), and Germany (Rote Armee Fraktion or Baader-Meinhop, 1970–96).

96   Colombia: FARC (Fuerzas Armadas Revolucionarias de Colombia) and Ejército de Liberación Nacional, Movimiento 19 de Abril; Costa Rica: La Familia; Chile: MIR (Movimiento de Izquierda Revolucionario), Frente Patriótico Manuel Rodríguez; Ecuador: Alfaro Vive ¡Carajo!; El Salvador: FMLN (Frente Farabundo Martí para la Liberación Nacional); Guatemala: Unidad Revolucionaria Nacional Guatemalteca; Honduras: Unificación Democrática; México: Liga Comunista 23 de Septiembre; Nicaragua: Frente Sandinista de Liberación Nacional; Perú: Sendero Luminoso, MRTA (Movimiento Revolucionario Tupác Amaru); Uruguay: MLN-Tupamaros (Movimiento de Liberación Nacional-Tupamaros); Venezuela: FALN (Fuerzas Armadas de Liberación Nacional).

97   Scholars are beginning to take into account the diverse nature of political participation by women in the various Latin American revolutionary movements throughout the second half of the twentieth century, including the more recent testimonial accounts by mothers who participated in logistical and/or combat roles in the leftist movements. See Tracy Crowe Morey and Cristina Santos, *"Las madres guerreras*: Testimonial Writing on Militant Motherhood in Latin America," in *Motherhood and War: International Perspectives*, ed. Dana Cooper and Claire Phelan (New York: Palgrave Macmillan, 2014), 61–84.

98   Members of the following organizations joined Montoneros: FAP (Fuerzas Armadas Peronistas/Peronist Armed Forces) and Descamisados/Shirtless. For more information, see Juan Gasparini, *Montoneros: Final de cuentas* (Buenos Aires: Puntosur Editores, 1988), 26–36.

99   Adriana Spahr, "Removing the Blindfold: Power, Truth, and Testimony," paper presented at the 12th Global Conference on Monsters and the Monstrous, Oxford, http://www.inter-disciplinary.net/at-the-interface/wp-content/uploads/2014/05/A.Spahr-m12-wpaper.pdf.

100   It is difficult to determine the number of people who integrated the social and guerrilla movements in the country. One of the most significant factors was their clandestine mode of operating. The majority of studies on this topic are based upon the number of disappeared people reported by relatives or acquaintances. The following study shows two numbers

in each category. The first number corresponds to the 1970s, when the repression was more indiscriminate. The second number corresponds to the last period of the dictatorship, when the repression was focused on the guerrilla organizations as well as on the dictatorship's allies, for example the murders of dictatorship diplomats (Elena Angélica Holmberg Lanusse, the ex-dictator's niece, and Ambassador Héctor Hidalgo Solá). Percentages of the wealthy bourgeoisie, 4.7 and 9.6; middle and petite bourgeoisie (professionals, university students), 8.8 and 4.1; self-employed, 13.2 and 21.8; qualified urban employees with the same conditions as the petite bourgeoisie, 21.0 and 22.0; qualified urban and rural workers, 50.8 and 45.9. Inés Izaguirre, "Los desaparecidos: Recuperación de una identidad expropiada," Programa de Investigaciones sobre Conflicto Social, Instituto de Investigaciones Gino Germani, Facultad de Ciencias Sociales, Universidad de Buenos Aires, 1–9, http://webiigg.sociales.uba.ar/conflictosocial/libros/izaguirre/losdesaparecidos/index.htm.

101 Débora D'Antonio, "Represión y resistencia en las cárceles de la última dictadura militar argentina," *La revista del CCC* 2 (2008): 3, http://www.centrocultural.coop/revista/articulo/29/represion_y_resistencia_en_las_carceles_de_la_ultima_dictadura_militar_argentina.html.

102 Eva Duarte de Perón (1919–52) was the second wife of Juan Domingo Perón. She was an important political figure in the country. During her husband's first presidency (1946–52), she ran the Ministries of Labour and Health, created the Female Peronist Party (women's wing of the Peronist Party), and championed suffrage for women (a law allowing women to vote was passed in 1947). In 1951, supported mainly by working-class and low-income people in the country, she announced her candidacy as vice-president of the nation. However, because of strong opposition by the bourgeoisie and military forces, she withdrew her candidacy. A year later she died from cancer at the age of thirty-three.

103 ESMA was one of the 610 clandestine detention centres of torture and extermination established in Argentina between 1975 and 1983 and through which passed 4,237 of the disappeared. Gasparini, *Montoneros*, 102. The exact number of survivors is unknown, but it is estimated at between 70 and 200. Calviero, *Poder y desaparición*, 29, maintains that out of the total of the disappeared—between 15,000 and 30,000—about 90 percent of them were killed. According to information from Liliana Gardella, out of "a hundred people two or three were part of the 'reintegration

program,'" and thus the number of 200 seems to be appropriate. Munú Actis et al., *Ese infierno: Conversaciones con cinco mujeres sobrevivientes de la* ESMA (Buenos Aires: Altamira, 2006), 152.

104 Gasparini, *Montoneros*, 102. Some marine officers protected Arrostito while in ESMA, but others did not. Lieutenant Commander Jorge Eduardo Acosta sent someone to inject her with a poison, telling her that she needed an anti-coagulant for her swelling leg because of the chains and shackles. Ibid., 32. Injection of pentothal was one of the methods used to kill detainees. Actis et al., *Ese infierno*, 118. For more information on the topic, see *Nunca Más: Informe de la Comisión Nacional sobre la Desaparición de Personas* (Buenos Aires: Eudeba, 2006).

105 Susana Jorgelina Ramus, *Sueños sobrevivientes de una montonera a pesar de la* ESMA (Buenos Aires: Colihue, 2000), 76.

106 Along with Acosta, the other authority in ESMA was Ruben Jacinto Chamorro.

107 Actis et al., *Ese infierno*, 136; Gasparini, *Montoneros*, 107; Ramus, *Sueños sobrevivientes*, 44. Furthermore, ESMA's prisoners were taken outside the camp to public places in the hope that they would point out to the military other guerrilla comrades. Some prisoners did so, while others did not. Actis et al., *Ese infierno*, 137; Gasparini, *Montoneros*, 106.

108 Actis et al., *Ese infierno*; Gasparini, *Montoneros*, 101; Ramus, *Sueños sobrevivientes*, 107.

109 Actis et al., *Ese infierno*, 93, 151; Viktor E. Frankl, *Man's Search for Meaning* (Boston: Beacon Press, 2006), 19–20; Ramus, *Sueños sobrevivientes*, 37.

110 Other similarities between ESMA and Auschwitz include the loss of identity of the prisoner by means of numbers instead of names. Actis et al., *Ese infierno*, 83–84. This procedure was also used in other CCDs not overseen by the army. In the place where María Consuelo Castaño Blanco was taken, controlled by the army, the numbers given to prisoners were those of the padlocks to which they were chained. In addition to shackles, prisoners always had hoods over their heads. María Consuelo Castaño Blanco, *Más que humanos* (Madrid: Ediciones de Cultura Hispánica, 1988, 32–35, 41–43.

111 Actis et al., *Ese infierno*, 123.

112 Frankl, *Man's Search for Meaning*, 19.

113 Ibid., 6.

114 At ESMA, women whose husbands occupied high ranks in the Montoneros organization were also kept alive, as hostages. The army believed that through them it would capture their husbands. Actis et al., *Ese infierno*, 135, 150.

115 The program included both men and women. Gasparini, *Montoneros*, 103. The program for men was based upon the grade of repentance—real or pretended—by the prisoners (e.g., giving information to the armed forces to facilitate the detention of comrades). It is important to add that this option was in the hands not of the captives but of the kidnappers. The selection was made according to the needs of the navy, as specified above. Even though Gardella said that "we do not know by what random criteria, two or three out of a hundred people that may have been at one time [in ESMA] became part of the project that included the possibility of survival." Actis et al., *Ese infierno*, 152.

116 The program failed. Because of continuous denouncement abroad of the systematic violations of human rights, Massera wanted to use his prisoners to clean up the image of the country. In 1977, he freed prisoners and let them leave the country; among them were Ana María Martí, Sara Solarz of Osantinsky, and María Alicia Pirlo. In Paris, they gave full testimony of the atrocities in ESMA. Ramus, *Sueños sobrevivientes*, 45. This was the first of many denunciations by prisoners from CCDs. These denunciations—along with relatives of *desaparecidos*, legal prisoners, and exiles, among others—allowed and still allow for charges in court against the security forces and their accomplices.

117 Actis et al., *Ese infierno*, 77; Ramus, *Sueños sobrevivientes*, 42–43, 67. Original: La tortura y la humillación era el rito de iniciación para los prisioneros.

118 Gasparini, *Montoneros*, 32.

119 Ramus, *Sueños sobrevivientes*, 55.

120 Ibid.

121 Gasparini, *Montoneros*, 223.

122 Brownmiller, *Against Our Will*, 33, 38; Groth and Birnbaum, *Men Who Rape*, 115.

123 Before the disappeared were chosen to be part of this program, prisoners were humiliated during interrogations, which included all types of harassment, even the rape of women and men. Calviero, *Poder y desaparición*, 65. For more information on the topic, see Miriam Lewin and

Olga Wornat, *Putas y guerrilleras* (Buenos Aires: Grupo Planeta, 2014). The book focuses on women illegally detained at ESMA.

124 The CCD operated in the attic, third floor, and basement of the building.

125 Ramus, *Sueños sobrevivientes*, 52, 75.

126 Actis et al., *Ese infierno*, 82–83, 86.

127 Ramus, *Sueños sobrevivientes*, 78.

128 Actis et al., *Ese infierno*, 93.

129 Ramus, *Sueños sobrevivientes*, 77.

130 Actis et al., *Ese infierno*, 13–14.

131 Ibid., 94; Ramus, *Sueños sobrevivientes*, 75. For the fictional exploration of this occurrence, see, especially, Luisa Valenzuela, *Other Weapons*, trans. Deborah Bonner (Hanover, NH: Ediciones del Norte, 1985).

132 Ramus, *Sueños sobrevivientes*, 37.

133 Actis et al., *Ese infierno*, 92.

134 Ibid., 74.

135 Ibid., 162. Original: Había que empilcharse, y si te pintabas mejor. Cuanto más revoque, más *recuperada* estabas. Nada de vaqueritos, zapatos de gamuza o mocasines. Muchos aros y cadenita, tipo arbolito de Navidad.

136 Ibid., 58. Original: Tratá de pedir ropa linda nosotras te vamos a prestar, vamos a darte maquillaje para que vean que estás mejor.

137 Ibid., 95. Original: O te vestís y vamos a bailar o significa que no sos recuperable, te aplico un pentanoval y te mando para arriba, ¡montonera de mierda!

138 Blank, *Virgin*, 193.

139 MacKinnon, "Rape," 43.

140 Wolf, *Vagina*, 136.

141 Valenzuela, "Dirty Words," 9.

REFERENCES

Actis, Munú, Cristina Aldini, Liliana Gardella, Miriam Lewin, and Elisa Tokar. *Ese infierno: Conversaciones de cinco mujeres sobrevivientes de la* ESMA. Buenos Aires: Altamira, 2006.

Allocco, Katherine. "Vampiric Viragoes: Villainizing and Sexualizing Arthurian Women in *Dracula vs. King Arthur* (2005)." In *The Universal Vampire: Origins and Evolution of a Legend*, edited by Barbara Brodman and James E. Doan, 149–64. Madison: Fairleigh Dickinson University Press, 2013.

Anzaldúa, Gloria. *Borderlands/La frontera: The New Mestiza*. San Francisco: Aunt Lute Books, 1999.

Beckstrand, Lisa. *Deviant Women of the French Revolution and the Rise of Feminism*. Madison: Fairleigh Dickinson University Press, 2009.

Bernau, Anke. *Virgins: A Cultural History*. London: Granta, 2007.

Blank, Hanne. *Virgin: The Untouched History*. New York: Bloomsbury, 2007.

Brownmiller, Susan. *Against Our Will: Men, Women, and Rape*. New York: Simon and Schuster, 1975.

Callan, Maeve B. "Of Vanishing Fetuses and Maidens Made-Again: Abortion, Restored Virginity, and Similar Scenarios in Medieval Irish Hagiography and Penitentials." *Journal of the History of Sexuality* 21, 2 (2012): 282–96.

Calviero, Pilar. *Poder y desaparición: Los campos de concentración en Argentina*. Buenos Aires: Colihue, 1998.

Castaño Blanco, María Consuelo. *Más que humanos*. Madrid: Ediciones de Cultura Hispánica, 1988.

Cox, Catherine S. "'An Excellent Thing in Woman': Virgo and Viragos in *King Lear*." *Modern Philology* 96, 2 (1988): 143–57.

Curbet, Joan. "Repressing the Amazon: Cross-Dressing and Militarism in Edmund Spenser's *The Faerie Queene*." In *Dressing Up for War: Transformations of Gender and Genre in the Discourse and Literature of War*, edited by Aránzazu Usandizaga and Andrew Monnickendam, 157–72. New York: Rodopi, 2001.

D'Antonio, Débora. "Represión y resistencia en las cárceles de la última dictadura militar argentina." *La revista del CCC* 2 (2008), http://www.centrocultural.coop/revista/articulo/29/represion_y_resistencia_en_la_carceles_de_la_ultima_dictadura_militar_argentina.html.

Ducat, Stephen J. *The Wimp Factor: Gender Gaps, Holy Wars, and the Politics of Anxious Masculinity*. Boston: Beacon Press, 2004.

Dworkin, Andrea. *Intercourse*. New York: Basic Books, 2007.

Einersen, Dorrit, and Ingeborg Nixon. "Virago and Lamia: Woman as Monster." *Angles on the English-Speaking World* 2 (1987): 3–29.

Feal, Rosemary Geisdorfer. "The Politics of 'Wargasm': Sexuality, Domination, and Female Subversion in Luisa Valenzuela's *Cambio de Armas*." In *Structures of Power: Essays on Twentieth-Century Spanish-American Fiction*, edited by Terry J. Peavler and Peter Standish, 159–87. Albany: SUNY Press, 1996.

Feinberg, Leslie. *Transgender Warriors: Making History from Joan of Arc to RuPaul*. Boston: Beacon Press, 1996.

Fernández, Delia. "From Soldadera to Adelita: The Depiction of Women in the Mexican Revolution." *NcNair Scholars Journal* 13, 1 (2009): 53–62.

Franco, Jean. *Critical Passions: Selected Essays*. Edited by Mary Louise Pratt and Kathleen Newman. Durham: Duke University Press, 1999.

Frankl, Viktor E. *Man's Search for Meaning*. Boston: Beacon Press, 2006.

Gasparini, Juan. *Montoneros: Final de cuentas*. Buenos Aires: Puntosur Editores, 1988.

Gibbons, Meghan. "Political Motherhood in the United States and Argentina." In *Mothers Who Deliver: Feminist Interventions in Public and Interpersonal Discourse*, edited by Jocelyn Fenton Stitt and Pegeen Reichert Powell, 253–78. Albany: SUNY Press, 2010.

Gratham Turner, James. *One Flesh: Paradisal Marriage and Sexual Relations in the Age of Milton*. Oxford: Oxford University Press, 1987.

Groth, A. Nicholas, and H. Jean Birnbaum. *Men Who Rape: The Psychology of the Offender*. New York: Plenum Press, 1979.

Halberstam, Judith. *Female Masculinity*. Durham: Duke University Press, 1998.

Horen, Berta. Interview. Buenos Aires. May 20, 2015.

Izaguirre, Inés. "Los desaparecidos: Recuperación de una identidad expropiada." Programa de Investigaciones sobre Conflicto Social, Instituto de Investigaciones Gino Germani, Facultad de Ciencias Sociales, Universidad de Buenos Aires, 1–9. http://webiigg.sociales.uba.ar/conflictosocial/libros/izaguirre/losdesaparecidos/index.htm.

Katz, Gregory. "For Modern Royal Bride, Virginity Doesn't Matter." Associated Press, April 8, 2011, http://www.today.com/id/42490092/ns/today-to-day_news/t/modern-royal-bride-virginity-doesnt-matter/#.VyOisjArLIU.

Kelly, Kathleen Coyne. *Performing Virginity and Testing Chastity in the Middle Ages*. New York: Routledge, 2000.

Lavrin, Asunción. "Masculine and Feminine: The Construction of Gender Roles in the Regular Orders in Early Modern Mexico." *Explorations in Renaissance Culture* 34, 1 (2008): 3–26.

Lewin, Miriam, and Olga Wornat. *Putas y guerrilleras*. Buenos Aires: Grupo Planeta, 2014.

Linhard, Tabea Alexa. "Adelita's Radical Act of Counter-Writing." In *Dressing Up for War: Transformations of Gender and Genre in the Discourse and Literature of War*, edited by Aránzazu Usandizaga and Andrew Monnickendam, 127–44. New York: Rodopi, 2001.

Luttfring, Sara D. "Bodily Narratives and the Politics of Virginity in *The Changeling* and the Essex Divorce." *Renaissance Drama* 39 (2011): 97–128.

MacKinnon, Catherine A. "Rape: On Coercion and Consent." In *Writing on the Body: Female Embodiment and Feminist Theory*, edited by Katie Conboy, Nadia Medina, and Sarah Stanbury, 42–58. New York: Columbia University Press, 1997.

Mallon, Florencia E. "*Barbudos*, Warriors, and *Rotos*: The MIR, Masculinity, and Power in the Chilean Agrarian Reform, 1965–74." In *Changing Men and Masculinities in Latin America*, edited by Matthew C. Gutmann, 179–215. Durham: Duke University Press, 2003.

Martin, Cheryl E., and Mark Wasserman. *Latin America and Its People*. 2nd ed. Vol. 2. Toronto: Pearson, 2008.

McNamara, Jo Ann. "The *Herrenfrage*: The Restructuring of the Gender System, 1050–1150." In *Medieval Masculinities: Regarding Men in the Middle Ages*, edited by Clare A. Lees, 3–29. Minneapolis: University of Minnesota Press, 1994.

Mendieta, Eva. *In Search of Catalina de Erauso: The National and Sexual Identity of the Lieutenant Nun*. Translated by Angeles Prado. Reno: Center for Basque Studies, 2009.

Miller, Maureen C. "Masculinity, Reform, and Clerical Culture: Narratives of the Episcopal Holiness in the Gregorian Era." *Church History: Studies in Christianity and Culture* 72, 1 (2003): 25–52.

Mirrer, Louise. "Representing 'Other' Men: Muslims, Jews, and Masculine Ideals in Medieval Castilian Epic and Ballad." In *Medieval Masculinities: Regarding Men in the Middle Ages*, edited by Clare A. Lees, 169–86. Minneapolis: University of Minnesota Press, 1994.

Moore, Alex. *Teaching and Learning: Pedagogy, Curriculum, and Culture*. New York: Routledge, 2012.

Moran, Lee. "Brazilian Student Who Auctioned Her Virginity for £485,000 Hopes to Sell It AGAIN after Claiming the Last Buyer Did Not Have Sex with Her." *Daily Mail* online, November 20, 2013, http://www.dailymail.co.uk/news/article-2510425/Brazilian-student-auctioned-virginity-hopes-sell-AGAIN.html.

Morey, Tracy Crowe, and Cristina Santos. "*Las madres guerreras*: Testimonial Writing on Militant Motherhood in Latin America." In *Motherhood and War: International Perspectives*, edited by Dana Cooper and Claire Phelan, 61–84. New York: Palgrave Macmillan, 2014.

Myers, Kathleen Ann. *Neither Saints nor Sinners: Writing the Lives of Women in Spanish America*. Oxford: Oxford University Press, 2003.

Nunca Más: Informe de la Comisión Nacional sobre la Desaparición de Personas. Buenos Aires: Eudeba, 2006.

Olcott, Jocelyn, Mary Kay Vaughan, and Gabriela Cano, eds. *Sex in Revolution: Gender, Politics, and Power in Modern Mexico*. Durham: Duke University Press, 2006.

Platía, Marta. "La peor herida: Terribles testimonios sobre los crímenes sexuales en la megacausa de Córdoba." *Página 12*, May 10, 2015, http://www.pagina12.com.ar/diario/elpais/1-272367-2015-05-10.html.

Ramus, Susana Jorgelina. *Sueños sobrevivientes de una montonera a pesar de la ESMA*. Buenos Aires: Colihue, 2000.

Rhodes, Cassandra. "'What, after All, Is a Male Virgin?' Multiple Performances of Male Virginity in Anglo-Saxon Saints' Lives." In *Representing Medieval Genders and Sexualities in Europe: Construction, Transformation, and Subversion, 600–1530*, edited by Elizabeth L'Estrange and Alison More, 15–32. Burlington, VT: Ashgate, 2011.

Robben, Antonius C. G. M. *Political Violence and Trauma in Argentina*. Philadelphia: University of Pennsylvania Press, 2005.

Salas, Elizabeth. *Soldaderas in the Mexican Military: Myth and History*. Austin: University of Texas Press, 1990.

Salih, Sarah. *Versions of Virginity in Late Medieval England*. Cambridge, UK: D. S. Brewer, 2001.

Salih, Sarah, Anke Bernau, and Ruth Evans. "Introduction: Virginities and Virginity Studies." In *Medieval Virginities*, edited by Anke Bernau, Ruth Evans, and Sarah Salih, 1–13. Toronto: University of Toronto Press, 2003.

Sillato, María del Carmen. *Huellas: Memorias de resistencia*. San Luis, Argentina: Nueva Editorial Universitaria, 2008.

Spahr, Adriana. "Removing the Blindfold: Power, Truth, and Testimony." Paper presented at the 12th Global Conference on Monsters and the Monstrous, Oxford, UK. http://www.inter-disciplinary.net/at-the-interface/wp-content/uploads/2014/05/A.Spahr-m12-wpaper.pdf.

Suarez-Orozco, Marcelo M. "The Treatment of Children in the 'Dirty War': Ideology, State Terrorism, and the Abuse of Children in Argentina." In *Child Survival: Anthropological Perspectives on the Treatment and Maltreatment of Children*, edited by Nancy Scheper-Hughes, 227–46. Dordrecht: D. Reidel, 1987.

Taylor, Diana. *Disappearing Acts: Spectacles of Gender and Nationalism in Argentina's "Dirty War."* Durham: Duke University Press, 1997.

Twinam, Ann. *Public Lives, Private Secrets: Gender, Honor, Sexuality, and Illegitimacy in Colonial Spanish America*. Stanford: Stanford University Press, 1999.

Valenti, Jessica. *The Purity Myth: How America's Obsession with Virginity Is Hurting Young Women*. Berkeley: Seal Press, 2010.

Valenzuela, Luisa. "Dirty Words." *Review of Contemporary Fiction* 6, 3 (1986): 9–21.

———. *Other Weapons*. Translated by Deborah Bonner. Hanover, NH: Ediciones del Norte, 1985.

Velasco, Sherry. *The Lieutenant Nun: Transgenderism, Lesbian Desire, and Catalina de Erauso*. Austin: University of Texas Press, 2000.

Warner, Marina. *Alone of All Her Sex: The Myth and the Cult of the Virgin Mary*. London: Weidenfeld and Nicolson, 1976.

Wogan-Browne, Jocelyn. "Virginity Always Comes Twice: Virginity and Profession, Virginity and Romance." In *Maistresse of My Wit: Medieval Women, Modern Scholars*, edited by Louise D. D'Arcens and Juanita Feros Ruys, 335–69. Turnhout: Brepols, 2004.

Wolf, Naomi. *Vagina: A New Biography*. New York: HarperCollins Publishers, 2012.

Zalaquett, Cherie. *Chilenas en armas: Testimonios e historia de mujeres militares y guerrilleras subversivas*. Santiago: Catalonia, 2009.

CONTRIBUTORS

JONATHAN A. ALLAN is the Canada Research Chair in Queer Theory and an associate professor of Gender and Women's Studies and English and Creative Writing at Brandon University. He is the author of *Reading from Behind: A Cultural Analysis of the Anus* (University of Regina Press, 2016).

AMY BURGE is a researcher in literature, women's studies, and cultural studies. Her research approaches modern discourses of love, relationships, gender, and sexuality from a comparative medieval perspective. She has published research on contemporary women's historical fiction, medieval and modern literary representations of masculinity, and gender, ethnicity, and religion in Middle English and modern popular romance.

TRACY CROWE MOREY is a doctoral student in educational studies at Brock University. Her dissertation is in the area of entrepreneurship training and women's economic development in Ontario. Current research interests include postcolonial contexts of education, feminist methodologies of research, and women's testimonial literature.

JODI MCALISTER is an honorary associate in the Department of Modern History, Politics, and International Relations at Macquarie University in Sydney. Her PhD dissertation was on the evolving representations of virginity and romantic love in anglophone popular literature. Her research interests include the histories of love, sex, romance, and popular culture.

KEVIN MCGUINESS is a Canadian academic currently enrolled in the Interdisciplinary Humanities PhD program at Brock University. His areas of scholarly research include medieval folklore, Egyptology, and film studies.

GIBSON NCUBE holds a PhD in French and francophone literatures from Stellenbosch University (South Africa). He is a postdoctoral fellow at that university, and his research interests are in queer and gender studies, comparative literatures, onomastics, and comparative cultural studies. His current work focuses on the role of literature in the creation of a queer archive. His latest research has been published in international journals such as the *Journal of Commonwealth Literature, Social Dynamics: A Journal of African Studies*, and the *Journal of Contemporary African Studies*.

CRISTINA SANTOS is an associate professor at Brock University. Her current research and scholarship reflect an interest in investigating the monstrous depictions of women as aberrations of feminine nature vis-à-vis the socioculturally prescribed norm. She also investigates political and social deviance and trauma in life narratives as the constructions of a personal and communal sense of identity that challenge official history and patriarchy. Her publications include *Bending the Rules in the Quest for an Authentic Female Identity: Clarice Lispector and Carmen Boullosa* (2004), *Defiant Deviance: The Irreality of Reality in the Cultural Imaginary* (2006), *The Monster Imagined:*

Humanity's Re-Creation of Monsters and Monstrosity (2010), and *Monstrous Deviations in Literature and the Arts* (2011), to name a few.

ASMA SAYED, PhD, is a scholar of comparative literature and film studies whose interdisciplinary research focuses on South Asian diasporas in the context of global multiculturalism, postcolonial literature and theory, and Islamic cultures. She has published research on gender dynamics, disability, and other social justice issues in Bollywood cinema, and her work has appeared in many academic journals and anthologies. Her books include *Screening Motherhood in Contemporary World Cinema* (2016), *M. G. Vassanji: Essays on His Work* (2014), *Writing Diaspora: Transnational Memories, Identities, and Cultures* (2014), and *World on a Maple Leaf: A Treasure of Canadian Multicultural Folktales* (2011).

ADRIANA SPAHR received her PhD from the University of Toronto. She is an associate professor in the Department of Humanities at MacEwan University in Edmonton. She explores the interdisciplinary connections between cultural and political components in Latin American literature, especially in Argentina. Her last co-authored book, *Madre de Mendoza/Mother of Mendoza* (2013), reflects her current research interest in testimonial literature.

JANICE ZEHENTBAUER holds a PhD in Comparative Literature from Western University in London, Ontario. Her research focuses on the history of medicine, particularly neurology, in nineteenth-century Europe and in British Victorian literature. Additional research interests include representations and theories of "monstrosity" in popular culture. She is writing a book entitled *Scintillating Scotoma: Migraine, Perception, and Double Consciousness in the Victorian Novel.*

INDEX

A

Abdellah (in *Une mélancolie arabe*), 152–56, 158–60

abstinence, 5, 20, 67, 70, 73, 75–76, 80–83, 85; cultural anxieties about, 7, 86; movements for, 7–8, 106

abstinence-only education, 68, 79, 82–85, 98, 105

Acosta, Commander Jorge Eduardo, 207

Acta sanctorum, 130

Adolescent Family Life Act, 83, 98

adolescent sexuality, 74, 83–85, 99, 108–9; as associated with danger and death, 68; and female sexuality, 67, 106

adulthood, 6, 58, 109, 148–49, 160

Allan, Jonathan A., 1, 7

anal sex, 68, 161

ancient Greece: and homosexuality, 161

Arab Muslim societies in North Africa: and queerness, 146–47, 150–51, 162

Arabian Mistress, The, 18, 23, 28, 31

Aradhana (Prayer), 174–75, 180–81

Argentina: gender politics of, 209; guerrilla women in, 10, 192, 204, 208, 210; sexual torture in prisons, 204–7

Arnold, J. H., 70

Arrostito, Esther Norma, 207–8

At the Sheikh's Bidding, 18, 23, 28

At Your Own Risk, 134–35

Auchinleck manuscript, 24

Auerbach, Nina, 98, 105, 109

Averett, Paige, 11

B

Band Baaja Baaraat (Wedding Planners), 174–75, 185
Bandidas, 203
Barthes, Roland, 2
Bazzi, Giovanni Antonio, 131
Bernau, Anke, 4, 26, 32, 50, 68, 99, 191, 200
Bernini, Gian Lorenzo, 131
Bersani, Leo, 161–62
Bevis of Hampton, 6, 18, 24, 27, 32
Beyond Heaving Bosoms: The Smart Bitches' Guide to Romance Novels, 6, 56
binaries: of gender, 12, 147, 156, 194; of good woman/bad woman, 175; of nation/gender, 183; of penetrator/penetrated, 161; of sexual identities, 153
Birnbaum, H. Jean, 196
bisexuality, 5, 105
Blank, Hanne, 19–20, 48, 68, 97, 102, 105, 111, 176, 179, 210
Bliss, Ann V., 72–73
blood: as authenticating the vampire, 105; of martyrdom, 128; and sexual rage in Jessica Hamby, 108–9
blood (of first intercourse): as sign of virginity loss, 47, 51, 100, 102, 105, 110; and stained sheets, 17, 19–20, 28, 32, 34
Bollywood cinema, 9, 176, 179–81, 183, 188; female film characters as good/bad women, 174; and sexually liberated women, 9, 185, 187; virginity in, 173–75, 177
Bowersock, G. W., 139
Boyhoods: Rethinking Masculinities, 149
boyish femininity. *See* boyishness
boyishness, 159–60; and adult male homosexuality, 129, 135, 146, 149; troping of, 145, 147–48
Breaking Dawn, 80–81
Burge, Amy, 6

C

Carmody, Dianne C., 71
Caron, Sandra L., 69
Carpenter, Laura M., 58, 101
Carvajal, Fray Augustín de, 197–98
castration, 105, 203, 205
CCD (centro clandestino de detención), 207–9
celibacy, 5, 8, 70, 72, 82
Charpentier, Isabelle, 150
chastity, 30, 70, 200, 210; cultural anxieties about, 7, 86; testing of, 17, 19
Chilenas en armas: Testimonios e historia de mujeres militares y guerrilleras subversivas, 201
Christianity: and female sex and virginity, 25, 98, 176, 193–94, 197, 200; and Sebastian, 8, 127, 129–30, 135, 137–38
Cleland, John, 51
Cohn, Jan, 33
Collins, Victoria E., 71
Compton, Bill (in *True Blood*), 103, 108–10
Confessions of a Mask, 134
Corbett, Ken, 149
Craft, Christopher, 105–6
cross-dressing, 195, 197
Crossen, Caryss, 72–73
Cuban Revolution, 205
Cullen, Edward (in *Twilight* saga): relationship to Bella, 74, 76–77, 85; as vampire, 79, 84; as virgin hero, 67, 70–73, 78, 80–82, 86

D

D'Cruze, Shani, 162
De secretis mulierum (Secrets of
    Women), 19–20
death, 139; and orgasm, 137–38; and
    sex, 128, 136
defiant deviance, 147–48
*Defiant Deviance: The Irreality of
    Reality in the Cultural Imaginary,*
    I
defloration, 47, 49–50, 52, 56–57,
    70, 76, 101, 111; as bloody/
    pornographic, 51, 53–54
deflowering. *See* defloration
Deleuze, Gilles, 82
Derek Jarman: Dreams of England,
    129
Derrida, Jacques, 45–46, 57, 59, 107
Desert Sheikh's Captive Wife, The,
    18, 28
Desperado, 203
*Dialogue between a Married Woman
    and a Maid, A,* 6, 51
Dilwale Dulhania le Jayenge (The
    Braveheart Will Take the Bride),
    174–75, 183
Diocletian, Emperor, 130, 137
disappeared, the: in Argentina, 204
Dissemination, 45
Djaziri, Eyet-Chékib, 8–9, 146–50,
    152, 155, 160–62
Duranti, Andrea, 158
Dworkin, Andrea, 196

E

Eclipse, 81
effeminacy: and homosexuality,
    149–50, 162; as state of halted
    development, 160; troping of,
    145, 147–48

effeminate boys/men, 145–46,
    148–49, 152, 156, 159–60; as
    substitute for women, 151
effeminophobia, 145–46, 152
electroshock: to genitals, 204
Elia, John P., 83
Eliason, Mickey J., 83
emasculation, 155, 203, 205
Epistemology of the Closet, 5, 73
Eppink, Andreas, 153
Erauso, Catalina de, 10, 192–95, 197,
    207; as *virago* and nun, 198–99
eroticism, 71, 76, 103, 105, 156; in
    depicting Sebastian's life/death,
    133–36, 138; in romance texts, 51,
    56, 75. *See also* homoeroticism
erotophobia, 7, 79, 83–85
Evans, Ruth, 26, 99, 191
Eve, 77; as antithesis of virgin,
    193–94
extramarital heterosexual relations,
    199

F

Falconer, Pete, 102–3
family honour, 177
fangs: as phallic symbols, 105–6
fellatio, 68, 205
female masculinity, 199, 201;
    discipline of it, 208; as
    rehabilitated, 192; subjugation
    of, 210
female sexuality, 8, 101, 113; male
    power over, 33, 185; patriarchal
    view of, 8, 10, 100, 112, 185; and
    performance, 192; politics of,
    193. *See also* sexuality
female soldiers. *See soldaderas*
female virginity, 7, 10, 20–21, 23,
    30, 69, 82, 84, 86, 98; anxieties
    about, 73, 100–101; fetishization
    of, 99, 113; importance in
    Arab Muslim societies, 150–51;

male conquest of, 99, 105; as performance, 191; symbolic of purity of Indian state, 174; value of, 33, 75. *See also* hymen; vagina; virginity

femininity: of boys, 149; gendered performances of, 201–2; as hypersexualized, 7; and motherhood, 184, 200; and virginity, 178–79, 192. *See also* effeminacy; effeminate boys/ men

Fetz, Wolfgang, 138

Fields, Jessica, 84

Floris and Blancheflur, 6, 18, 24, 26–28, 32

Fortenberry, Hoyt (in *True Blood*), 103, 105, 110–12

40-Year-Old Virgin, The, 2, 69

Foucault, Michel, 161–62

Frankl, Viktor E., 207

Freud, Sigmund, 1–2, 103–5, 135, 203

Fruit Machine: Twenty Years of Writing on Queer Cinema, The, 129

fuckability: of female soldiers, 204, 208

fucking: as political and social act, 208

G

Gate Cinema in Notting Hill, 129

gay child. *See* proto-gay child

gay identities, 5, 150, 157–58; and civil liberties, 106. *See also* homosexuality

gay movement, 145, 150

Gay News, 129

gay pornography. *See* pornography

gay sexuality: in Arab Muslim societies of North Africa, 9

gender: binaries of, 12, 147, 156, 183, 194; expectations in India,

173–74, 177–78, 187; fluidity of, 106; norms of, 18, 33–35, 100, 152, 185, 193–94; roles of, 70, 76, 102, 111, 161; and sexuality, 79, 101, 150, 155, 161; traditional forms of, 9, 148, 156

Glantz, Margo, 191

Graham, Lynne, 18

green-sickness, 47–48

Greer, Germaine, 128

Gresh, Lois H., 79

Greslé-Favier, Claire, 83

Groth, A. Nicholas, 196

Gubar, Susan, 32

guerrilla movements, 205–6

guerrilleras, 10, 192, 205–6, 208–10

Gwilliam, Tassie, 46, 49

H

Halberstam, Judith, 10

Halperin, David M., 153–54

Hamby, Jessica (in *True Blood*): as perpetual virgin, 99–102, 108, 111, 113; and regenerating hymen, 100, 102, 106, 110; as virgin/ vampire, 7–8, 98, 102–7, 109–10, 113

Harlequin Mills & Boon, 18, 21, 55

Harol, Corrinne, 49

Haywood, Eliza, 49

heteronormativity, 6, 18, 210

heterosexuality, 33, 83–84, 107, 148, 152, 161, 199

Hilderbrand, Lucas, 9, 149

Hill, Fanny (in *Memoirs of a Woman of Pleasure*), 51, 54

Hindi cinema. *See* Bollywood cinema

Hindu religious texts: on sexuality, 176

Hinman, Sarah P., 69

Hirschbein, Ron, 101

Hirschman, Celeste, 84

History of Sexuality, The, 161
HIV/AIDS, 20, 83–86, 154
Holtzman, Deanna, 101
homoeroticism, 8, 129–30, 134, 136, 139, 151. *See also* eroticism
homophobia, 146, 160
homosexual intercourse, 158
homosexuality, 161, 204; as forecasted in effeminacy, 150; in francophone North Africa, 152; as passive, 154–56, 158, 161. *See also* effeminacy; passivity
Hoogland, Renée C., 147
hymen, 2, 19, 53, 68, 97, 111; as barrier of virginity, 28, 45, 51, 57, 112; as a consummation, 45–46; as imperforate, 6, 51–52, 55–58; as intact, 18, 26, 191, 198; as proof of woman's virginity, 4, 45–47, 69, 100, 106; as regenerating, 99–100, 102, 106, 110; rupturing of, 6–7, 105, 107; and virginity loss, 49–50, 59, 80, 103. *See also* virginity, loss of
hymenoplasty, 112
hysteria, 78, 178

I

identity politics, 9, 150, 174
India: and roles of women, 173–74, 177, 187; and sexual purity and virginity, 176, 183–84
innocence, 5, 21–22, 28, 46, 108, 133, 159
Interview with the Vampire, 109
Irvine, Janice, 68
Islam: and sanctions on premarital sex, 176

J

James, Barney, 132
Jarman, Derek, 8, 127–35, 138–40
Jerome, Saint, 194–95
Joan of Arc, 199, 207, 210; military prowess of, 194; and testing of her virginity, 195–96; torture and rape of, 196, 206; as witch, 197
Jordan, Penny, 18

K

Kaye, Richard A., 128, 136
Kelly, Kathleen Coyne, 19–20, 25–31, 46, 51, 194
Kimmel, Michael, 82
Kleinpaul, Rudolf, 104
Ku, Chung-Hao, 149
Kulish, Nancy, 101

L

La vie sexuelle d'un Islamiste à Paris, 147
Laqueur, Thomas Walter, 52
L'Armée du salut (The Salvation Army), 146
Latin America, 193–94, 201, 204–5; female sexuality in, 192, 200; military women in, 10, 199, 210. *See also* Argentina; Chilean military women
Le roman de la rose, 6, 50, 53
Le rouge du tarbouche (The Red of the Fez), 146
Leitner, Paul Albert, 133
lesbianism, 106, 199
Levéel, Eric, 146
liberation: of females in Bollywood films, 9, 175, 177, 182, 185, 187; of vampire Jessica, 99, 101, 108, 112; of *viragos,* 193
Lichtenstein, Mitchell, 105
lily: as symbol of purity, 133–34
Luttfring, Sarah, 112

M

MacKinnon, Catherine A., 210

Maghreb region: Arab Muslim societies in, 147, 150, 152, 162; literature of, 146, 158

Maguire, Laurie, 19

Mahabharata, 176–77, 184

Majumdar, Neepa, 182

Making Sex: Body and Gender from the Greeks to Freud, 52

male sexual penetration. *See* penetration

male virginity, 7–8, 68–70, 73, 78, 82, 84, 86, 128; in Arab Muslim societies, 9; gap in research on, 146; as performative, 192

Malek, Doreen Owens, 32

Mallarmé, Stéphane, 107

Manley, Delarivier, 49

Mann, Bonnie, 76

mansos. See castration

Manusmriti, 176

Marouane, Leïla, 147

marriage, 47, 71–72, 78, 112, 160, 173, 185, 202; as arranged, 187; as compensation for virginity loss, 186; as ideal state, 48; as monogamous, 83–84; and virginity, 200

martyrs/martyrdom, 8, 127, 129–31, 134, 200; and masochism, 138–39

Marxist-Leninist ERP (Ejercito Revolucionario de Pueblo), 206

Marxist-Leninist FAR (Fuerzas Armadas Revolucionarias), 206

Mary Magdalene, St., 200

masculine queer virginity: in Arab Muslim North Africa, 9, 146, 150–54, 161–62; as defiant form of deviance, 147; in Maghrebian novels, 145, 153, 157–59; troping of, 145, 148

masculinity, 69, 72, 147, 178, 192–93, 203–4; as homosocial enactment, 82; performance of, 192, 194, 202. *See also* female masculinity

masochism, 134, 137, 157; and martyrdom, 138–39

Massera, Admiral Emilio, 207–8

masturbation, 5, 81

Mavor, Carol, 145

McAlister, Jodi, 6–7

McDonald, Tamar Jeffers, 31, 178

McGuiness, Kevin, 8

McNamara, Jo Ann, 194

medieval romances, 6, 17–21, 24, 26, 28, 33–34

Memoirs of a Woman of Pleasure, 51–52, 54

men: abstinence of, 70, 83; feminization of, 105, 145; rape of other men, 204–5; role in woman's virginity, 74–75, 100, 102, 175. *See also* male virginity; masculinity

Mexican female soldiers: and virgin/whore paradigm, 203. *See also* soldaderas

Meyer, Stephenie, 7, 70, 84–85

Midnight Sun, 80

military women: in Chile, 10, 192, 201–2, 210; as romanticized, 203. *See also soldaderas*

Mishima, Yukio, 133–34

Mon Maroc (My Morrocco), 146

Monroe, Lucy, 18

Montoneros, 206–7, 209

Moore, Amy, 11

Morey, Tracy Crowe, 10

Morgan, Sarah, 18

motherhood, 200, 202; as ideal state, 54

mumblecore films, 72

Murray, Stephen O., 147

Myers, Kathleen Ann, 198–99

N

Navy School of Mechanical
    Engineering, 207–9
Ncube, Gibson, 9
New Moon, 80
New York Times, 150
non-heterosexual sex, 68
nymphomaniac, 49, 99

O

Oblon, Jim, 109
*One Flesh: Paradisal Marriage and
    Sexual Relations in the Age of
    Milton,* 193
O'Pray, Michael, 129, 133
orgasm: and death, 128, 137–38
Our Vampires, Ourselves, 98

P

pain, 6, 58; of first intercourse, 102;
    of penetration, 51–52, 157; as sign
    of virginity, 110; as transformed
    into pleasure, 57; from virginity
    loss, 55, 57, 59
Pardes (Foreign Land), 174–75
Parla, Ayse, 34
parthenophilia, 111
passivity, 101, 135, 205; of females,
    54, 196, 202; in homosexuals,
    155–56, 158, 161
patriarchy, 20, 75, 109, 202;
    constructs of, 33, 77, 102, 112,
    174–75, 178, 200, 209–10; as
    controlling women, 10, 99–100,
    185–86, 193, 196, 201, 206; and
    gender norms, 34, 100, 152, 185,
    193–94; in society, 9, 100, 108,
    146–47, 176, 182, 199; values of,
    8, 24, 76, 78, 104, 160, 177, 207
Pearl, 6, 53
pederasty, 154

penetration, 19, 27–28, 32, 46, 50,
    54, 56, 68, 97; in male-male
    contexts, 153–54; and pain, 157;
    and power, 161; symbolized by
    arrows into Sebastian's flesh, 128,
    135–36
penis envy, 1–2
performances: of gender, 192, 194,
    198, 202; of virginity, 31, 67, 71,
    73, 86, 102, 178, 191, 199, 208
Perón, Eva (Evita), 207
Perón, Isabel, 204
Peronist Movement, 206
perpetual virginity, 99–100, 102, 108,
    111, 113. *See also* virginity
Perrault, Charles, 110
phallus, 2, 33, 101, 107, 112, 203
Phillips, Adam, 2
Phillips, Anita, 138
Phillips, Kim M., 24
physical gratification, 80–81
physical intimacy: in Bollywood
    films, 180
Pinochet, Augusto, 201
Platt, Carrie Anne, 67–68
*Political Violence and Trauma in
    Argentina,* 205
Pollack, Daniel, 18
pornography, 49, 51, 53–54, 129
Possessed by the Sheikh, 18, 23, 28, 31
Powell, Anastasia, 83
power, 77–78, 198, 202, 208; of
    gender relations, 70, 76, 102,
    109, 111, 161; of the patriarchy,
    33, 206; as political, 195–96; of
    the vampire, 104, 107–8; of the
    virgin, 100, 102, 104, 107, 153,
    155–56
pregnancy, 70, 78–79, 83–86
premarital sexual activity, 178; in
    Arab-Muslim societies, 151; and
    loss of virginity, 185–86. *See also*
    taboos

premature ejaculation, 69
Price, Lindsay, 11
procreation, 81, 105; cultural
    meaning of, 162; and exclusivity,
    20; as rite of passage, 160
promiscuity, 23, 31, 111–12
Protestantism: as emphasizing
    marriage, 48
proto-gay child, 9, 148–49
Purab aur Paschim (East and West),
    174–75, 182–83
purity, 7, 68, 72–73, 79, 85,
    132–33, 180, 183; as ideal, 106;
    movements for, 84, 101, 109;
    signs of, 70, 112. *See also* chastity
purity balls/clubs, 7, 72, 98

Q

queer children, 9, 148–49
queer cinema, 127–29
queer virginity. *See* masculine queer
    virginity
queerness, 78, 147–48, 152, 160–62;
    as affirmed in homosexual
    intercourse, 158; rehabilitation
    of, 146. *See also* masculine queer
    virginity

R

Ramayana, 176–77
Rao, Anupama, 162
rape, 8, 107, 127, 136, 192, 196, 204–5
recovery process: from leftist
    ideology, 209
rehymenization: of Jessica Hamby in
    True Blood, 106
religion: beliefs of, 11, 72, 127, 138–
    39; in cultural context, 152, 173,
    176–77, 181; and virginity, 8, 178,
    194–95, 198. *See also* spirituality
Remedy for Green Sickness, A, 6
Reni, Guido, 131

revirginization, 112
Rice, Anne, 109
Robben, Antonius, 205
romance East. *See* sheikh romance
    novels
romance fiction, 71, 82; explicit
    defloration scenes in, 54; and
    heteronormative gender system,
    18, 33–35; and transformation of
    heroine, 57; and virgin heroes,
    72; virginity loss in, 56. *See also*
    sheikh romance novels
Roscoe, Will, 147
Rosello, Mireille, 147
Rubin, Gayle S., 74
rupturing of hymen. *See* hymen

S

Sabbadini, Andrea, 102
Salih, Sarah, 19, 26, 99, 191
same-sex sexuality. *See*
    homosexuality
Santos, Cristina, 1, 7, 97–98, 147
Savonarola, Michael, 47
Sayed, Asma, 9
Schwarz, Kathryn, 102, 112
scold's bridle, 210
Sebastian, Saint: depictions in
    history, 128–31, 135
Sebastian, Saint (in *Confessions of a
    Mask*): homoerotic images of,
    134; and symbol of lily, 134
Sebastian, Saint (in *Sebastiane*):
    erotic death of, 130, 132–37; as
    martyr and masochist, 138–39;
    virginity of, 132–34, 136, 139
Sebastian: Love, Death, and Paradise,
    133
Sebastiane, 8, 128–30; execution
    scene in, 127, 131, 135–36, 139
Sedgwick, Eve Kosofsky, 5, 73, 81,
    145, 162
sexual agency, 97, 107, 109, 112, 178

sexual intercourse, 72, 78–79, 111, 128, 136, 201. *See also* homosexual intercourse; penetration

sexual orientation, 150

sexual penetration. *See* penetration

sexual purity. *See* purity

sexual reproduction. *See* procreation

sexuality, 2, 75, 155; and gender, 79, 101, 150, 155, 161; and spirituality, 132; traditional forms of, 9, 148; traumatic experiences of, 79, 84. *See also* female sexuality; heterosexuality; homosexuality

sexually transmitted diseases, 83, 86

shame, 8, 81–82, 180

Shaw, Chantelle, 18

sheikh romance novels, 17–18, 23–24, 26, 28, 32, 35; and medieval virginity, 34; virgin heroines in, 21–22; and virginity testing, 31

Sheikh's Bartered Bride, The, 18

Shuddh Desi Romance (A Random Desi Romance), 174–75, 185–87

Silver, Anna, 71–72, 78, 84

slut shaming, 8, 81

Smith, Lacey Baldwin, 138, 154–55

sodomy, 154, 205

Sofiène (in *Un poisson sur la balançoire*), 146, 149, 151, 155–60

soldaderas, 10, 192, 203–5, 210

Song of Songs, 51

Spahr, Adriana, 1, 10, 147

spirituality, 129, 132–33, 182, 194, 200; as fulfillment, 138–39; and virginity, 46–47, 49–50. *See also* religion

Stackhouse, Jason and Sookie (in *True Blood*), 103

Stockton, Kathryn Bond, 9, 162

Stradling, Matthew, 137

straight men: and loss of virginity, 5

Sultan's Virgin Bride, The, 18, 28

Swan, Bella (in *Twilight* saga), 74–77, 81–82; pregnancy of, 78, 85; as virgin heroine, 67, 70–73, 80, 86

T

taboos, 103–4, 160–61, 180, 187

Taïa, Abdellah, 8–9, 32, 146–50, 152, 160–62

Tan, Candy, 56

Teeth, 105

Tel Quel, 146

time, to grow to maturity: non-normative use of, 160

Totem and Taboo, 104

transformation: from human to vampire, 76–77, 99, 107–8; through virginity loss, 6, 46–49, 51, 57–58, 102, 179

transgenderism, 11, 106, 198

Treichler, Paula A., 85

Treviglio, Leonardo, 131–32

True Blood television series, 7, 98–99, 101, 103–4, 106, 112

Tumini, Angela, 105

Turner, James Gratham, 194

Twilight saga, 7, 67–68, 70–75, 78–80, 83–86

Twinam, Ann, 200

Tyndall, Farrah (in *The Sultan's Virgin Bride*), 28

U

Un poisson sur la balançoire (A Fish on a Swing), 146

Une mélancolie arabe (An Arab Melancholia), 146, 152

Une promesse de douleur et de sang (A Promise of Pain and Blood), 146

Universal Spectator, 49

University of Western Ontario, 97

Urban VIII, Pope, 199

uterus: as signifier of virginity, 47

V

vagina, 10, 204; as intact, 191–92, 197; rejuvenation of, 112
vagina dentata, 105, 203
Valenti, Jessica, 7, 98–101, 105
Valenzuela, Luisa, 210
vampires, 7–8, 74, 76, 79–80, 84, 98; as liberated, 99, 108; mouths, as gender ambiguous, 106; as sign of sexual excess, 105
vampirism, 79, 85, 101, 109
Velasco, Sherry, 199
verbal testimony: of virginity, 27, 29–30. *See also* virginity testing
Versions of Virginity in Late Medieval England, 191
Vida i sucesos de la Monja Alférez, 197
viragos, 10, 192, 195–96, 203, 210; performative nature of, 199; as perversion of male sex, 193; as protected in monastery, 194
Virdi, Jyotika, 176, 181, 183
virgin heroes/heroines, 6, 18, 21, 55–56, 67, 72
Virgin Mary, 2, 133, 176, 193, 200, 205
Virgin Territory: Representing Sexual Inexperience in Film, 102
Virgin: The Untouched History, 68, 97, 210
virginity, 5, 9, 12, 48, 69–70, 73, 81, 98, 181; as cultural concept, 2, 49–50, 68, 71, 86, 102, 150, 178; and marriage, 74, 200; as performative, 30–31, 67, 208; signs and proofs of, 4, 23, 27–28, 100, 105–7, 112; value of, 18, 24–25, 32, 76, 82, 177. *See also* female virginity; male virginity
virginity, loss of, 2–6, 32, 69, 71, 76–77, 106, 201; as belonging to the woman, 74, 100, 102; and hymen, 58–59; and intercourse/

penetration, 50, 54, 101; and pleasure and pain, 55, 57; social consequences of, 56; through premarital sex, 185–86; as transformative, 34, 46–49, 58, 179. *See also* hymen; penetration
virginity testing, 6, 10, 17–19, 23, 25–27, 35, 191; as loss of virginity, 32–33; of religious men, 194; as tool of female oppression, 20, 32; as unreliable, 20–21, 28–31, 34
Virgins: A Cultural History, 4, 68
virility: anxiety over being drained of, 106

W

Warner, Jessica, 80
Warner, Maria, 200
Waugh, Thomas, 129
wedding night, 20, 70; and loss of virginity, 179
Wendell, Sarah, 56
Western decadence: in Bollywood films, 181–82, 184
Western femininity: as promiscuous, 23
whore, 196, 200, 205
witch, 196–97, 200
Wogan-Browne, Jocelyn, 69, 200
Wolf, Naomi, 108
women: agency of, 107–8, 177, 187; in clandestine detention centre, 207–9; male ownership of, 6, 18, 24, 31, 34; marginalization of, 174; as recuperated, 209; rights of, 109; in submissive roles, 9, 202; trafficking of, 75; and transition through virginity loss, 6–7, 57, 74; as virgins, martyrs or mothers, 173, 200. *See also* liberation; military women; patriarchy

Women's Military School: as
    feminizing recruits, 202
wound, 8, 106; as symbol of vagina,
    105
Wyke, Maria, 130–31

Z

Zalaquett, Cherie, 201
Zehentbauer, Janice, 7